"An excellent summ〔...〕 for the modern reader. With the aid of diagrams, tables, and a very clear prose style, the author organizes a tremendous amount of esoteric material in an understandable form . . . an excellent introduction to the field. . ."

—*East West Journal*

Witness the wondrous blending of Mind and Matter . . . Body and Spirit . . . Science and Mysticism

A Kabbalah for the Modern World was the first book to present the Kabbalah from a scientific orientation and show how it clearly relates to such modern scientific models as Quantum Theory, Relativity and the Big Bang.

It is also a highly spiritual book. The Kabbalah has been identified as the single most important esoteric system on the evolution and importance of each human being. It also shows that the Kabbalah, a prime source for both Judaism and Christianity, does not have a patriarchal concept of the Godhead, and goes on to prove the equal importance of the feminine principle in both the creation of the macrocosmic universe, and the microcosmic individual person.

Now this classic has been revised and expanded to include a larger bibliography and new section: "The Kabbalah of Wisdom," which explores Chaos, Dark Matter, Black Holes, and how to prepare for the time when, according to Kabbalah, God will finally show His/Her face to the world.

This book is not merely a "magical manual." It is far more than that. It is a journey into new dimensions of being, self-discovery and spiritual development. Above all, it is a search for "devekkut" (also known as Nirvana or Samadhi), the true union with the Godhead. Reading *A Kabbalah for the Modern World* is a unique experience. You will grow inwardly as you read, as your spirit comprehends the message . . . and you will never, ever be the same again.

About the Author

Migene González-Wippler was born in Puerto Rico and has degrees in psychology and anthropology from the University of Puerto Rico and from Columbia University. She has worked as a science editor for the Interscience Division of John Wiley, the American Institute of Physics and the American Museum of Natural History in New York, and as an English editor for the United Nations in Vienna, where she lived for many years. She is the noted author of many books on religion and mysticism, including the widely acclaimed *Santería: African Magic in Latin America.*

To Write to the Author

If you wish to contact the author or would like more information about this book, please write to the author in care of Llewellyn Worldwide, and we will forward your request. Both the author and publisher appreciate hearing from you and learning of your enjoyment of this book and how it has helped you. Llewellyn Worldwide cannot guarantee that every letter written to the author can be answered, but all will be forwarded. Please write to:

Migene González-Wippler
c/o Llewellyn Worldwide
P.O. Box 64383, Dept. L294-2,
St. Paul, MN 55164-0383, U.S.A.

Please enclose a self-addressed, stamped envelope for reply, or $1.00 to cover costs. If outside the U.S.A., enclose international postal reply coupon.

LLEWELLYN'S NEW AGE SERIES

A KABBALAH FOR THE MODERN WORLD

Third Edition, Revised and Enlarged

Migene González-Wippler

1997
Llewellyn Publications
St. Paul, Minnesota 55164-0383, U.S.A.

THIRD EDITION
Third Printing, 1997

Cover Painting: Randy Asplund Faith

Library of Congress Cataloging-in-Publication Data

González-Wippler, Migene.
    A Kabbalah for the modern world / Migene González-Wippler.—3rd ed., rev. and enl.
        p.   cm.—(Llewellyn's new age series)
    Includes bibliographical references.
    ISBN 0-87542-294-2
    1. Cabala. 2. Religion and science. 3. Spiritual life—New Age movement.   I. Title   II. Series.
BM525.G58   1993
296.1'6 — dc20   23-18497
                                                                CIP

Publisher's note:
Llewellyn Worldwide does not participate in, endorse, or have any authority or responsibility concerning private business transactions between our authors and the public.
    All mail addressed to the author is forwarded but the publisher cannot, unless specifically instructed by the author, give out an address or phone number.

Printed in the United States of America

Llewellyn Publications
A Division of Llewellyn Worldwide, Ltd.
P.O. 64383, St. Paul, MN 55164-0383

ABOUT LLEWELLYN'S NEW AGE SERIES

The "New Age"—it's a phrase we use, but what does it mean? Does it mean the changing of the Zodiacal Tides, that we are entering the Aquarian Age? Does it mean that a new Messiah is coming to correct all that is wrong and make Earth into a Garden? Probably not—but the idea of a *major change* is there, combined with awareness that Earth *can* be a Garden; that war, crime, poverty, disease, etc., are not necessary "evils."

Optimists, dreamers, scientists . . . nearly all of us believe in a "better tomorrow," and that somehow we can do things now that will make for a better future life for ourselves and for coming generations.

In one sense, we all know "there's nothing new under the Heavens," and in another sense that "every day makes a new world." The difference is in our consciousness. And this is what the New Age is all about: it's a major change in consciousness found within each of us as we learn to bring forth and manifest "powers" that Humanity has always potentially had.

Evolution moves in "leaps." Individuals struggle to develop talents and powers, and their efforts build a "power bank" in the Collective Unconsciousness, the "soul" of Humanity that suddenly makes these same talents and powers easier access for the majority.

Those who talk about a New Age believe a new level of consciousness is becoming accessible that will allow anyone to manifest powers previously restricted to the few who had worked strenuously for them: powers such as Healing (for self or others), Creative Visualization, Psychic Perception, Out-of-Body Consciousness and more.

You still have to learn the 'rules' for developing and applying these powers, but it is more like a "relearning" than a *new* learning, because with the New Age it is as if the basis for these had become genetic.

The books in the New Age series are as much about ATTITUDE and AWARENESS as they are about the "mechanics" for learning and using Psychic, Mental, Spiritual, or Parapsychological Powers. Understanding that the Human Being is indeed a "potential god" is the first step towards the realization of that potential: expressing in outer life the inner creative powers.

Other Books by Migene González-Wippler

Santeria: African Magic in Latin America
The Complete Book of Spells, Ceremonies & Magic
Rituals and Spells of Santeria
The Seashells
Tales of the Orishas
The Complete Book of Amulets and Talismans
Dreams and What They Mean to You
Legends of Santeria
La Magia de Las Piedras y Los Cristales (in Spanish)
La Magia Y Tu (in Spanish)
Peregrinaje (in Spanish)
Santeria the Religion
The Santeria Experience
Suenos (in Spanish)
What Happens After Death

To ALPHA

And OMEGA:

With LOVE

CONTENTS

ILLUSTRATIONS

TABLES

PREFACE TO THE THIRD EDITION

A year after A KABBALAH FOR THE MODERN WORLD was first published, I wrote a book entitled *God and the Body Electric*. It was not a treatise on magic, but rather a compilation of scientific data, all of which clearly indicated that science had already proven the existence of God. The year was 1975 and my editor looked at me and told me that although the premise was interesting and the science was sound, no one would be interested in reading the book. It is too far fetched and rather fantastic, he said. No one wants to speculate about God's existence, he said. It's a subject best left to religion. It's not the sort of topic scientists are likely to discuss seriously.

After listening to his comments, I reread the book and tried to determine, as honestly as any writer can when reading his or her own work, how far fetched and fantastic were my claims. But after careful perusal of the manuscript, I was more convinced than ever that I was correct in my belief that God's reality as a sentient, omniscient force had already been determined through the scientific method. Not that it had been the intention of science to prove God's existence. The proof had followed as an aftermath, a sort of corollary to other more tangible scientific endeavors.

Undaunted by that particular editor's opinion, I took the book to a second editor and then to a third and a fourth. They all liked the book. They just did not feel it would find a readership. An editor from Doubleday liked the book so much she urged me to find a publisher as she felt the book needed to be published. Not by Doubleday, though. It was just too specialized for their list. This, incidentally, is a standard excuse publishers give authors when they don't want to publish their books.

Finally, growing weary of doing my own leg work, I placed the manuscript in the hands of an agent. He read the book in one night and gave me raving reviews of the contents. Chapter Six, he said, nearly "blew his mind." (This chapter presented my speculations on who, or rather what, God is and how He came into being.) The agent, however, was as unsuccessful as I was in trying to place the manuscript. After almost a year of searching in vain for a publisher, I sadly put the manuscript in my filing cabinet and tried to forget about it.

But the book would not rest in peace. It haunted me constantly. I knew, with the certainty of the absolute, that it was an important book, that it was necessary, that it was a major work. I had a vision and I wanted to share it with the world, but no one was willing to help me share that vision.

Many years have passed and suddenly belief in the existence of God is no longer unfashionable. Highly respected scientists the world over do not hesitate to express their belief that the universe could not have come into being through an evolutionary accident. There must be an Ultimate Cause, they say, there must be a Creator. God is now a fashionable reality that science is quite willing to sustain.

Everything I wrote in that book is now quite feasible. If I had written it last year it would have already been published, but it would have been old news. When I first wrote it, it was fresh and original, so much so that no one dared to publish it. Now the science in that book is dated and it would have to be thoroughly revised before it could be published. It was simply written too far ahead of its time. And I wonder what kind of impact it would have had on the world at a time when it most needed it.

Some, but not all, certainly not the kernel, of that book has been used in Part IV of this book, specifically because of recent scientific discoveries about the origin of the universe and human consciousness. The new material has been added because I want to stress the fact that the more science delves into the origins of humanity, the closer it comes to the face of God.

In Part I of this book, I presented various scientific premises that are in accordance with kabbalistic principles. When the book was first published very few scientists would have agreed with my views. Part IV closes and substantiates my initial argument with the evidence of some of today's most brilliant scientific minds, the same minds that would have undoubtedly refuted Part I when the book was originally published.

This book is now complete. And I now realize that each of its four parts corresponds to one of the four kabbalistic worlds. Part I corresponds to Atziluth, the World of Emanation; Part II to Briah, the World of Creation; Part III to Yetzirah, the World of Formation; and Part IV to Assiah, the world of Action. I did not plan this originally, at least not consciously, but it is now obvious that the book was incomplete when it was first published. All it presented was the World of Emanation, Atziluth. The second edition "emitted" the second and third worlds of Creation and Formation, Briah and

Yetzirah. And this third and last edition "emits" the last world, that of Action, Assiah. Part IV concludes the book and, at the same time, the seed that was planted in Part I is finally harvested.

I still grieve over my unpublished manuscript, *God and the Body Electric*. I still wonder and ponder about it. But now I feel that part of my message, or Somebody's message, has at last been delivered. Maybe someday the whole of the message will be given.

Migene González-Wippler
New York City
October, 1992

PREFACE TO THE SECOND EDITION

When A KABBALAH FOR THE MODERN WORLD was first published in 1974, the reviews were mixed. On one side it received the enthusiastic endorsement of many of the critics; on the other, the acerbic condemnation of some members of the Jewish orthodoxy, who could not tolerate the idea of a woman—and a gentile woman at that—writing about the kabbalah, a field traditionally reserved for male rabinnical students. But the final and most important judgment is always that of the readers, and *they* seemed to love the book. I received many letters from all over the world thanking me for the book or asking me where it could be bought. A reader from Yucca Valley, California, wrote to tell me she used the book daily as a "reference and guide book." Since she traveled constantly from Ventura County to Whittier, from there to Yucca Valley and thence to Rancho La Costa, with much use the front cover and the first nine pages had come apart. Also, purple ink and yellow felt markers had soaked into some pages obliterating them. She wanted to know where she could purchase a large quantity of the book so she could make it available to other people, as well as have a new copy for herself.

Many of the readers who wrote were Jews who were rediscovering their spiritual roots. They were mostly concerned with the "practical" aspects of kabbalah. A young Hassidic Jew wrote to ask how he could use the kabbalah to make "spiritual contact" with other people. Another Hassidim, this one a young woman, wanted to know how to nullify the kabbalistic magic that she felt a member of her congregation was using against her.

Non-Jewish readers were also interested in the practical kabbalah. When Carl Weschcke, the president of Llewellyn, and I talked about the possibility of a new edition of the book, we discussed this reader interest in the practical aspects of kabbalah. Carl suggested we put out an expanded version of the original work, with a new section dedicated to the practical kabbalah. That is how this edition came into being.

At first I greeted Carl's suggestion with some reluctance because kabbalah is too lofty a system to be used mostly for material considerations, but since the readers obviously wanted it, I agreed to write the new material. What we did was to divide the text into three parts. The first part comprises the original book in its entirety with some minor corrections. The second part is a study of the practical kabbalah, while the third part deals with the kabbalah of understanding. It will be noted that whereas I discuss kabbalistic rites and kabbalistic magic in some detail, I place a greater emphasis on *devotion,* and on the observance of the Law. Students who adhere to this principle will find their efforts amply rewarded.

One of the questions most often asked of me is why I am so deeply interested in the kabbalah. Why should a Puerto Rican woman, born and raised a Catholic, become so fascinated with Jewish mysticism? The answer to this question is two-fold. First of all, a large part of my ancestry originated in Spain which was the birthplace of the first kabbalists, notably Moses de Leon, the reputed author of *The Zohar.* Jews lived in Spain for many centuries before the infamous machinery of the Inquisition forced them to migrate to other countries, and eventually to the New World. It is entirely possible that some of these ancient Jews were part of my ancestry. On the other hand, I have always been fascinated by roots. One of the many statements attributed to Jesus by the scriptures is the following: "I am the Way. No one can reach the Father except through me." And in truth, the entire Christian world is based on the scriptures and the Torah—the Law—as given in the teachings of Jesus. These teachings are rooted in the Old Testament and therefore in the Jewish tradition. Jesus was the "Way" into the Torah for all Christians. To the kabbalist, the Torah is the "Way" to God.

When I realized the importance of my Judeo-Christian background, I became determined to learn more about Jewish religious and mystical traditions. That is how I discovered the kabbalah.

In the beginning I was mostly interested in the "magical" aspects of kabbalistic teachings. I wanted more knowledge about the transformation of cosmic energies for "practical" purposes. I wanted "power." I devoted many years to this study. I had very little help in my quest. At the time there were very few books available on the subject. There were also few people knowledgeable enough on the mystical traditions. Those who knew were not talking. I was therefore quite alone in my search. One day I came across an old book based on the kabbalistic teachings of Rabbi Isaac Luria. On the inner cover of the book was the telephone number of an obscure kabbalistic sect in the Hassidic section of Brooklyn. I called the number and was invited to meet with several members of the group. I was surprised by the invitation as I knew the Hassidim are not usually interested in outsiders, but welcomed the opportunity to meet with them. The place of the meeting turned out to be the back of a shoemaker's shop. There were four bearded Hassidim waiting for me. We talked for some time about my interest in the kabbalah, and then one of them produced a large typewritten manuscript. It was an original, unpublished work of anonymous authorship about the creation of the universe according to kabbalistic tradition. The author related how, when God was ready to start the creation, the twenty-two letters of the Hebrew alphabet came to Him to ask that He choose one of them to begin His work. Each letter argued convincingly on its behalf, describing its especial qualities and abilities. After careful consideration, God decided to use the letter *Beth* because of its capacity to "contain." That is why the first word in the Hebrew version of Genesis starts with Beth; that is, Berashith, meaning "In the beginning."

I asked the Hassidim why they were confiding these things to me, a non-Hassidim, a woman, and a Christian. They explained that it was necessary that these teachings were given now to the world, and that they had every reason to believe that I was the person to do this work. They gave me the manuscript, and I never saw them again.

After receiving this manuscript, the way of kabbalah seemed to open to me. Much of what I learned, I learned through "inner levels," but what had been obscure before was suddenly clear. One of the things I learned was that "power" can be a very dangerous commodity if it is not properly founded in wisdom and understanding, two of the most important qualities desired by the true kabbalist. At this point, I made an even more important discovery. I no longer wanted power. I knew how to gather it, I knew how to work with it, but I no longer wanted it.

As I said before, many people write to ask me how to accomplish material things through the kabbalah. My answer is always the same. The use of "magic" can be exciting and sometimes rewarding, but it is only a transitory phase on the way to bigger and better things. It is like the few steps a child takes on his own. He's thrilled by his prowess, unaware that in time he will be able to run, to jump, to swim and to somersault through the air. Likewise, the one who does "magic," as he continues to delve deeper into the mysteries, will find that there are greater things to be accomplished. These things are only possible through the total identification with the All and a complete surrender to Its will. That is why this book is not a magical manual. This book is about self-discovery, about spiritual development, about awareness, about love. The true kabbalist never searches for power. He does not even search for truth, because even the ultimate truth is unknowable. All he searches for is love. If this book can help you in this search then my own search has not been in vain.

Migene Gonzalēz-Wippler
New York City
October, 1986

Part
I

A KABBALAH FOR THE MODERN WORLD

How God Created the Universe

What is Kabbalah?

The word Kabbalah is a derivation of the hebrew root KBL (Kibel), which means "to receive it." It aptly describes the ancient tradition of "receiving" the secret doctrine orally.

The Kabbalah is a philosophical and theosophical system that was originally designed to answer man's eternal questions on the nature of God and of the universe, and the ultimate destiny of mankind. As a practical system, it is based on the numerical correspondences between the various aspects of human life and the universal laws.

1 The Creation

"In the beginning God created the heaven and the earth. . . ."
This is the opening sentence of the Book of Genesis,
according to the King James Version of the Bible. The
familiar words have been part of the heritage of mankind
for countless centuries. Upon their reverberating echoes
have been built religions and empires. The ancient words
were even heard across the vacuum of interstellar space
when man first walked on the moon. Yet Hebrew scholars
and Kabbalists claim that these words, revered and
cherished by so many, for so long, are esentially false. They
contend that the original Hebrew in which the Scriptures
were actually written has been hopelessly misinterpreted
by translators, and that the real message is of far greater
spiritual significance and psychological impact.

Genesis means "In the beginning," and is a direct translation of the Hebrew word *Berashith,* which we will discuss
in detail later on. Unfortunately, Hebrew began to die out as
a spoken language around 500 B.C. and was replaced by
Aramaic, the ancient tongue spoken by the Jews during
their captivity in Babylon and during the time of Jesus.

During their seventy years' captivity in Babylon, the
Jews lost the knowledge of their original Hebrew tongue.

1

When they were finally allowed by King Cyrus of Persia to return to Palestine, the only men who understood Hebrew were Esdras and Daniel. Esdras revised the first five books of the Scriptures, known as the Pentateuch and reputed to have been written by Moses. When these teachings were reintroduced into the synagogues, they had to be interpreted by means of a series of books known as the Targums ("interpretations"), which gave a translation of some parts of the Hebrew text into Aramaic for the common people. From 70 A.D., when the dispersion of the Jews from Palestine began, until modern times, Hebrew once more became the language of religion and culture. At the end of the 19th century, the Zionist movement revived Hebrew as a spoken language. It is now the official tongue of the state of Israel.

About 300 B.C. Ptolemy II, who ruled Palestine after the death of Alexander, ordered that the Hebrew Scriptures be translated into Greek. The work was undertaken by a group of Essene* scholars who lived in seclusion outside Alexandria, and who were the only people at the time with a competent knowledge of the original Hebrew in which the Old Testament had been written, as well as of Greek. The Essene initiates, however, were reluctant to reveal the secret doctrine of the Hebrew Faith to non-initiates, and therefore disguised, with the use of similes and symbolical imagery, the mysteries given by Moses. The stories of Adam and Eve, the serpent, and of Adam's rib, which were introduced in the Greek version of Genesis, have no corresponding passages in the Hebrew original. The seventy rabbis who formed the Supreme Council of the Priesthood in Jerusalem, known as the Sanhedrin, and who were not familiar with the abstruse quality of the Hebrew text, accepted this misleading translation as accurate and appended their

---

*The Essenes were a Hebrew sect of ascetics and mystics that existed from 200 B.C. to 200 A.D.

signatures to it, whereupon it became known as the Septuagint. The Essene translators remained anonymous. Thus, since 300 B.C. the Septuagint has been accepted as the correct Greek translation of the Old Testament.

In spite of common acceptance of the Septuagint, many biblical scholars and theologians have regarded its veracity with growing skepticism. Notable among these was Saint Jerome, who even engaged a Hebrew rabbi to teach him the ancient tongue, but to no avail. Saint Jerome spent twenty years translating the Septuagint into Latin. The Latin version became known as the Vulgate and is considered to be one of the foundations of the Roman Catholic Church since 400 A.D. In 500 A.D. the books of the Old and the New Testaments were first published together as the Bible, as we know it. They became known as the Holy Scriptures and have been since then accepted without question by the large majority of the Christian world.

One of the first translations of the Bible into the English language is ascribed to John Wycliff (d. 1384), but the best translation has been that of William Tynsdale (d. 1536), to which the famous Authorized Version of King James owes much of its phraseology. The standard King James Version is generally ranked in English literature with the works of Shakespeare, in poetic beauty and clarity of speech.

In 1515 a book entitled *The Polyglot of Paris* was published by Cardinal Ximenes, with the permission of the Vatican. This book was extraordinary in the fact that it presented the Book of Genesis printed in three different languages. Each page was set in three columns. The first column presented the original Hebrew text, the second column had the Latin Vulgate, and in the third was printed the Greek Suptuagint. The Cardinal's intention was to show that the Vulgate had been "crucified" between the other two versions, but that it was nevertheless the true word of God. The fact that the Vulgate had been the adulterated product of the Greek and Hebrew versions did not occur to the good Cardinal, who nevertheless did the world a great service by presenting it with a rare copy of the Mosaic Hebrew text, which had been zealously guarded for over three thousand years.

It was not until 1810 that a French scholar named Fabre d'Olivet discovered an old copy of the Cardinal's book. D'Olivet was quite a polyglot himself and had a considerable knowledge of several Eastern languages, including ancient Hebrew. It was with considerable excitement that he set out to study the Hebrew text given in *The Polyglot of Paris*. After several years of deep study, during which he compared the Hebrew original with Samarian, Arabic, and other translations, he wrote his erudite masterpiece, *La Langue Hebraique Restituee* (The Hebraic Tongue Restored). The book is a thorough study of the Hebrew language and contains a complete copy of the first ten chapters of Genesis in the original version, as well as literal translations into French and English. Thus for the first time since Moses reputedly wrote the Book of Genesis, European scholars were able to delve into the mysteries of the secret doctrine of the Hebrews, the true Torah, as the Mosaic books are known among the Jews.

Although the book was very expensive to print, d'Olivet was able to get it published with a subsidy from the French Government, who considered the work of such vast importance that they agreed to pay all publishing expenses, providing d'Olivet would send copies to all the universities and academies in France. D'Olivet did send copies of his book to the various university heads throughout France and requested that they criticize or otherwise correct the work should they deem it necessary. At the end of six years, since no one came forth to question the erudition of his work, he announced that his book had been found free from error and therefore should be acknowledged as totally correct. D'Olivet's work shows without a doubt that both the Vulgate and Septuagint, upon which the Authorized Version of King James is based, are complete travesties of the original Hebrew text.*

The work of Fabre d'Olivet made it possible for modern Kabbalists to reinterpret the Book of Genesis in its true Kabbalistic and mystical content.

The cosmological concepts that are such an intrinsic part of Genesis can be seen, in the light of the original Hebrew text, to have a significant correlation with modern theories on the creation of the universe and the evolution of man.

Perhaps one of the biggest dilemmas in the acceptance of the account of creation (as given in Genesis) by logicians and scientists is the fact that the whole process was completed in six days. That for God a day may last for thousands or maybe millions of years has occurred to many philosophers and theologians, but the answer to the enigma lies in Genesis itself. And the secret doctrine of the Hebrews, which is known as the Kabbalah, is the key that unlocks the mysteries of Creation, as given in Genesis.

The Kabbalah teaches that God is pure immanence. He is the ever-pervading energy that fills the universe. He is All, and greater than All. His essence is intangible, unknowable, yet the source from which all things are known. In His ultimate manifestation God is light. In Genesis 1:3, when God says "Let there be light," He is referring to this manifestation. For before the creation of the universe, God existed as the Unmanifested Principle. The purpose behind God's Creative Action was that of willfully manifesting His essence in the physical universe.

Light is a form of radiant energy that has no mass and no electrical charge, but can create protons and electrons,

---

*See Shabaz Britten Best. *Genesis Revisited*. London, 1970.

the building blocks of the atom and thus, of the universe. According to Planck's quantum theory, light is transmitted in "whole pieces" or quanta of action, also known as photons. These "whole pieces" of action are nonphysical, and yet they are the basis of the physical world. And despite the intense abhorrence that teleology, or purposive design in nature, awakens in scientists, the photon or unit of light seems to be motivated by a definite purpose. This startling fact was first discovered by Leibniz, who noticed that the photons that form a ray of light always select a path through the atmosphere that will take them most quickly to their destination. In the words of Planck, "Photons... behave like intelligent human beings." This observed phenomenon is known as *the principle of action or least action.* It was also Planck who said that the development of theoretical physics has led to the formulation of the principle of physical causality that is explicitly teleological in character. In other words, physics has proved that there is a definite purpose behind the causes of the material world, which is something that the ancient Kabbalists knew long before the advent of physics.

The theory of relativity presented to the world a new, interesting fact about the properties of light, namely, that time does not exist in the world of photons. Clocks stop at the speed of light. Even space is an insignificant concept for light because photons can go through space without any loss of energy. Furthermore, light cannot be really "seen." It simply makes seeing possible. It is an unintelligible force whose existence is proven mostly by the phenomena it creates.

Thus by the logic of scientific discovery, we have a concept of light that categorizes it as a force that is pure energy, timeless and spaceless, pervading the whole universe in an infinity of purpose and action.

All the characteristics that science has attributed to

light are remarkably similar to those that the Kabbalists, who see God as light, attribute to God. And if we also take into consideration that according to Planck there is a definite purpose behind physical causality, we can say, without stretching either the truth or the imagination, that science has proved the existence of God.

The two most innate qualities of the human mind are intuition and logic. Intuition is the mystical insight that makes a fact known before it is proved. Logic is the process of analytical reasoning that validates intuition. If we use logic to work with, instead of against, intuitive or mystical knowledge, we create a system that encompasses both the three–dimensional world of pure reason and the multi-dimensional world of mystical experience. Such a concept is not an innovation of this writer. Long before Bacon, and before Aristotle, the basis for this "higher" transcendental logic was given in ancient Hindu scriptures. Unfortunately, the formulas that made possible the use of this system were lost with the passage of time. Nevertheless, the "idea" of this concept persisted. Ouspensky, in his monumental work *Tertium Organum*, says that:

> New thinkers again discovered these principles, and expressed them in new words, but again they remained incomprehensible, again they suffered transformation into some unnecessary ornamental form of words. . . . The higher logic existed before *deductive* and *inductive* logic was formulated. This higher logic may be called *intuitive* logic— the logic of infinity, the logic of ecstasy.

The fact that the concept of intuitive logic had been clearly formulated in my mind long before reading Ouspensky underlines the noumenal quality of this higher logic.

Inevitably science must seek in mysticism a new theory of knowledge, particularly the methods of the Kabbalah, since only the Kabbalah possesses a classification system that enlightens equally the phenomenal and the noumenal worlds. This system, which is known by Kabbalists as the Tree of Life, is based on the harmonious union of opposites for the purpose of manifestation. This concept of opposites differs distinctly from the dualism of Aristotle and Bacon. The general axiom of the Aristotelian logic is that every thing has some thing opposite to it. Thus every thesis has its antithesis, object is opposed to subject, truth to falsehood, good to evil. This concept of duality is the foundation of our logic. The essential difference between the opposites of dualism and the Kabbalistic opposites is that the latter are in harmonious balance with each other. Their nature is either positive or negative, male or female. The result of their union is an Act of Creation in itself.

The Aristotelian logic contrasts sharply with the intuitive insight of Plato, who conceived of Creation in Kabbalistic terms. In the *Timaeus,* Plato describes the Creation of the universe.

> God, the all-perfect ruler of the spiritual world, though himself lacking nothing, beheld the sphere of non-being, or, as it was to be called later, matter, and found it lifeless, dark, and chaotic. Himself all goodness, he desired all things to be like himself, good and not evil. So he looked to the spiritual world of Ideas about him and framed a mterial world after its model, bringing down spirit to unite with matter, making it rich and diversified and endowing it with life, soul and intelligence. He created first the lesser gods, the Olympian deities, Zeus, Apollo, Athene and the rest, and after them the beasts, birds, fishes, and land animals, bestowing on each an appropriate soul. Last of all he poured what was left of matter into the cup in which he had mixed the world's soul and from this diluted mixture created the throng of human souls.

The Platonic concept of the Creation of the Universe, based as it is upon the idea of monism; i.e., the fundamental unity of everything that is, is diametrically "opposed" to the dualism of Aristotelian logic. Only the Kabbalah can reconcile these contraries with its fundamental tenet that opposites unite for the purpose of manifestation. This places the Kabbalah in the realms of intuitive logic; that is, the harmonious union of logic and intuition. Having shown that Kabbalah functions validly in the world of "higher logic," we may quote Ouspensky further:

> And then, beginning to understand all this, we shall grasp the separate ideas concerning the essentials of the noumenal world, or *the world of many dimensions* in which we really live. In such case, the *higher logic,* even with its imperfect formulae, as they appear in our rough language of concepts, represents in spite of this a powerful instrument of knowledge of the world, our only means of preservation from deceptions. The application of this instrument of thought gives the key to the mysteries of nature, to *the world as it is.*

We have shown earlier how the Kabbalistic concept of God as light agrees in principle with the concept of light, as proved by science. We have also seen that time does not "exist" for light. This means that all events must exist together, before and after their manifestation, in the world of light. All given *moments* must exist simultaneously and may be in contact with one another, even when divided by great intervals of "time." Thus for God, who Is light, all time processes blend together into an infinite sequence of events. This provides a valid basis for the reconciliation of the Creation of the Universe in six "days," or stages, with the Darwinian theory of the Origin of Species. The long process of evolution, which for man is measured in millions of years, was a simultaneous occurrence for God. Moreover, science recognizes six stages in the Creation of the Universe. Genesis says, "And the earth was without form and void." Science tells us that in the beginning the material out of which the earth was to be formed was scattered about in utter chaos throughout the original nebula. According to Genesis, God says, "Let there be light, and there was light."

Science states that the initial molecules were set in motion throughout the nebula giving rise to light. This was the *first stage.* Genesis says that the firmament was created during the second "day." Science claims that during the second stage the earth settled down into a spherical shape and the atmosphere (firmament) was formed. Genesis speaks of the creation of land and water and the vegetable kingdom on the third day. Science says that in the third stage, while the atmosphere was still dense, the waters began to settle in the low places. While Genesis speaks of the creation of the sun, the moon, and the stars on the fourth day science says that the stmosphere thinned out allowing the sun, the moon, and the stars to be seen. Genesis says that great whales and fowls were created on the fifth day. Science tells us that mammals (whales are mammals) were among the last species to be developed on the earth. Genesis says that man was created on the sixth day, and science confirms this by saying that man is the highest form of animal life.

So far I have been showing how the Creation of the Universe according to Genesis can be verified by scientific data. But a closer look at the first two chapters of Genesis, in the light of the original Hebrew text, reveals an evolutionary principle that is of far greater significance than that implied in the nature of God as light. For in fact there are *two* Creations. The first chapter of Genesis speaks of the universal plan *as conceived in the mind of God.* As such this first Creation is only an ideological plan of the cosmos. It existed only in potentiality to be followed by actual evolutionary development. What God does in the first chapter of Genesis is to manifest His essence as the spark of light from which the universe would evolve. He then ideates a cosmic plan for the Creation of the Universe that is to be carried out in an extensive process of physical evolution. The material source from which the cosmos would eventually evolve was the radiant energy that was God's initial *willful* manifestation. Saint Augustine, who was familiar with ancient Hebrew, gives the same interpretation of this "first" creation. He said: "In the beginning God created the Heavens and the Earth, though this was not in reality, because at first they only existed in potentiality of being." Herein lie the deep motivations for Saint Augustine's ideas on predestination.

Thus our universe was preconceived in the mind of God and as such, predestined. From this can be seen that evolutionary development was part of the initial cosmic plan. Therefore, in the light of the original text of Genesis, the Darwinian theory of evolution is a definite part of the Divine Order of things.

The second chapter of Genesis carries out the conceived Divine Plan on the material plane, as the physical universe. This is the "second" Creation. In chapter 1, Genesis speaks of GOD, the Creator, on a mental plane. In chapter 2 the Creator is no longer GOD but THE LORD GOD. Very often in the Scriptures the Supreme Being is referred to in various ways, such as God, The Lord God, The Lord, and so on. Each title given to the Godhead in Hebrew has a special meaning and refers to an aspect of the Deity. In Hebrew GOD is ELOHIM, the Being of Beings, the Creator on a spiritual level. THE LORD GOD is Jehovah (IHVH), the actual manifestation of the Elohim in the phenomenal world as the first spark of light whence the universe evolved. The meaning of these two names or aspects of the Supreme Being will be described later on in this book.

In order to grasp some understanding of the Kabbalistic doctrines hidden in Genesis it is necessary for the reader to become a little familiar with the Hebrew alphabet and with some of the characteristics of the Hebrew letters. We will study these characteristics in the next pages, and we will also see an analysis of the most significant passages of Genesis along Kabbalistic lines. It is important for the reader to understand the subtleties of the Hebrew alphabet, because according to Kabbalists, the first five chapters of Genesis were written in code and cannot be interpreted without the proper keys, which are the Hebrew letters. Each Hebrew letter has a specific meaning and also represents a certain number. The numbers ascribed to the letters have no mathematical significance. Each letter, and thus each number, is simply an "ideogram," a symbol of a cosmic force. The interaction between these cosmic energies is taking place simultaneously in the universe as well as in man. The biblical message is thus intended as a means of awakening all our centers of awareness, acting in this sense as a spiritual revelation.

It is an accepted fact that the whole universe is based upon numbers. Pythagoras said, "Nature Geometrizes." And Carl G. Jung went one step further and said that numbers were pre-existent to consciousness. He believed numbers were not invented by man, but rather they were discovered, for they always existed. According to Jung, numbers are probably the most primitive element of order in the human mind and are used by the unconscious as an ordering factor. He further stated that it is not an audacious conclusion to define numbers psychologically as "archetypes of order" that have become conscious. Jung's theory of synchronicity, which may be defined as the simultaneous occurrence of two or more "meaningfully" connected events, has a distinct parallelism with numbers. And Jung himself asserted that numbers and synchronicity have always been brought in contact with one another. Bertrand Russell was expressing the same thought when he said that "It must have required many ages to discover that a brace of pheasants and a couple of days were both instances of number two."

A number is a symbol used to convey an idea, an abstraction. Many scientists agree that all possible knowledge is present in the mind in an abstract form. In the abstract world of the mind there is no time or space, for nothing in it ever changes. In this purely abstract world knowledge is Absolute, and past, present, and future blend together into eternity.

The study of the abstract comes under the jurisdiction of mathematics, especially number theory, which teaches, among other things, that numbers have characteristics and that no two numbers have exactly the same ones. On the other hand, number is also language, a means of communication. Man communicates his thoughts and ideas by using languages based on numerical symbolism. Leo Stalnaker, in his work, *Mystic Symbolism in Bible Numerals*, says that

> The importance of numerical symbolism to the ancients perhaps arose from the fact that the letters of the Hebrew language were originally numerals, and the entire Bible being composed of different groups or combinations of Hebrew letters, it came to be the common belief that the true meaning or proper interpretation of difficult passages of scripture could best be ascertained or reached only be resorting to the numerical value of those letters.

The Kabbalah teaches that God created the universe by means of the Hebrew alphabet. The twenty-two letters that form the alphabet are really twenty-two different states of consciousness of the cosmic energy, and are the essence of all that exists. Although they represent numbers, symbols, and ideas, they cannot be easily classified because they are virtually all the things they designate. In order to clarify the preceding statement, let us use the following example. Our ordinary languages are sensually derived; that is, they have been designed to express our sensory perceptions, what we see, touch, hear. The word "house" in English means dwelling, the same as "casa" in Spanish or "haus" in German. In Hebrew, the letter Beth *means* more than house. It is the *essence* of house. It is the archetype of all dwellings or containers.

Tradition teaches that the essence of the Kabbalah cannot be comprehended without a perfect understanding of the Hebrew alphabet. Thus to understand the act of creation the Hebrew letters are an indispensable tool. Table I presents a list of the twenty-two letters with their names, their numerical values, the Roman characters with which they are commonly identified, and their esoteric meanings. The Hebrew alphabet is mostly composed of consonants, the vowel sounds being often indicated by a series of small dots underneath the letters.

The *Sepher Yetzirah,* or *Book of Formation,* which is the oldest and one of the most important Kabbalistic treatises, says that the twenty-two sounds and letters of the Hebrew alphabet are the foundation of all things. It divides the letters into three mothers, seven doubles, and twelve simples. The three mother letters are Aleph, Mem, and Shin. The seven double letters are Beth, Gimel, Daleth, Caph, Pe, Resh, and Tau. The twelve simple letters are He, Vau, Zayin, Cheth, Teth, Yod, Lamed, Nun, Samekh, Ayin, Tzaddi, and Qoph.

The three mother letters, Aleph, Mem, and Shin, are a trinity from which proceeds everything that is in the world. Mem and Shin are opposite forces and Aleph is the balancing force. They represent Air, Fire, and Water. The heavens were created from the Fire; the earth from the Water; the Air is spirit, a mediator between the Fire and the Water. The three mother letters are found in the year. The hot season was made from Fire, the cold season from Water, and the temperate seasons from Air, which is again a reconciling factor between Fire and Water. Again, the three mother letters, Fire, Water, and Air, can be found in man. Fire was used to form the head; Water was used to form the belly; and Air was used to form the chest, which again is found

Table 1.   The Hebrew Alphabet*

ALEPH (A) Ox	BETH (B) House	GIMEL (G) Camel	DALETH (D) Door	HE (H) Window	VAU (V) Peg, Nail	ZAYIN (Z) Weapon	CHETH (CH) Enclosure	TETH (T) Serpent
1	2	3	4	5	6	7	8	9
YOD (I) Hand	CAPH (K) Palm of the Hand	LAMED (L) Ox-Goad	MEM (M) Water	NUN (N) Fish	SAMEKH (S) Support	AYIN (O) Eye	PE (P) Mouth	TZADDI (TZ) Fishing Hook
10	20	30	40	50	60	70	80	90
QOPH (Q) Back of Head	RESH (R) Head	SHIN (SH) Tooth	TAV (TH) Sign of Cross	Final Caph	Final Mem	Final Nun	Final Pe	Final Tzaddi
100	200	300	400	500	600	700	800	900

* Although there are only twenty-two letters in the Hebrew alphabet, five of these letters have final versions, which are also of importance.

between the preceding two.

The seven double letters are called double because they have each a hard and a soft sound, and they also have a set of double qualities. Thus,

> Beth—Wisdom and Folly
> Gimel—Grace and Indignation
> Daleth—Fertility and Solitude
> Caph—Life and Death
> Pe—Power and Servitude
> Resh—Peace and War
> Tau—Riches and Poverty

The seven double letters symbolize seven directions: above, below, east, west, north, south, and center. They also represent the seven planets, the seven days of creation, and the seven orifices of perception in man, namely, the two eyes, the two ears, the two nostrils, and the mouth.

The twelve simple letters are the foundations of twelve human properties:

> He—Sight
> Vau—Hearing
> Zayin—Smell
> Cheth—Speech
> Teth—Taste
> Yod—Sexual love
>
> Lamed—Work
> Nun—Movement
> Samekh—Anger
> Ayin—Mirth
> Tzaddi—Imagination
> Qoph—Sleep

The twelve simple letters also represent the twelve months of the year, the twelve signs of the Zodiac, and the twelve organs of man; that is, the two hands, the two feet; the two kidneys, the spleen, the liver, the gall, the sexual organs, the stomach, and the intestines.

According to Kabbalists, the twenty-two letters are also archetypes of different states of consciousness, as follows:

1 ALEPH

is the dual principle that represents all that exists and all that does not exist, the positive and negative, life and death.

2 BETH

is the symbol of all habitations and receptacles, of anything that "contains."

3 GIMEL

is the activity, the motion of contained, limited existence or nonexistence; it is Aleph in Beth.

4 DALETH

is the archetype of physical existence.

5 HE

is the principle of universal life.

6 VAU

is the archtype of all fertilizing substances.

7 ZAYIN

is the completed fertilizing act.

8 CHETH

is the "enclosure" of all unevolved cosmic energy.

9 TETH

is the symbol of the initial female energy.

10 YOD

is the opposite of Aleph; it is a steady-state, continuity.

20 CAPH

is the archetype of receivers.

30 LAMED

is the principle of the conscious, connecting link.

40 MEM

is the archetype of the maternal creative principle.

50 NUN

is the archetype of all individual existences.

60 SAMEKH

is the archetype of female fertility, the ovum.

70 AYIN

> is the illuminating principle behind the act of impregnation (Zayin).

80 PE

> the same as Cheth.

90 TZADDI

> is a symbol of womanhood in a social sense.

100 QOPH

> is an exalted state of Aleph, transcending the negative or death aspect.

200 RESH

> is the archtype of universal or cosmic "containers."

300 SHIN

> is the "spirit" of God.

400 TAU

> is the archetype of all cosmic existence.

500 Final CAPH

> is the cosmic final attainment of individual existences.

600 Final MEM

> is the cosmic state of fertility in man, both in mind and body.

700 Final NUN

> is the symbol of interplay of cosmic energies.

800 Final PE

> the same as Pe and Cheth.

900 Final TZADDI

> is the archetype of womanhood, in a mythical sense.

Aleph (1), Beth (2), Gimel (3), Daleth (4), He (5), Vau (6), Zayin (7), Cheth (8) and Teth (9) are the archetypes of numbers one to nine. These first nine letters project themselves into various stages of manifestations always in multiples of ten. That is, the next series of letters from Yod (10) to Tzaddi (90) are exalted states of the first nine letters. The third series, from Qoph (100) to Final Tzaddi (900), represent the most advanced cosmic state that may be reached by the first nine.

According to Kabbalistic tradition, when God created the universe He used the letter Beth to begin His creation. Since Kabbalistic teachings are mostly based in allegories and metaphors, one must not take them literally, and must search for their hidden meanings in the symbolism of the Hebrew letters. The letter Beth, as we stated before, is the representation of all dwellings and "containers." In this total sense, it symbolizes the cosmic energy as it became contained and projected into actual manifestation. The shell, the "container" of this radiant energy is the created universe. This is the intrinsic meaning of the letter Beth. But let us now look at the opening sentence of Genesis* in the original Hebrew in which it was written, and let us seek its hidden meaning according to the letter code.

"In the beginning God created the heaven and the earth...." The transliteration of the Hebrew characters into Roman letters would render the original version of this passage as: *Berashith Bera Elohim Ath Ha Shamaim Va Ath Ha Aretz.*

Berashith

> "In the beginning." This word is made of the letters Beth, Resh, Aleph, Shin, Yod, and Teth. According to the preceding letter code, this initial word would be interpreted as follows. The "spirit" of God brought into continuous expression the dual principle of life and death, the pulsation of existence, by containing and realizing it in an infinite array of cosmic manifestations.

---

*See also the interesting work by Carlo Suares entitled *The Cipher of Genesis,* New York, 1971, for a detailed interpretation of the Book of Genesis.

Bera

"created." There are three letters in this word, Beth, Resh, and Aleph. Its intrinsic meaning is creation, but in a perpetual, infinite sense.

Elohim

"God." This word is composed of Aleph, Lamed, He, Yod, and Mem. It symbolizes a process by means of which the cosmic energy can be brought into realization.

Ath

"the." Aleph and Teth. The essence of the act of creation has now been given. Aleph (1) and Teth (9) are the first and the last characters of the first nine letters of the Hebrew alphabet (see Table I). The meaning of this word is then clear. Through the initial manifestation of the cosmic energy, the first nine archetypes of all existence (Aleph through Teth) came into being.

Ha Shamaim Va Ath Ha Aretz

"heaven and the earth." The cosmic energy is in gestation, and creation is under way. The act of manifestation is dual. For, in the process of creating the external, phenomenal universe, the cosmic principle brings itself also into manifestation. This cosmic principle is "heaven" and the phenomenal universe is "earth."

Thus, we see that the real meaning of the first sentence of Genesis, "In the beginning God created the heaven and earth," in the light of the Hebrew text, is as follows:

The Spirit of God brought into continuous expression the dual principle of life and death by "containing" it in an infinite array of cosmic manifestations. This creation is a perpetual process by means of which the Cosmic Principle is eternally brought into realization. Through this initial manifestation the first nine archetypes of existence came into being. The creation was dual, for in the process of crea-

ting the exteral universe, the Cosmic Principle brought
Itself also into manifestation.

By the preceding analysis we have reached a deeper
understanding of the first sentence of Genesis. We have
become aware of a far more urgent message. For we are
now able to form an idea of the principle of creation and of
the nature of the creator.

So far, we have been delving in the realm of the Literal
Kabbalah. This aspect of the Kabbalah is divided into three
parts, all of which deal with the hidden meanings of Hebrew letters.

1 Gematria

According to this principle, Hebrew words of similar
numerical values are considered to be identical with
each other. For instance, the words *achad* (unity) and
Ahebah (love) both add up to thirteen. They are therefore considered to be symbols of one another.

2 Notarikon

There are two forms of Notarikon. In the first, every
letter of a word is taken to represent the initial of
another word. Thus from the letters of one word a
whole sentence may be formed. A very common
example is the word *Berashith,* which we have already
discussed. From each of the letters of this word a new
word may be formed, thus: *Berashith Ra Elohim Sheye-
quebelo Israel Torah:* "In the beginning God saw that
Israel would accept the law." The second form of
Notarikon is the exact opposite of the first. That is,
from the initials or final letters of a sentence, a word
may be formed.

3 Temura

According to certain special rules, one letter is substituted for another that follows or precedes it in the
alphabet, thus forming an entirely new word.

But the Kabbalah has other teachings that go beyond the actual meaning of words, to imply even deeper things. For instance, ancient Kabbalistic tradition teaches that sound is power. *The sound of the Spoken Word.* It was by means of Sound that the universe was created.

The *Sepher Yetzirah,* or *Book of Formation,* says that the twenty-two "sounds *or* letters" are formed by the voice, impressed on the air, and audibly modified in the throat, in the mouth, by the tongue, through the teeth, and by the lips. So strong is the power of the spoken word, according to the Kabbalah, that the mighty four-letter name of God, the Tetragrammaton—IHVH—is never pronounced by devout Hebrews. The name is usually substituted for by another four-letter name, ADNI, which is pronounced Adonai and means Lord. The true pronunciation of IHVH is known to very few, as it is believed to be a great secret, and "He who can rightly pronouce it, causeth heaven and earth to tremble, for it is the name which rusheth through the universe." IHVH is commonly spelled out as Jehovah, but it is extremely dubious, say the Kabbalists, that this is the correct pronunciation of the Name.

The intrinsic meaning of the Tetragrammaton—IHVH—is "to be," and it is a symbol of existence. It also represents the four cardinal points, the four elements, (fire, air, water, and earth), and the four worlds of the Kabbalists, among other things. The Name may be transposed in twelve different ways, all of which mean "to be." The twelve transpositions are known as the "twelve banners of the mighty name," and are said to represent the twelve signs of the Zodiac. The are IHVH, IHHV, IVHH, HVHI, HVIH, HHIV, VHHI, VIHH, VHIH, HIHV, HIVH, HHVI. The Deity has three other four-letter names, which are AHIH (existence), ADNI (Lord), and AGLA; the latter is a Notarikon version of the following sentence; Atoh Gebor Leolahm Adonai (Thou are mighty forever, O Lord).

I

18	17	16	15	14	13	12	11	10	9	8	7	6	5	4	3	2	1
K	L	H	H	M	I	H	L	A	H	K	A	L	M	O	S	I	V
L	A	Q	R	B	Z	H	A	L	Z	H	K	L	H	L	I	L	H
I	V	M	I	H	L	O	V	D	I	Th	A	H	Sh	M	T	I	V

H

36	35	34	33	32	31	30	29	28	27	26	25	24	23	22	21	20	19
M	K	L	I	V	L	A	R	Sh	I	H	N	Ch	M	I	N	P	L
N	V	H	Ch	Sh	K	V	I	A	R	A	Th	H	L	I	L	H	V
D	Q	Ch	V	R	B	M	I	H	Th	A	H	V	H	I	K	L	V

V

54	53	52	51	50	49	48	47	46	45	44	43	42	41	40	39	38	37
N	N	O	H	D	V	M	O	O	S	I	V	M	H	I	R	Ch	A
I	N	M	Ch	N	H	I	Sh	R	A	L	V	I	H	I	H	O	N
Th	A	M	Sh	I	V	H	L	I	L	H	L	K	H	Z	O	M	I

H

72	71	70	69	68	67	66	65	64	63	62	61	60	59	58	57	56	55
M	H	I	R	Ch	A	M	D	M	O	I	V	M	H	I	N	P	M
V	I	B	A	B	I	N	M	Ch	N	H	M	Tz	R	I	M	V	B
M	I	M	H	V	O	Q	B	I	V	H	B	R	Ch	L	M	I	H

The *pronunciation* of the seventy-two names is as follows:
1. Vehu; 2. Yeli; 3. Sit; 4. Aulem; 5. Mahash; 6. Lelah;
7. Aka; 8. Kahath; 9. Hezi; 10. Elad; 11. Lav; 12. Hahau;
13. Yezel; 14. Mebha; 15. Heri; 16. Haquem; 17. Lau; 18.
Keli; 19. Levo; 20. Pahel; 21. Nelak; 22. Yiai; 23. Melah;
24. Chaho; 25. Nethah; 26. Haa; 27. Yereth; 28. Shaah;
29. Riyi; 30. Aum; 31. Lekab; 32. Vesher; 33. Yecho;
34. Lehach; 35. Keveq; 36. Menad; 37. Ani; 38. Chaum;
39. Rehau; 40. Yeiz; 41. Hahah; 42. Mik; 43. Veval; 44.
Yelah; 45. Sael; 46. Auri; 47. Aushal; 48. Miah; 49. Vaho;
50. Doni; 51. Hachash; 52. Aumem; 53. Nena; 54. Neith;
55. Mabeh; 56. Poi; 57. Nemem; 58. Yeil; 59. Harach; 60.
Metzer; 61. Vamet; 62. Yehah; 63. Aunu; 64. Machi; 65.
Dameb; 66. Menak; 67. Aiau; 68. Chebo; 69. Raah; 70.
Yekem; 71. Haiai; 72. Moum.

The similarities between IHVH (Jehovah) and AHIH (Eheih) are very marked. To begin with, they are both symbols of existence. Also, the letter He (the archetype of universal life) is the second and fourth character in both names. Kabbalistically, AHIH (Eheih) is the unmanifested cosmic principle, God before the Creation, while IHVH is the manifested cosmic principle, the Creation itself. This will be seen in greater detail later on, when we discuss the Kabbalistic Tree of Life.

Another powerful name of God, and one by means of which great things may be accomplished, according to Kabbalists, is the Schemhamphoras, or the Divided Name. This name is hidden in the Book of Exodus, chapter 14, versicles 19, 20, and 21. Each of these three versicles is composed of seventy-two letters (in the original Hebrew). If one writes these three verses one above the other, the first from right to left, the second from left to right, and the third from right to left, one would get seventy-two columns of three letters each. Each column would be a three-letter name of God, making seventy-two names in total. This is the Schemhamphoras or Divided Name. These seventy-two names are divided into four columns of eighteen names each. Each of the four columns falls under the aegis of one of the letters of the Tetragrammaton, IGVH. *(See Table II for a presentation of the Schemhamphoras.)*

From the preceding discussion we see the great importance that words and sounds have in the Kabbalah, and how secret messages, often of vast significance, are hidden in the Scriptures. It is also evident that the message of the Bible is vastly Kabbalistic in context.

The next sentence of Genesis that is to be considered here is the first act of creation, where the Will of God first comes into effect by means of Sound. "... And God said, Let there be light and there was light." The original Hebrew reads: *Viamr Alhim Ihi Aur Vihi Aur.* The fact that this sentence is composed of six words is significant in Kabbalistic symbolism, for six is the number usually associated with the created universe. An analysis of this sentence would render the biblical meaning as follows:

Viamr (Vau, Yod, Aleph, Mem, Resh) "And said." This word represents an act, a volitive projection of power by means of which Will is brought into manifestation. It implies sound. The fertilizing agent (Vau) projects into continuity (Yod) the dual principle of life and death (Aleph) into the maternal womb (Mem) which embraces and contains its cosmic substance (Resh) and starts the gestation process that will bring forth the created universe.

Alhim (Aleph, Lamed, He, Yod, Mem) "God."
The creative, immanent principle in actual manifestation.

Ihi (Yod, He, Yod) "Let there be."
The principle of universal life (He) is encompassed by continuous existence (Yod and Yod).

Aur (Aleph, Vau, Resh) "Light."
The essence of spirit that is the duality of life and death (Aleph) is fertilized (Vau) and expressed in universal manifestation.

Vihi (Vau, Yod, He, Yod) "And there was."
This word is a repetition of the third (IHI) conjoined in cosmic copulation with Vau, the male, fertilizing principle.

Aur (Aleph, Vau, Resh) "Light."
This is a repetition of the fourth word. This repetition is intended and it has a hidden purpose. The first *Aur* is inner light, soul. The second *Aur* is outer light, body. The result of the fertilizing action of the creative principle is the greatest speed of which the universe is capable, which, according to an ancient tradition, is the speed of light.

We see then that the proper translation of the phrase: "And God said, Let there be light, and there was light," should be:

> The Divine Fertilizing Agent projected in continuity the dual principle of life and death into the cosmic womb, and started the gestation process which brought forth the spiritual essence of the Created Universe. The Manifested Cosmic Principle was then surrounded by continuous existence. The essence of spirit was fertilized and expressed in universal manifestation through the cosmic copulation between the male and the female Cosmic Principles. This brought forth the Creation of the Physical Universe in the form of a vast explosion of light.

Thus by the pictorial splendor of this sentence we can envision an explosion of light and sound, and therefore of life, through the volitive act of an unknown principle that gave birth to the primordial substance from which worlds and galaxies were formed.

But how does this Kabbalistic rendition of the act of creation compare with the scientific theories concerning the evolution of the universe?

2 The Cosmic Egg

The first scientist who proposed an effective theory of the beginning of the universe was Belgian astronomer Georges E. Lemaitre. In 1927 he advanced the idea that the universe was the result of a gigantic conglomeration of matter and energy that became condensed into a huge mass of the approximate size of thirty of our suns. He called this mass the *cosmic egg* because it was formed from the cosmos (universe).

The cosmic egg was unstable and burst in a gigantic explosion that set its fragments hurtling in all directions. As the primeval matter of the cosmic egg emerged from the "Big Squeeze," it cooled rapidly through expansion, and its elementary particles began to stick together thus forming the prototypes of atomic nuclei. During this time cosmic space was full of vast amounts of high-energy X rays and Gamma rays. There were very few atoms of ordinary matter. In the words of astrophysicist George Gamow: "One may almost quote the Biblical statement, *In the beginning there was light,* and plenty of it." This radiant energy, which at the beginning played such an important part in the evolutionary process, eventually receded and was replaced by atomic matter. In the wake of atomic matter came the gravitational force that broke up the homogeneous gas of the universe into huge clouds, which became the protogalaxies. From the condensation of the gaseous material of the protogalaxies, the stars were formed. Some of the gas that was left over gave birth to the planetary systems. The Lemaitre model of the universe is known as the "theory of the exploding universe" or as the "big-bang theory."

According to Lemaitre's theory, the fragments of the cosmic egg were hurtled outward at different velocities, depending on where in the egg they were originally situated and how much they were slowed down by collision with each other. The fragments that reached higher velocities would gain constantly on those that had low velocities. This would give rise to an expanding universe, in which the galaxies recede from each other at a rate of recession proportional to the distance.

In 1915, Albert Einstein presented to the scientific world his General Theory of Relativity, in which he described the overall properties of the universe. According to Einstein's calculations the universe is spherical in shape, and finite; in other words, it is confined. Einstein based his views on the form of the universe on a system first described by German mathematician Georg Riemann, according to which, three-dimensional space curves itself in every direction in a constant curvature. This means the universe is a four-dimensional analogue of a sphere. A ray of light traveling on the Riemannian-Einstein universe curves back on itself. It can go on endlessly only by going over its same path. Thus we have a view of a universe that is unbounded, but finite.

All the tests that have been made of Einstein's theory of relativity have proved his model of the universe to be undeniably accurate, and astronomers have generally agreed that the universe is spherical.

The only flaw in Einstein's theory was that he had conceived the universe as being essentially static, without undergoing any significant change. The individual components might move about but the over-all density of matter would remain the same. This concept did not allow for either expansion or contraction, and scientists were not satisfied. In 1922 a Russian astronomer, A. Friedman, showed that the static nature of Einstein's universe was the result of an algebraic mistake in the process of mathematical calculations, where there had been an erroneous division by zero. Friedman was able to prove that the correct application of Einstein's basic equations led to a concept of an expanding or contracting universe.

These were all theoretical conjectures, however, without any material evidence as to their accuracy. Proof was not long in coming, however, and in 1925 Edwin P. Hubble, an astronomer at Mount Wilson Observatory, discovered that the entire space of the universe, filled with billions of galaxies, is in a state of rapid expansion and that all the galaxies are receding away from each other at incredible speeds.

Hubble based his discovery on the fact that what had been believed to be spiral nebulae (large clouds of gas floating in interstellar space) were in reality independent galaxies scattered throughout the universe. The spectral lines in the light emitted by these bodies showed a shift toward the red end of the spectrum. According to an accepted law of physics (the Doppler effect), when the source of light is approaching the observer, light waves are shortened and all colors are shifted to the blue end of the spectrum. When the source is receding, light waves are lengthened and all colors shift to the red end.

Lemaitre was quick in realizing that Hubble's discovery of the expansion of the universe agreed with the cosmological conclusions of Einstein's theory of relativity, as modified by Friedman. Based upon these discoveries, he evolved his theory of the cosmic egg.

The universe conceived on the principle of the cosmic egg can be of two different types. In the first type, the universe starts filled with a very thin gas, which contracts to maximum density, explodes, and then expands into eventual emptiness. This model is known as the *hyperbolic universe*. It lasts through "eternity," at the same time undergoing a permanent and irrevocable change. In this concept of the universe, there is a beginning and a definite end, and "we inhabit the brief interval of time during which the universe deviates for an instant from its eternal emptiness."

In the second model of the universe based on the concept of the cosmic egg, the force of universal gravitation is taken into consideration. If the universe is pictured as being blown into pieces by a tremendous cosmic explosion, it is conceivable that the forces of gravitation that rule the cosmos might eventually pull the pieces back together again. If this were to happen, the universe would be compressed together again, and a new explosion would take place, which would be followed by another contraction, ad infinitum. The result would be a "pulsating" or "oscillating" universe.

Although scientists are not altogether certain as to which of these two models may fit our universe, modern calculations indicate that at the present time the gravitational pull between galaxies is comparatively small as compared with their inertial velocities of recession. It is a case similar to that of a rocket ship breaking away from the earth's gravitational field as it moves away into outer space. All seems to indicate that the distances between galaxies are bound to increase beyond all limits, and that there is no chance that the present expansion will ever stop or regress.

There is another theory on the "creation" of the universe, which does not take into consideration the concept of a cosmic egg. This theory is known as the "steady-state universe" and it was propounded by Bondi, Gold and Hoyle. According to this theory, the galaxies are gradually receding from each other, but meanwhile, new galaxies are being formed by the condensation of "newly created matter" in the spaces left vacant by the receding ones. This theory postulates that this new matter is created at the rate of approximately one new hydrogen atom every billion years. Even at such a slow rate, this concept does violate the law of conservation of energy, which says that matter cannot be created or destroyed, and therefore it is not satisfactory to many scientists.

Thus, so far, by scientific evidence, we have a concept of a cosmos, unbounded, but finite, spherical in shape, with a definite beginning and a definite end; a universe that is expanding at a gigantic rate into eventual emptiness, as a result of a gigantic explosion or cataclysmic happening that took place "in the beginning," or, in astronomical terms, at "zero time."

But, where did the cosmic egg come from? Scientists answer this question by falling back on the law of conservation of energy. In other words, if matter cannot be created or destroyed, it follows that the substance of the universe was always there; it is "eternal."

The next question that comes to mind is, what was the cosmic egg made of? What was the primordial substance from which the universe sprang? At the present time, the universe seems to be composed of approximately 90 percent hydrogen, 9 percent helium, and 1 percent more complex atoms. As the universe evolves, the hydrogen atoms fuse into helium, and from helium into more complex atoms. (These latter are formed mostly within stellar cores.). If we go backwards in time to the beginning of the universe, the quantity of helium and other atoms diminishes, while the quantity of hydrogen increases. Thus, at "zero time" the universe must have been made almost entirely of hydrogen. This is the primordial substance.

Hydrogen is the simplest of all elements. It is composed of two particles, a central proton carrying a positive electric charge and an outer electron carrying a negative electric charge. As long as the two particles are separated there is a limit as to how compressed a mass of hydrogen may become. But if the electrons and protons are pressed together, they form a mass of electrically uncharged particles called neutrons. This mass of compressed neutrons is known as "neutronium," although astrophysicist George Gamow renamed it "ylem," a Latin word used to denominate the substance from which all matter was formed.

At the time of the "big bang," the neutronium cosmic egg disintegrated into separate neutrons, which in turn separated into protons and electrons. The protons formed became the nuclei of hydrogen-1 atoms. The hydrogen-1 atoms conglomerated to form helium atoms, which in turn aggregated to form more complex atoms, from which eventually sprang the galaxies and the planetary systems. According to the α, β, γ theory, this entire atom-building process was completed during the course of one hour. Scientists estimate that the beginning of the universe took place approximately 15-25 billion years ago; but this is only an assumption based on geological and astronomical calculations. The real date lies shrouded in the inter-galactic dust of the ages.

The Kabbalistic Universe

According to the Kabbalistic concept of the universe, the cosmos has a dual quality, that is, it is composed of a positive (masculine) and a negative (feminine) principle, which are balanced by a third, which is the result of their union. This resulting, balancing essence is known as *Methe-qela*, and is a perfect analogue of neutronium, the substance of which the cosmic egg was originally made. Just as neutronium is the result of the union of a proton (positive particle) and an electron (negative particle), the Metheqela is the result of the union of the positive and negative principles that rule the universe.

The Kabbalah teaches that the universe is an "emanation" of the divine cosmic principle. The essence (neutronium-Metheqela) of which the cosmos was created issued from God as the result of the union of the feminine and the masculine principles. As such it is a parallel of the sexual act.

Thus the initial proton may be viewed as a form of cosmic sperm that fertilized the cosmic ovum (initial electron) and formed the cosmic egg, from which, after a period of gestation of several billion years, was "born" the universe.

The prodigious concept of a universe created as the result of a cosmic copulation on a divine plane need not stagger the imagination. All we have to do is observe the natural laws around us to realize how everything in the observable universe responds to an essential union of two opposites, a male and a female principle. From the miracle of electricity to the duality of night and day, everything is harmoniously based on a negative-positive principle. And, if as the Scriptures say, man was made "in God's image," the sexual act must be also an attribute of the Creator, albeit on a higher cosmic plane.

In this Kabbalistic view of the nature of man and of the universe, which agrees so completely with the cosmological principles of the cosmic egg, the universe is "contained." (We must remember it was started with the letter Beth—container.) Therefore, it has a beginning and perforce an end. But, if we are "contained" in this manner, it follows by analytical reasoning that there must be something beyond the rim of the universe in which we are "contained." In this respect, the Swedish astronomer C. V. L. Charlier has propounded a very interesting concept that has been called the hypothesis of "unlimited complexity." Charlier suggested that,

> Just as the multitude of stars surrounding our sun belongs to a single cloud known as our galaxy, galaxies themselves form a much larger cloud, only a small part of which falls within the range of our telescopes. This implies that if we could go farther and farther into space we would finally encounter a space beyond galaxies. However, this super-giant galaxy of galaxies is not the only one in the universe, and much, much farther in space other similar systems can be found. In their turn these galaxies of galaxies cluster in still larger units, ad infinitum.

Although this hypothesis lies outside the scope of empirical science, and thus cannot be proved by observational study, it is a concept that has fascinated many scientists. For, is it so astonishing to conceive that we are a "world within a world"? Hermes Trismegistus (Thoth the thrice great) was a legendary Egyptian philosopher who was identified by the early Greeks with Thoth, the Egyptian god of wisdom. It is unlikely that the Hermetic books that are ascribed to Hermes Trismegistus were indeed written by the mythical Thoth. What we know for sure is that the central theme recurring throughout Trismegistus' teachings was the unity of all things. Trismegistus is said to have engraved a message, based on this concept, in a fabled emerald tablet. The message read thus:

> True, without falsehood, certain and most true, that which is above is the same as that which is below, and that which is below is the same as that which is above, for the performance of the miracles of the One Thing. And as all things come from One, by the mediation of One, so all things have their birth from this One thing, by adaptation . . . So thou hast the glory of the whole world—therefore let all obscurity flee before thee. This is the strong force of all forces, overcoming every subtle and penetrating every solid thing. So the world was created . . .

The "One Thing" in Trismegistus's message could be the description of the hydrogen atom, as well as that of the divine essence that emanated from God, according to the Kabbalah. What then is this principle, this force unnamed and unidentified, in the face of which empirical science stands mute and irresolute, unable to deny its immutable, eternal essence? What, then, is the Creator?

3 The Creator

Most of the concepts that man has built across the centuries on the nature of God have been based on the biblical descriptions of the Deity. In the West the Hebraical concept of God has become the most accepted idea of the Divine Being. Man has come to see God as an omnipotent, omniscient entity, jealous and demanding, exacting and severe, a father image of noble countenance and wise ways. This idea of God became more widespread with the advent of Christianity. To the Christians God became the merciful Father, the perfect all-knowing omnipresence, generous and just, demanding strict obedience to his commandments, extolling the virtues of chastity and humility, exalting poverty over riches and deprivation over pleasure. Yet, this vision of a sempiternal, perfect, omniscient, pleasuring-abhorring, age-old Father does not adhere completely to the biblical story. For, according to the Scriptures, God created man in His own image. To quote directly from Genesis: "And God said, Let *us* make man in *our* image, after *our* likeness . . ." (Genesis 1:26) "So God created man in his own image, in the image of God created he him; male and female created he them." (Genesis 1:27) According to these passages, God was not alone when he created man. For he spoke in the plural; he said, *us* and *our*. Furthermore, he created man and woman in "his own image." It is therefore obvious that there were at least two beings present at the time of creation, a male and a female.

As we have already seen, Kabbalists do not accept the standard translation of the Bible. In reference to this passage, they state that the translators of Genesis purposely obliterated every reference to the fact that the Deity is both masculine and feminine. The Hebrew word used to denominate God in Genesis is Elohim. This word is a plural formed from the feminine singular ALH (Eloh) by adding IM to it. Since IM is the termination of the masculine plural, added to a feminine noun it makes ELOHIM a female potency united to a male principle, and thus capable of having an offspring. The same intended misconception is given in the Christian idea of the Holy Trinity: Father, Son, and the Holy Ghost. In the Kabbalah the Deity manifests simultaneously as Mother and Father and thus begets the Son. We are told that the Holy Spirit is essentially masculine, but the Hebrew word used in the Scriptures to denote spirit is Ruach, a feminine noun. The Holy Spirit is really the Mother, and thus the Christian Trinity properly translated should be Father, Son and Mother.

The feminine principle of the Deity is also known in the Kabbalah as the Shekinah, the Great Mother in whose fertile womb the universe was conceived.

The tendency to smother all references to the creative power of a feminine principle is evident throughout both the Old and the New Testaments. God is consistently represented as a totally unisexual being, who persistently denies "his" own nature by creating a whole world populated by creatures of two genders.

The Kabbalah teaches that the Deity are dual in nature. There are a male and a female principle that are evident in all creation. How could the Elohim create man in the

Elohim's own image, male and female, unless the Elohim were male and female also? And how could the Deity tell man to reproduce and be fruitful (Genesis 1:28) if the Deity could not reproduce and be fruitful THEMSELVES? And why should the Elohim provide man and woman with a sensorial apparatus by means of which they could derive pleasure from their union if the Elohim did not have the same ability to experience pleasure?

Throughout the Kabbalah there is always the veiled allusion to the creative power of God, which becomes manifested through the union of the male and the female principles. Therefore the idea of sex, so maligned and purposely repressed by the translators of the Bible, becomes, by the proper understanding of the Scriptures, the most sublime and perfect symbol of the Divine Being. For, according to the Kabbalistic doctrines, the entire universe is based upon the principle of sex, that is, the harmonious union of two opposites, a positive and a negative principle, proton and electron, male and female, fruitfully conjoined to create new life.

4 The Body of God

In the beginning, according to Genesis, ". . . The earth was without form and void; and darkness was upon the face of the deep. And the Spirit of God (Elohim) moved upon the face of the water. And God said, Let there be light: and there was light." (Genesis 1:2, 3) Again, there is a misconception here. For God does not necessitate to "create" light. He is all light Himself. In the beginning this light was undifferentiated, unrestricted. For the purpose of Creation, that is, of manifestation, the light had to be "contained." In order to manifest Himself, the Infinite, unrestrained Light (the male principle) confined His essence within a Vessel (the female principle). The Kabbalists call the two principles, the Light and the Vessel, *He and His Name*. This is the secret of the Elohim, the Creative Principle.

The Infinite Light, as yet unmanifested, is called by Kabbalists, AIN (Negativity). The Vessel that contains it is AIN SUP, *Ain Soph* (The Limitless). The restricted Light that is the result of the union of AIN and AIN SUP is AIN SUP AUR, *Ain Soph Aur* (The Limitless Light). These three planes of unmanifestation are known as the Veils of Negative Existence.

The states of Negative Existence cannot be defined

because being as yet unmanifested they are outside the realm of human experience. Thus they cannot be conceived in terms of anything we know. Nevertheless, this unmanifested Negative Existence carries within itself the seed of Positive Existence, and thus of life as we know it.

The main characteristics of the Infinite Light (AIN) is "bestowal." This trait of bestowal is defined by the Kabbalists as the intention of receiving for the purpose of imparting. But as AIN is unconfined, He does not receive, He only imparts. His will is to bestow His essence. Hence His willful restriction of His own Light in the Vessel of AIN SUP.

The AIN SUP, being the perfect Vessel, has within Herself the desire to receive for the purpose of bestowing. In order to bestow the Light, the AIN SUP restrained Her will to receive, causing the entire Light to depart from within Her. She then became a vacant circle within the Infinite Light, which surrounded Her evenly, also in the form of a circle. A thin ray of light was extended from the Infinite Light and traversed the vacant circle of the AUN SUP, making a series of concentric circles, which are the varying degrees of the entire creation.

The beginning of this shaft of Light forms the Primordial Point, whence sprang the created universe. It is the AIN SUP AUR.

From the pinpoint of Light that is the AIN SUP AUR was formed the "archetypal man" or "world of archetypes," known as Adam Kadmon, or Body of God. This may be likened to the differentiated cosmic energy that composed the cosmic egg at the time of the "big bang," for it had within it the seed from which all the worlds of the universe would eventually evolve.

The Primordial Point (AIN SUP AUR) that traverses the circle that is the AIN SUP is a perfect analogy of the male sperm's head as it breaks through the outer circle of the

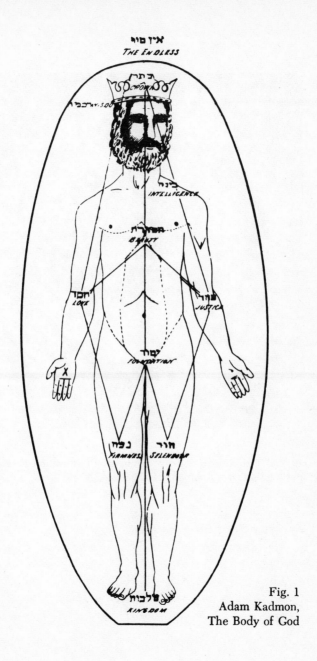

Fig. 1
Adam Kadmon,
The Body of God

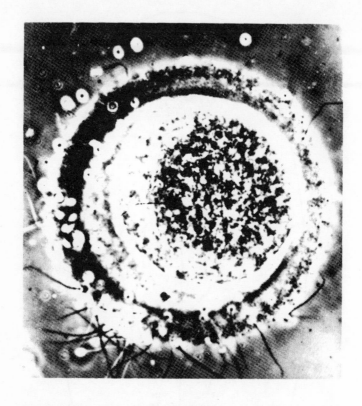

Fig. 2(a) The human ovum at moment of fertilization by male
sperm (*Courtesy of Landrum B. Shettles, M.D.*)

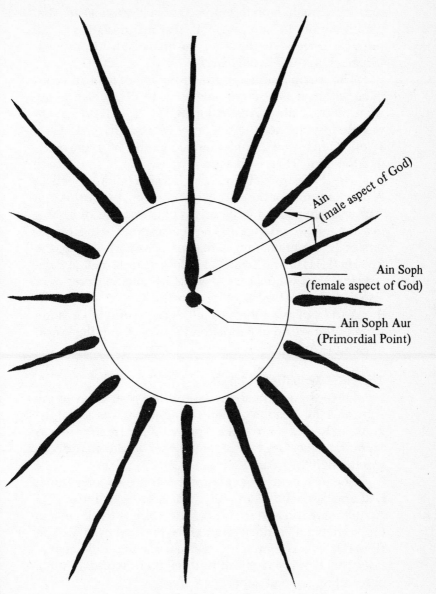

Fig. 2(b) God, at the moment of Creation

female ovum. In both instances, the final result is creation, manifestation. In one case, the final manifestation is the physical universe. In the other, the final result is human life *(See accompanying illustrations.)*

The Adam Kadmon is the prototype of man and contains within it the Tetragrammaton, IHVH, which is the same numerically as Adam or man. The "I" of IHVH is represented by the head of the Body of God, the first "H" is symbolized by the shoulders and arms, the "V" is the body, and the final "H" are the legs.

The Primordial Point, which was circumscribed in Adam Kadmon for the purpose of creation, broke through four apertures that are the origin of the senses of seeing, hearing, smell, and speech. They correspond to the four letters of Tetragrammaton, as follows: Yod (I) is seeing, the first He (H) is hearing, Vau (V) is the sense of smell, and the last He (H) is the quality of speech. The four apertures were also the origin of the Four Worlds of the Kabbalists, namely, the World of Emanation (Atziluth), the World of Creation (Briah), the World of Formation (Yetzirah), and the World of Action (Assiah).

The Four Kabbalistic Worlds

Since the eventual purpose of the restriction of the Light was the creation of man, the light that was contained in Adam Kadmon was still too powerful for creation. It was therefore necessary to emanate further worlds in order to veil the light of Adam Kadmon.

The next degree of light to be manifested after Adam Kadmon was the World of Emanation (Atziluth). The Atziluthic World is the plane of Pure Spirit and is known as the Archetypal World. It is under the presidency of the Yod (I) of IHVH. It is commonly associated with the element of Fire. This world gave birth to three other worlds, all in a descending scale of light.

The Second World is that of Creation (Briah). This

world corresponds to the plane of archangels and falls under the regency of the first He (H) of IHVH. It is associated with the element of water.

The Third World is that of Yetzirah, which proceeds directly from Briah. It is also known as the World of Formation, and is the plane of angelic forces. It is ruled by Vau (V) of the Tetragrammaton and is commonly associated with the element of air.

The Fourth World is known as Assiah, and is the World of Action, which is the plane of matter and man. It is also the world of "shells," made up of the denser elements of the first three worlds. In this world have their habitation the evil spirits, known by Kabbalists as the Qlippoth. This world is ruled by the last He (H) of IHVH and its element is earth.

Each of these worlds encloses the one preceding it like "the layers of an onion." Thus the Archetypal Man (Adam Kadmon) surrounds and covers, as "a garment," the Primordial Point of Light that emanates from the Infinite. The World of Emanation, in turn, surrounds Adam Kadmon; the World of Creation surrounds that of Emanation; the World of Formation surrounds that of Creation; and the World of Action surrounds that of Formation.

There are four secret names assigned to the Four Worlds, as follows: Atziluth—Aub; Briah—Seg; Yetzirah—Mah; and Assiah—Ben. Again, IHVH is said to be written in a special way in each one of the Four Worlds.

The use of a vast array of names to designate the Deity is characteristic of the Kabbalah. As we have seen, the Bible gives some of the translations of the names as Lord, the Lord God, the Lord of Hosts, and so on. These names are not used indiscriminately or to avoid repetition. Each title or appellative given to the Deity is an exact "metaphysical term," and is used to designate a particular aspect of the Divine force and the plane on which it is functioning.

The Four Kabbalistic Worlds have also been compared to the various elements in Ezekiel's vision; "And I looked, and, behold, a whirlwind came out of the north, a great cloud, and a fire infolding itself, and a brightness was about it, and out of the midst thereof as the color of amber, out of the midst of the fire. Also out of the midst thereof came the likeness of four living creatures. . . ." (Ezekiel 1:4-5) "And above the firmament that was over their heads was the likeness of a throne, as the appearance of a sapphire stone: and upon the likeness of the throne was the likeness as the appearance of a man above upon it." (Ezekiel 1:26) According to Kabbalistic symbolism, the man upon the throne is Adam Kadmon, the Body of God. This figure is the World of Emanation, Atziluth. The throne is the World of Creation, Briah. The firmament is the World of Formation, Yetzirah. And the "four living creatures," also known as the Kerubim, are the World of Action, Assiah.

Purpose of the Creation

The Kabbalah has three categories of ideas on the motives of the Supreme Being in creating the universe. The first category is concerned with the principal reason of the Creator for His creation. The first motive was to make manifest His three basic attributes: Mercy, Justice, and Compassion.

The second category of ideas deals with the intention of the Deity of creating the world in order to benefit man, and bestow upon him His Infinite Light.

The bestowal of God's Infinite Light upon man can only occur when man succeeds in removing the obstruction between himself and the Light. This obstruction is the evil spirit that is incarnate in him. When he accomplishes this he receives the Light as a reward for his effort.

As we have already seen, one of the main attributes of the Divine Light is the bestowal of its essence. But bestowal in the Kabbalistic sense is the will to receive in order to give, to bestow. Man, who is part of the last of the worlds of emanation, the World of Action, is a mixture of spirit and matter. The nature of matter is essentially "evil," and its will is only to receive, never to give, to bestow. Thus man desires only to acquire, without sharing what he receives. As long as man refuses to share, to give, he will be confined in the material world. When he learns this ultimate truth, and joyfully gives of himself, he will vanquish the evil nature in him and will be able to identify with his Creator. The Divine Light that he will then receive as a reward for his merits will be bestowed by him on the Creator because the World of Action is the last of the Four Worlds. Therefore the Light will return to the Infinite Source whence it sprang, forming a luminous circle that will encompass the universe throughout eternity.

The third category of ideas concerning the motives of the Deity in creating the world deals with the ultimate of His intentions; that of revealing His absolute unity, to manifest "that He is first and He is last; that all things are effected by His will alone. That ultimately every curse will be transformed into a blessing and every evil will be transmuted into good."

Proof of God's Existence

To the Kabbalist the best proof of God's existence is the created universe. The creative will is seen in the seed and in the fruit, in the four seasons of the year, in the mating call of animals, in a tender new leaf. To the Kabbalist, God is everywhere. He is in the mineral, in the vegetable, and in the animal kingdoms, always in different stages of differentiation.

One of the most interesting analyses of the Kabbalistic concept of God was given by Dr. Jellinek* in his definition

---

*Jellinek, J. *Beitrage zur Geschichte der Kabbalah, Erstes Heft.* Leipzig, 1852.

of the Deity, according to Spinoza's ethics. Following is an abstract of the analysis.

1. DEFINITION

By the Being who is the cause and governor of all things I understand the *Ain Soph,* i.e., a Being infinite, boundless, absolutely identical with itself, united in itself, without attributes, will, intention, desire, thought, word or deed.

1. *Proposition*

The primary cause and governor of the world is the Ain Soph, who is both immanent and transcendent.

a) Proof

Each effect has a cause and everything which has order and design has a governor.

b) Proof

Everything visible has a limit, what is limited is finite, what is finite is not absolutely identical; the primary cause of the world is invisible, therefore unlimited, infinite, absolutely identical, i.e., he is the Ain Soph.

c) Proof

As the primary cause of the world is infinite, nothing can exist *without* (extra) him; hence he is immanent.

Macrocosmus Versus Microcosmus

In the Kabbalistic ideology God is seen as the macrocosmus, while man is the microcosmus, God on a lower level. The Kabbalists despise idolatry, yet they ascribe the human form to the Deity because man was created in God's image. But this human form is an abstraction, a purely hieroglyphical figure. God is a loving, living, Infinite being, a supreme Intelligence, cognizant and aware. He is in All, different from All, and greater than All. His essence is expressed in the Name that, according to the Scriptures, he gave to Moses from the "burning bush": *Eheieh Asher Eheieh,*

"I am that I am." A clearer translation would be "Existence is Existence." Existence is "the absolute of reason, existence exists by itself and because it exists." One may ask, why does a particular thing exist, but not why existence exists. For existence is the very essence of being. It is the Absolute. But, since the Absolute is undefinable, can we say, logically speaking, that it is absurd? Not so, for if we could define it we would be limiting and containing it by our reason, and then it would not be Absolute any longer.*

This name of the Deity, "I am that I am," is the first principle of the Kabbalah and has various titles attributed to it, which are quite descriptive in nature:

Temira De-Temirin—The Concealed of the Concealed
Authiqa De-Authiqin—The Ancient of the Ancient
Authiq Iomin—The Ancient of Days
Authiqa Qadisha—The Most Holy Ancient One
Nequdah Rashunah—The Primordial Point

Before the Deity conformed himself as male and female, the worlds of the universe could not subsist. Or, in the words of Genesis, "The earth was formless and void." With the manifestation of the male and the female principle was established an "equilibrium of balance." Equilibrium is the harmony that results from the union of two opposite forces, *equal* in strength. It is rest after motion, counterbalanced power. In the Kabbalah, the term "balance" is applied to two opposite natures, which are equilibriated by a third one, which is the result of their union. Again, we see here the principle of the Trinity, Father, Mother, and Son: He-God, She-God, and the Created Universe. So were man and woman created, according to Kabbalah, in God's image and "equal before God."

---

*See also S. L. MacGregor Mathers. *The Kabbalah Unveiled.* New York, 1971.

5 God and Sex

The Shekinah, also known as the Matrona, is the female aspect of God. As the male aspect, God manifests as Jehovah. The name ELohim denotes the union of the male and female aspects of the Deity. In this context, we must also mention the great Archangel Metatron, who is said to be the "vesture" of the Deity under His, Her, or Their various aspects.* Metatron may be male or female, depending on the aspect of the Godhead with whom he comes in contact. He is in constant attendance on the Supreme Being, and is the most powerful of the archangels.

The mystery of the Shekinah is one of the most zealously guarded in the Kabbalistic doctrine. Her essence is intensely sexual, and She is said to hover over the marriage bed when a husband and wife are having sexual intercourse. She resides only in a house where a man is united to a woman, that is, where the sex act may take place between man and wife.

The Shekinah is the Divine Bride, the beloved of Jehovah. From their union as Elohim came forth the manifested universe. It was the Shekinah who walked in the Garden of Eden under the guise of Jehovah, the Lord

---

*Metatron is also believed to be one of the aspects of the Shekinah.

God. That the Shekinah, who is essentially feminine, may be transformed into Jehovah who is a male principle is explained by the Kabbalists by the fact that during the union between a male and a female there is only one body and one flesh. This is one of the deepest secrets of the Kabbalah, which is revealed only to a select few. From this can be seen that according to the Kabbalah the Divine Being not only have a dual sexual nature but that They copulate on a higher cosmic level for the purpose of manifestation. This explains why mankind was created male and female, why they were given sexual organs and told to reproduce. As Genesis so clearly states, they were simply created in God's image.

To the Kabbalists the sexual act is a most divine and sacred sacrament. Men and women who are not sexually active and unable or unwilling to procreate are considered spiritually barren. A man who does not unite with a woman in this life must return in another life and carry on this sacred duty to his Creator. The concept of virginity as a blessed state is unthinkable to a Kabbalist or to a devout Hebrew. The only virgins in heaven are those who are the handmaidens of the Shekinah, and they are not real souls. The ancient Hebrews placed an extreme importance on marriage at an early age because they believed, as do the Kabbalists, that the marital act brings man closer to God and that the pleasure that is felt by a man and a woman during their sexual embrace is shared by the Shekinah who hovers over their marital couch.

The Shekinah is called alternately the Daughter of the King and the Divine Bride, but She is also the Sister *and* the Mother of man. She is the architect of the created universe, acting in virtue of the Word that God uttered to Her at the time of the Creation. The Word was conceived and begotten into action by the Shekinah, just like a child is conceived and given birth by a woman.

The mystery of the Shekinah is also hidden in the Ineffable Name of Jehovah (Yod-He-Vau-He). Yod is the Father and the first He is the Mother. From the infinite and divine love that He has for Yod is born Vau, who is conceived, nourished, and brought forth by He. Vau, who is the male child or the Son, has a twin sister named Grace. Of the affirmed union of Vau and Grace was conceived the second He of the Divine Name. The second He is seen by Kabbalists as a transition from the metaphysical to the physical world, and within it is the seed of the created universe.

The Shekinah is connected very strongly with the patriarchal age. Most of the divine visions that Abraham had were manifestations of the Shekinah, who dwelt in the tent of Abraham's wife, Sarah. That is why Abraham described Sarah as his sister to Pharaoh. Because, as we have already seen, the Shekinah is also known as "sister" in respect to man. She also abode with Jacob and Rachel, and it is said that when Jacob was seeking a wife he "united his intention with the Shekinah." According to the Zohar, when Jacob married Rachel, "he united heaven and earth."

When Jacob lost his son Joseph, the Shekinah abandoned him because in his sorrow he ceased to cohabit with his wife. Not until Joseph was reunited with Jacob did the Shekinah return to Jacob. She remained with Israel all the time Joseph was alive. When he died She departed and did not return until the birth of Moses. She is said to have been attracted to Moses because his father and mother invoked the Shekinah at the time of his conception. In Moses' case the intimation is that their union was of a far deeper nature than with the other patriarchs, just as God revealed Himself to Moses under a new name (Eheieh—I Am that I Am). It is also believed by Kabbalists that this was the reason of Moses' separation from his wife, Zipporah. This is a peculiar connotation of the Kabbalistic teachings, particularly in the light of the fact that the Shekinah is said to abide with a man only if he is cohabiting with a woman. Another account goes even further and says that the "Holy One of Israel spoused Matrona to Moses, and this was the first time that She made contact with the world below."*

From the preceding it can be seen that the mystery of the Shekinah is the mystery of sex on a Divine Plane. But the Zohar also says that the union between the male and the female is Modesty and Purity. This Purity is symbolized by the circumcision of the male children of Israel. By the act of circumcision Israel is purified and enters under the Divine protection of the Shekinah.

The Kabbalah teaches, as we have seen, that a man who is "incomplete," that is, unmarried or one who never engenders a child, does not enter paradise after death. By paradise is meant in Kabbalistic terms the reunion of man's soul with his Creator. God's command to increase and be fruitful implies the procreation of children for the purpose of spreading the Light of God's Name, which is accomplished by allowing other souls to be born and made in God's image.

The Kabbalah teaches that souls descend to the world in pairs, male and female. This is the concept of "soul mates." The souls are separated during their descent to earth. But sometimes, if they are in a sufficient state of purity, they are reunited on the earth.

According to the Kabbalah there are specific times when sexual intercourse should be undertaken for the exaltation and glory of God. For ordinary persons the conjugal relations should be set after midnight because tradition says that it is then that God descends to paradise, and therefore at that time sanctification is plentiful. The "sons of the doctrine," that is to say, orthodox Jews and Kabbalists, should defer their marital relations until the night of the Sabbath, when the Deity is united with Israel. The principle

---

*See also A. E. Waite. The Holy Kabbalah. New York, 1960.

behind this belief is that since God is One, it pleases Him to be in contact with a unified people. Man may be called *one* only when he is united with a woman for the sanctification of God. And both man and woman should think of uniting, not just their bodies but also their souls, in order to blend together with their Creator.

Just as there is a specific time preferred by Kabbalists for the sexual act, there is a rule that makes it imperative that the man and the woman should be face to face during the act. This refers back to Genesis when Adam and Eve were created side by side. Only when they came face to face could they unite.

As we have seen, the male must always be united with the female for the Shekinah to be with him. The Shekinah, being a female principle, abides with the woman, and thus, only through the woman can man achieve union with the Shekinah. If a man does not keep this precept, it does not matter how serious and devoted he may be to his sacred studies and religious practices: The Spirit of God is not with him. For this reason the Shekinah is known by Kabbalists as the Indwelling Glory.

The Kabbalists explain this intensely sexual doctrine by saying that there must be a union on the material plane between a man and a woman in order to "offer a point of contact" for the union between the man and the Shekinah. The man is thus said to be surrounded by two females at the time of sexual intercourse; one on the spiritual and the other on the material planes. The blessings of the Shekinah then pour onto both man and woman in equal measure.

According to the Kabbalah, when a child is conceived, the Heavenly King and His Shekinah provide the soul, while the man and the woman provide the body. There is therefore a dual union taking place at the time of conception. In the metaphysical plane that of the male and the female aspects of God, and in the phenomenal plane, that of man and woman.

The Shekinah is said to be in exile, away from Her Heavenly Spouse, since Adam's fall. When Adam left the Garden of Eden, the Shekinah left with him, so that there might be hope for mankind. Thus it is said in the *Zohar*, the most important of the Kabbalistic books, "Therefore the man was driven out and the Mother was driven out with him." The light of the Shekinah was diminished by Adam's trespass, and thus She must wait until man purified himself to regain all Her splendor. At this time all the souls will unite with God in eternal joy, the devil and all the infernal legions will become angels of light, and hell will be dispersed. Infinite bliss will reign throughout the universe and there will be light forevermore.

The secret of the Shekinah and of the Creation of man as male and female is known in Kabbalah as a Mystery of Faith.

6 Kabbalah

According to an ancient tradition the Kabbalah was originally taught by God to a group of angels, who formed a theosophic school in Paradise. After Adam's fall, the angels taught the secret doctrine to the children of man to help them regain the grace of God.

Another version teaches that Abraham received the secrets of the Kabbalah directly from God, at the time of the covenant. The pact was of a double nature. First, he received the knowledge of the Holy Name (IHVH), in which is hidden the entire wisdom of the Kabbalah. And second, he was taught the hidden meaning of the circumcision of male children after the eighth day. The circumcision is a symbolic purification of the body and emphasizes its importance in carrying out the divine purpose. The Kabbalah, hidden in the Divine Name, is designed to awaken the mind and all the cognitive powers latent in man.

Abraham transmitted the secret doctrine to his son Isaac, who gave it to Jacob in turn. The last on the patriarchal line to receive it was Jacob's favorite son, Joseph.

The fact that Joseph had been initiated in the Kabbalah by Jacob (Israel) is seen in various passages of the Scriptures. In one of the most significant parts, Israel transfers his powers to Joseph by asking him to put his hand under Israel's thigh and to "deal kindly" with him (Genesis 47:29). This place under Israel's thigh was the seat of Israel's powers, for therein was the patriarch wounded by the Elohim when they wrestled together all night (Genesis 32:25). Joseph, however, was not destined to transmit the Kabbalah further, and its secrets died with him and thus were lost to the world.

After several generations, during which the children of Israel suffered unaccountable misfortunes by the hands of the Egyptians, the next link in the Kabbalistic chain—Moses—was born.

Moses is seen by Kabbalists as having both a symbolical and a historical personality. He is a symbol of the transmutation of the Hebrew people—from slavery to spiritual freedom. His name in Hebrew is Mosheh, and is composed of three letters: Mem, Shin, and He. The esoteric meaning of the letters renders the "mythical" Moses as a new breath of cosmic life that compelled the Hebrews to break their chains through divine inspiration.

When Moses went to Mount Sinai and confronted the Deity in the "burning bush," he received the Kabbalistic knowledge in the form of God's name: Eheieh Asher Eheieh. "I am that I Am." God then said to Moses, "Go and say that Eheieh (AHIH) sent you. Tell them that Jehovah (IHVH) sent you." Here we see the fusion of the two four-letter names of the Deity, which is the key to the entire Kabbalah, as we will see when we discuss the Tree of Life.*

Moses veiled the precepts and the teachings of the Kabbalah and gave them, thus distorted, in the first four books of the Bible. The fifth book, Deuteronomy, does not have any Kabbalistic traces in it.

The Kabbalistic tradition teaches that the Torah Moses received on Mount Sinai is dual in nature, for it comprises

---

*See C. Suares. *The Cipher of Genesis.* New York.

both "nigleh," the codes of law, and "nistor," the secret mysteries. Moses passed on "nigleh" to the people, but saved "nistor" for the elect.

According to tradition, a controversy developed between the angels and God against Moses. The angels demanded that the Torah should remain with them in heaven instead of being given to man. They contended that since they are purely spiritual beings and the secret mysteries are also spiritual in nature, it was only right that the Torah should be kept in heaven instead of being given to man, who has a gross, material body in spite of the spiritual essence of his soul. Moses pleaded with God, saying that since the Torah consists of, in addition to the secret doctrine, positive as well as prohibitive precepts, which can only be fulfilled on the material plane, it was more proper to give the Torah to man and not to the angels because the Torah is one and indivisible.

The Kabbalistic Books

The oldest book written on the Kabbalah is the *Sepher Yetzirah, the Book of Formation.* Tradition has attributed this book to Abraham, but modern Kabbalists believe that its probably author was Rabbi Akiba, who lived in the time of Emperor Hadrian, A.D. 120. Heinrich Graetz places the *Sepher Yetzirah* in early gnostic times. Most scholars, however, agree that the book may have been written at any time between 500 B.C. and 500 A.D., with Rabbi Akiba being the most likely source.

Many commentaries have been written on this short treatise (its length is less than ten pages), but the most illuminating are those of Judah Halevi (A.D. 1150) and Saadia Gaon (A.D. 920), who translated the *Sepher Yetzirah* into Arabic, with an elaborate commentary upon the text.

The *Sepher Yetzirah* is mostly concerned with the origin

of the universe and of mankind. It describes, by means of the Hebrew alphabet and its numerical correspondences, the "gradual evolution of the Deity from negative into positive existence." The twenty-two letters and numbers one to ten are called "paths," and symbolize all the archetypal ideas that correspond to the manifested universe. Together they are known as the "Thirty-two Paths of Wisdom."

Hebrew scholars believe that the work is the consolidation, by one single writer, of centuries of esoteric Kabbalistic tradition, although there have been sporadic additions and revisions by later authors. There are several Latin versions of the original Hebrew text, chief among which are those of Postellus (1552), Pistorius (1587), and Rittangelius (1642). The small treatise was first translated into the English language by the English Kabbalist W. Wynn Westcott, about forty years ago.

The other significant work of the Kabbalah is the *Zohar, the Book of Splendor,* which is reputed to be the greatest storehouse of Kabbalistic knowledge in existence.

The *Zohar* deals with the essential attributes of the Deity, and with the various emanations that issued from the Infinite Light. These emanations form the Tree of Life, which is the kernel of the Kabbalistic doctrine.

According to Hebrew tradition, the oldest parts of the *Zohar* date before the building of the second temple, but Rabbi Simon ben Jochai, who lived during the time of Emperor Titus (A.D. 70-80), was the first to put them into writing.

Rabbi Simon ben Jochai was a disciple of Rabbi Akiba, who is the accepted author of the *Sepher Yetzirah.* Rabbi Akiba taught the Torah (the Hebrew Divine Law) in spite of the persecution of the Romans, until they had him executed for sedition. Rabbi Simon ben Jochai condemned the Romans for their murderous action, and he also was condemned to death. He was forced to flee from Roman persecution, and sought refuge in a cave in the mountains of Israel. During thirteen years he hid there in the company of his son, Rabbi Eleazar. The years that Rabbi Simon spent in this cave were not wasted."In the safety of darkness, with no text to read, Rabbi Simon drew on the deep levels of memory and vision stored in his unconscious from years of study with his masters of the past."* This was the birth of the *Zohar,* which was to become the classic text of Kabbalah, the "unwritten doctrine," coming directly from Moses to be finally transmitted to those who were there to receive it.

During many generations, the *Zohar* was guarded and transmitted by the followers of Rabbi Simon ben Jochai. Then, finally, in fourteenth-century Spain, an obscure rabbi named Moses de Leon published the *Zohar.* This is what tradition, and indeed, what the *Zohar* itself, tell us.

Hebrew scholars, however, were not entirely satisfied with the origins of the *Zohar* as given in the *Zohar* itself. There was much speculation as to whether Rabbi Simon ben Jochai really existed, or whether he was an invention of Moses de Leon. For many years, Moses de Leon was regarded "as the redactor of ancient writings and fragments to which he may perhaps have added something of his own." But many modern Kabbalists believe that Moses de Leon was the sole author of the most important parts of the *Zohar.*†

After the *Zohar* was written, it was brought to the Hebrew community of Safed, where the ancient teachings grew and flourished again. Two major trends of Kabbalistic thought were developed there during the sixteenth century. One was started by Moses Cordovero, who wrote several lucid commentaries on the *Zohar.* The other was the school of Isaac Luria, whose works assumed a "leading position" among Kabbalists during the last two centuries. Luria's

---

*See Rabbi L. I. Krakovsky. *Kabbalah, The Light of Redemption.* Israel, 1970.
†See also Gershom Scholem, ed. *The Zohar,* New York.

writings on the Tree of Life and the eight "gates" are the most complete commentary on the *Zohar*. His interpretations are accepted among Kabbalists as the most authoritative on the Kabbalistic doctrines. So great has been Luria's influence in the Kabbalistic movement that two of the books of the *Zohar* are based on his teachings. One of them is the *Beth Elohim*, which is a discourse on the nature of angels, demons, and of souls. The other is the *Book of the Revolutions of Souls*, a further commentary on Luria's ideas.

The three most important books of the *Zohar* are:

1. *The Siphra Dtzenioutha*, or *Book of Concealed Mystery*, which is the foundation of the *Zohar*;

2. *The Idra Rabba*, or *The Great Assembly*, which describes the mystical "Body of God" in the form of Adam Kadmon;

3. *The Idra Zutta*, or *The Small Assembly*, which is a monologue of Rabbi Simon ben Jochai before his death, on the same subject as that treated in the Great Assembly.

Besides the *Sepher Yetzirah* and the *Zohar* there are two other books on the Kabbalah that are of great spiritual significance. They are:

1. *The Sepher Sephiroth*, which describes the evolution of God from a negative to a positive existence;

2. *The Aesch Metzareph*, which is an abstruse chemico-Kabbalistic treatise.

What is Kabbalah?

The word Kabbalah is a derivation of the Hebrew root KBL (Kibel), which means "to receive." It aptly describes the ancient tradition of "receiving" the secret doctrine orally.

According to modern Kabbalist S. L. MacGregor Mathers, the Kabbalah may be classified under four divisions:

1. The Practical Kabbalah
2. The Literal Kabbalah
3. The Unwritten Kabbalah
4. The Dogmatic Kabbalah

The *Practical Kabbalah* is concerned with talismanic and ritual magic.

The *Literal Kabbalah* is divided into three parts: Gematria, Notarikon, and Temura.

The *Unwritten Kabbalah* is the part of the esoteric knowledge that is transmitted orally and had never been put into writing until recent times. It is closely linked with the Practical Kabbalah.

The *Dogmatic Kabbalah* may be classified also as the "written Kabbalah," and comprises the various works we have discussed, and others not mentioned because of their obscurity.

The Kabbalah is a philosophical and theosophical system that was originally designed to answer man's eternal questions on the nature of God and of the universe, and the ultimate destiny of mankind. As a practical system, it is based on the numerical correspondences between the various aspects of human life and the universal laws.

The correspondences between allied subjects is found by means of the three divisions of the Literal Kabbalah, especially Gematria. When a Kabbalist wishes to know the intrinsic nature of anything, he finds the numerical value of the name of the subject of his interest by substituting each letter of the name for its corresponding numerical value according to the Hebrew alphabet. By the laws of numerology he then reduces the resultant sum to one of the archetypal numbers, 1-9. For example, if the resulting sum equals 4 2 4, he adds $4+2+4$, which equals 10, which is the same as $1+0=1$. The nature of the subject, then, is to be found in the esoteric properties of archetypal number 1. The essence of any of the numbers may be ascertained by means of the correspondences of the Hebrew alphabet, the Tree of Life, as well as through astrology, alchemy, and various other allied systems.

The law of correspondences is such an important part of the Kabbalah that hidden meanings are found by Kabbalists in words of similar construction. An interesting example is the word "dam," which means blood in Hebrew. This word is "hidden" in the name Adam, which means man. The Kabbalists therefore see a distinct correlation in the union of *dam* and the letter Aleph(A), which is the principle of life and death, the "spark" of creation. They see in the union of A and *dam*, which results in Adam, a blood pact between mankind and the Deity.

From the preceding example we see that the symbolism of blood in the relations between man and God is very significant. This is the reason why men have always offered blood sacrifices to the Divine Being. In Hebrew tradition, all the covenants between the Hebrews and IHVH were ratified with a blood sacrifice, notably circumcision.

Water is seen by the Kabbalist as the potential seed of blood, capable of transformation into that precious life symbol.

According to the Scriptures, Moses changed the waters of the Nile River into blood, and thousands of years later, Jesus changed water into wine at the wedding in Canaan. The correlation between wine and blood is well-known. Jesus himself, who is recognized in the esoteric tradition as a master Kabbalist, made this fact obvious during the Last Supper, when he filled a goblet with wine and offered it to his disciples, saying, "Drink ye all of it. For this is my blood of the new testament, which is shed for many for the remission of sins." (Matthew 26:27-28) This "blood sacrifice" is still enacted in the Catholic "sacrifice" of the mass. During the ceremony the officiating priest presents to the congregation a goblet filled with wine and repeats the words of Jesus, "Drink, for this is my blood . . ."

Animal sacrifices also serve to achieve union with God. When an animal offering was made by the priests at the time of the temple, only the fat and certain organs of its body were burned at the altar. By burning the flesh and the fat of the animal the powers of the World of Action were bound. The spirit within the body of the animal bound the angels in the World of Formation. The "higher spirit" bound the archangels of the World of Creation. And the priest's intention bound the World of Emanation. Thus through the act of sacrifice, the Divine essence of the Four Kabbalistic Worlds was united. The Infinite Light would then bestow some of His Light to the World of Emanation, and from there the light would shine to the other worlds, including the World of Action, which is man.

Kabbalistic tradition teaches that prayer and the observance of the Divine precepts serve the same function as the ancient sacrifices. The reason why prayers and sacrifice achieve the binding of the Four Worlds may be explained as follows.

As we have already seen, the World of Emanation is the origin of the other three worlds. Kabbalah teaches that God willed that a portion of His Light, known as "sparks" of the World of Emanation, be sent into "exile" and caused to descend to the World of Action, where they are "clothed in matter" so that man may have the opportunity of redeeming them, causing the sparks to return to their source. The aim of creation is that all the essence that issued from the Infinite Light shall return whence it came. Thus when man, by means of prayer or sacrifices and the observance of the precepts, causes the sparks to return to their source, great "love and joy" are awakened in the higher worlds, and by virtue of this love and joy the Four Worlds are united. This is known as the raising of M'N by man, who then gets M'D (the bestowal of Infinite Light) as a reward. M'N means "mayin nukvah," and represents the "waters" of the feminine or passive principle. M'D stands for "mayin dchurin," the "waters" of the masculine or active principle. The great "love and joy" that result from the union of the sparks (the feminine principle) with the Infinite Light (the masculine principle) is analogous to the pleasure resulting from the sexual union between man and woman, on a higher, cosmic plane.

According to the Kabbalistic doctrine, man's soul stems from God, for it originates in the World of Emanation, which is all purity. Through the original fall of Adam, the soul of man was polluted by the evil spirit, symbolized by the serpent in paradise. God stripped the serpent of its skin, which represented its power for evil. With this skin, He fashioned "garments" for Adam and his wife. "Unto Adam also and to his wife did the Lord God make coats of skins, and clothed them." (Genesis 3:21) The "coats of skin" symbolize the corrupt, material nature of man. The power of man, however, is similar to the power of angels. "It is a Godly spirit which shines in man to help him, when he repents, to divest himself of his own evil, thus to remove this alien garment in which he was dressed because of Adam's sin." For this purpose, from the World of Emanation are extended 613 channels through which the Divine Light is either bestowed on man or withdrawn from him. The 613 channels are also used to "supervise" man's actions in the material world. They are the origin of the 613 precepts of the Torah, which are divided into 248 positive and 365 prohibitive commandments. The body, which is formed after the imprint of the soul, is also composed of 248 organs or limbs and 365 veins. The 248 positive precepts are so many "gates" in the pillar or source of Mercy, while the 365 prohibitive precepts are the same number of gates in the pillar or source of Judgment. When man performs a positive precept, one of the gates in the pillar of Mercy opens and the Light of the Infinite shines upon the World of Emanation, and thence to the other three worlds. Conversely, when man trespasses against a prohibitive commandment, he causes one of the gates of the pillar of Judgment to open, allowing the evil powers to seize hold of Judgment and "visit punishment upon the world."

As we have already seen, the feminine principle or Divine Presence is known in Kabbalah as the Shekinah. By Divine decree the Shekinah was sent into "exile" to abide with man, until that time when he purifies himself.

When the Shekinah is in Her full glory, she manifests from Her source, which is the World of Emanation, bestowing Her light on man through the 613 channels or precepts. When She is in exile, however, Her light is diminished by prearranged order. The restoration of Her full light can only come through the perfect observation of the 613 precepts.

During Her exile, the Shekinah manifests Herself where the shells or evil spirits abide (Qlippoth). When the diminished light of the Shekinah radiates through the shells, the light reflects on man very dimly, for the shells surround the light, appropriating most of it for themselves. This causes everything in the material world to become defective, so that Judgment increases and gains power over Mercy. This is the reason why there is not enough love and harmony in the world, and in contrast, there is so much sorrow and strife.

When man, by his good actions, purifies himself, the light of the Shekinah is restored and She then bestows Her bounty of light upon man's soul.

The sages tell us that truth, "Emet," is the Maker's "signature." Creation is in principle the "blueprint" of the Creator's wisdom and greatness. Genesis tells us that man appeared last at the time of Creation, the same as a signature at the end of a letter or decree. The numerical value of Adam (man) is nine, the same as Emet (truth). Thus, by Kabbalistic correspondence, they are one and the same.

Tradition asserts that Kabbalah is total truth. Therefore, if in essence man is also truth, it follows logically that the Kabbalistic truths may be found in man. Kabbalah, then, must provide the answers to all the questions that man has asked from his beginnings about his origin and the purpose of his existence. According to Kabbalists, since the Kabbalah is a synthesis of man, it must also embody all the studies known to man, such as biology, chemistry, philosophy, psychology, astronomy, medicine, and so on. The eminent French scholar and Kabbalist, Adolf Franck, said that Kabbalah is the only system known to man that explains the concept of God and the universe both mystically and scientifically.

According to English Kabbalist, S. L. MacGregor Mathers, the principal doctrines of the Kabbalah are concerned with providing a solution for the following problems:

1. The Supreme Being, His nature and attributes
2. The Cosmogony
3. The creation of angels and man
4. The destiny of man and angels
5. The nature of the soul
6. The nature of angels, demons, and elementals
7. The import of the revealed Law
8. The transcendental symbolism of numerals
9. The peculiar mysteries contained in the Hebrew letters
10. The equilibrium of contraries

The Kabbalah teaches that the manifestation of the deity may be expressed in five phases as follows:

1. Source or Seed—The Ain Soph Aur or Adam Kadmon
2. Root—World of Emanation or Atziluth

3. Tree—World of Creation or Briah
4. Branch—World of Formation or Yetzirah
5. Fruit—World of Action or Assiah

Rabbi L. I. Krakovsky, in his work, *Kabbalah, The Light of Redemption,* states that each phase in this allegory is

> the root or source of the phases that follow it. Thus for instance the branch is the source for the fruit, that is, the World of Action; the tree is source to the branches and fruit, thus the World of Creation is the source for both the Worlds of Formation and Action; the root of the tree is source to the tree, branches, and fruit, thus the World of Emanation is source to the Worlds of Creation, Formation, and Action; and lastly, the seed is source for root, tree, branches, and fruit, thus Adam Kadmon is the origin of the Worlds of Emanation, Creation, Formation, and Action.

These five phases form a schema of the Tree of Life, which is the essence of the Kabbalistic teachings.

7 The Tree of Life

Etz Hayim, the Tree of Life, is a glyph, a composite symbol that represents both the Heavenly Man, Adam Kadmon, conceived as the macrocosmus, and man in the material world, seen as the microcosmus. It resembles, in essence, Yggdrasil, the mythological tree of Scandinavians.*

The Tree of Life (Figure 3) is composed of ten spheres known as "sephiroth" (sephira is the singular form). The spheres are interconnected by lines that are called "paths." There are twenty-two paths, which represent the twenty-two letters of the Hebrew alphabet. In Kabbalah the ten sephiroth and the twenty-two paths are known as the thirty-two Paths of Wisdom. The sephiroth are different stages of manifestation of the Infinite Light, and thus of evolution. The paths are phases of "subjective consciousness" by means of which the soul becomes aware of cosmic manifestation.

The sephiroth are known as "numerical emanations," and are representative of the abstract forms of numbers one to ten. Each sephira symbolizes a development and an attitude of the Deity, as well as of man.

The ten sephiroth are also called the Ten Holy Emana-

*See also S. M. L. MacGregor Mathers. *The Kabbalah Unveiled.* New York, 1971.

tions, and are representative of the abstract forms of numbers one to ten. Each sephira symbolizes a development and an attitude of the Deity, as well as of man.

The ten sephiroth are also called the Ten Holy Emanations, and are divided into three columns or "pillars." (See Fig. 1.) The right-hand column is the Pillar of Mercy, to which is ascribed the male-active potency. The left-hand column is the Pillar of Judgment or Severity, to which is ascribed the female-passive principle. The Middle Pillar or Pillar of Mildness or Equilibrium is the harmonizing factor that blends and unites the Pillar of Mercy and the Pillar of Judgment.

From the preceding can be seen that the sephiroth on the right-hand column or Pillar of Mercy have masculine-positive qualities, while those on the left-hand column or Pillar of Judgment have feminine-negative properties. The sephiroth that form the Middle Pillar are transmitters or depositories of the other sephiroth, and as such have in them the seeds of both the male and the female potencies. Their essential quality is union, synthesis.

Each of the sephiroth is in a way androgynous or "bisexual" in essence, for it is feminine or receptive to the sephira that precedes it, and masculine or transmissive to the sephira that follows it.

According to an ancient Kabbalistic tradition, the reason why the Deity placed the Pillar of Mildness or Middle Pillar between the Pillar of Mercy and the Pillar of Judgment was to control the outpouring of the positive or negative qualities of each sephira. An analogy may be given of a water faucet from which may flow hot or cold water. One may graduate the water temperature by simply turning the proper handle. When the necessary amount of water has been accumulated, another turn of the handle will halt the flow. The Middle Pillar may be likened to the handle of the water faucet, without which the water would flow uncontrollably, eventually causing a flood. The Pillar of Mercy has the quality of

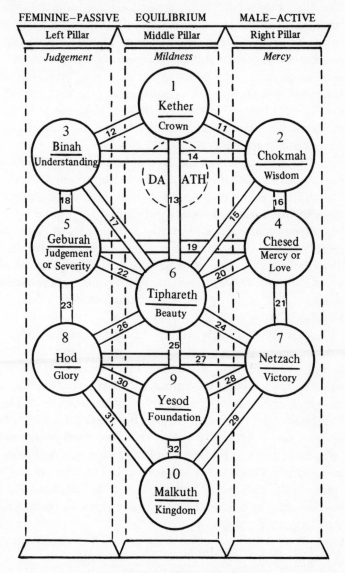

Fig. 3   The Tree of Life and the Paths

"limitless bestowal"; the Pillar of Judgment, on the other hand, is "unlimited restraint." Therefore, if a man by virtue of a good action deserves Mercy, the Pillar of Mercy would bestow of its essence endlessly. However, since there is no man so perfect as to deserve such bounty, the Pillar of Judgment would come into action and neutralize and restrain the Pillar of Mercy. Therefore the Pillar of Mildness or Middle Pillar must act as a mediator to allow only that measure of Mercy that is necessary.

The three pillars of the Tree of Life are comparable to Ida, Shushumna, and Pingala of the Yoga system, where Shushumna is the channel of ascent of kundalini, placed between the male and female potencies of Ida and Pingala. The three pillars may be also likened to Yin and Yang, the female and male principles of Chinese philosophy, with Tao (the way) being analogous to the Middle Pillar. Modern Kabbalists, however, see the left and the right pillars as positive and negative phases of manifestation, while the Middle Pillar is seen as consciousness.*

As we have already stated, the Tree is seen as both the macrocosmus (the divine essence) and the microcosmus (man). When one looks at a diagram of the Tree, it is being observed as an objective symbol, and thus, as the macrocosmus. In order to see the Tree as the microcosmus, that is, as a blueprint of man's soul, one must "back into the Tree," so to speak, and project outwardly. The Tree then becomes a subjective symbol, for one is *in* it, the same as a figure in a photograph. When the Tree is seen as the microcosmus, the order of the columns is reversed, and the left-hand Pillar becomes the right-hand Pillar and vice versa, the same as in a photographic negative.

The Ten Holy Emanations

Before the sephiroth were emanated, there was only

---

*See Dion Fortune. *The Mystical Qabalah*. London, 1935.

the Infinite Light. According to the Kabbalah, before the present universe was created, "certain primordial worlds" were formed from the Light, but could not subsist as the Light had not yet been "restricted" and expressed as the female and male aspects of the Deity. These ancient pre-Creation worlds are the "kings of Edom," which are mentioned in the Bible. (Genesis 36:31)

As we have already seen, at the time of the restriction of the light, a point of light issued from the Infinite Source, forming the Archetypal Man, Adam Kadmon. This may be likened to a point within a circle. All the ten sephiroth were included in this point of light, or Primordial Point. As we know, although a point is imperceptible and undivisible, nevertheless it has three dimensions. If this were not so, we could not even conceive of it. The three dimensions are length, breadth, and depth. Each of these dimensions is also divided into three parts, beginning, middle, and end. We then have nine parts within this point, with the point itself making the number ten. The point and its nine dimensions are the ten sephiroth before emanation or manifestation was completed.

The three pillars are also encompassed in the Primordial Point, as follows:
1. Breadth—Pillar of Mercy
2. Depth—Pillar of Judgment
3. Length—Pillar of Mildness or Middle Pillar

It must be born in mind that when we speak of such terms as breadth, depth, length, beginning, middle, and end, we are referring to abstract concepts, as varying states of consciousness on different levels, that exist simultaneously in time and space.

From the Primordial Point the ten sephiroth were emanated in succession in the following order:

1. Kether—Crown:
This first sephira is the source of the other nine. To it is

ascribed number 1, which encompasses within itself the other nine numbers of the decimal scale. Number 1 is the "monad" of the numerical symbolic ideas of Pythagoras. It is undivisible, but definable. And since definition projects an image or duplicate of the object defined, we find that by reflection of itself number 1 projects the other numbers. Thus it may be called the "father of all numbers" and a fitting image of the Father of all things.

Among the various titles given to Kether are Concealed of the Concealed, the Vast Countenance, the Primordial Point, the Point within a Circle, Macroprosopos, Ancient of Ancients. The Divine Name ascribed to this sphere is AHIH (Eheieh). Its archangel is Metraton. The angelical order, Chaioth ha Qadesh or Holy Living Creatures. Its correspondence in man is the cranium or skull.

Kether is outside human experience. Its essence cannot be comprehended by the human mind. In this sephira there is no form, but only "pure being" because in it there is no differentiation into a pair of opposites as yet.

The name of God ascribed to Kether is Eheieh, which means Existence. And that is what Kether is, the purest essence of existence, without any form or definition. In order to obtain an adequate concept of this formless state of latent existence, we may visualize it as void, formless, interstellar space, which nevertheless harbors in it all the potentials of life.

Another title given to Kether is The First Swirlings. This implies the activity of the cosmic energy at the time of the creation of the universe. It is a fitting title because from the "first swirlings" sprang the second sephira, which is the first to be differentiated in one of the two modes of existence, male and female.

2. Chokmah—Wisdom:

To this sephira is ascribed the numeral 2. It is a masculine-active potency that is also known as Aba, the Father image, to whom the mother, the third sephira, is united.

Among the titles given to Chokmah are The Supernal Father, Power of Yetzirah, Yod of Tetragrammaton. The Divine Name of this sephira is Jehovah, the archangel is Ratziel, and the angelic order is the Auphanim, or Wheels. Its correspondence in man is the left side of the face. This sphere is identified with the Zodiac.

If we can compare Kether to a point, we can compare Chokmah to a line, which is an extension of the point into space. This straight line or "uplifted rod of power" may be equalized with the phallus, which is one of the esoteric symbols of this sephira. Chokmah is essentially dynamic, for within it is the seed of all creation. Its quality is Wisdom, which implies perfect knowledge and understanding. It is significant that the quality ascribed to the third sephira is understanding.

The phallus as a symbol of this sephira represents the dynamic, positive essence of Chokmah, for maleness is dynamism, just as femaleness is latency or potential force.

3. Binah—Understanding:

To this sephira is assigned the numeral 3. Binah is a feminine-passive potency, which is also called Ama, Mother, and Aima, the Fertile Mother, who is eternally "conjoined with Aba, the Father (Chokmah), for the maintenance of the universe in order." This sephira is also called Marah, the Great Sea, which is a root for Mary, and is known as the Mother of All Living. She is the supernal Mother, the feminine aspect of God, the Elohim. She is seen by Kabbalists as the archetypal womb through which all life comes into manifestation.

Some of the titles given to Binah are Ama, the dark, sterile mother; Aima, the bright, fertile mother; Khorsia, the Throne. The God name of this sephira is Jehovah Elohim, the archangel is Tzaphkiel, and the angelic order is the Aralim, or Thrones. Its correspondence in man is the right side of the face.

Whereas Chokmah is dynamic force, Binah is form, which is the container of force. The first letter of Binah is "Beth," which is the archetypal symbol of all containers.

In Binah and Chokmah we have two polarizing aspects of manifestations, the Supernal Father and Mother, from which the universe sprang. Together, Chokmah and Binah are the Elohim, the Creator Genesis speaks about. They are the two primordial blocks of life, proton and electron, that constitute all aspects of creation. In this first pair of sephiroth lies the key to sex, for they represent the biological opposites, however, do not occur just in "space." They also occur in "time." We see them in the alternating periods in our lives, in the tides of the sea, in our physiological processes, and in international affairs. The alternating currents of activity and passivity, construction and destruction are the interplay of the two eternal opposites. It is interesting to note in this context that one of the symbols of Binah is the planet Saturn, also identified as Kronos, or Time. These cosmic tides are beautifully expressed in Shakespeare's words, "There is a tide in the affairs of men, which taken at the flood leads on to fortune."

While Wisdom is the quality of Chokmah, understanding is the essence of Binah. Wisdom suggests complete and infinite knowledge, while Understanding conveys the impression of the ability to grasp the concepts that are inherent in Wisdom. The Father knows all, but the Mother understands everything.

4. Chesed—Mercy:

To this sephira is ascribed the number 4. Chesed is a masculine potency, emanated from Binah as a result of her union with Chokmah. Chesed is also called Gedulah, which means Greatness or Magnificence. Its quality is Mercy or Love on a higher, cosmic scale.

Among the titles given to Chesed are Gedulah and Majesty. The God name is El, the archangel is Tzadkiel, and the angelic order is the Chasmalim or Brilliant Ones. Its correspondence in man is the left arm, and it is also identified with the planet Jupiter.

Chesed is the first sephira that may be conceived by the human mind, for it is the concretion of the abstract concepts formulated by the three Supernals, Kether, Chokmah, and Binah.

Whereas Chokmah may be likened to the All-knowing Father, the "All-Begetter," Chesed is the loving, protecting father, forgiving and generous.

Between the three supernals and the other seven sephiroth there is a chasm, which is known by Kabbalists as the Abyss. This pit is a demarcation of varying degrees of consciousness. The three supernals symbolize those higher states of consciousness that transcend human awareness. The lower sephiroth function within the realm of ideas and as such are the only ones we can apprehend with our normal consciousness. In order to grasp the abstract essence of the higher sephiroth, we have to cross the gulf of the Abyss which implies leaving the confinement of our personalities, to reach our Higher Self, the great unconscious.

5. Geburah—Strength, Severity:

To this sephira is ascribed the numeral 5. Geburah is a

feminine potency, emanated from Chesed.

The titles given to this sephira are Din, Justice; and Pachad, Fear. The God name is Elohim Gebor, the archangel is Khamael, and the angelic order is the Seraphim or Fiery Serpents. Its correspondence in man is the right arm. It is identifed with the planet Mars.

Geburah is the most forceful and disciplined of the sephiroth. Its force is not an evil force unless its essence overflows from justice into cruelty. This is the symbolism of Mars, which is also the Roman god of war and strife. To Kabbalists, Geburah is essentially a conciliatory force, a restriction of the merciful love of Chesed. Without the strong arm of Geburah the mercies of Chesed would degenerate into folly and cowardice.

Geburah may be likened to fire, which may be used constructively or destructively. Its power for destruction may be curtailed by careful control of the flame. In Geburah we find the element of awe, the "fear of God," which, according to the Scriptures, is necessary for salvation.

6. Tiphareth—Beauty:

To this sephira is ascribed the number 6. Its position is in the middle of the Tree of Life, in the Pillar of Mildness or Equilibrium. It is an emanation of Chesed and Geburah.

The titles given to Tiphareth are Zoar Anpin, the Lesser Countenance; Melekh, the King; Adam; the Son; and the Man. The God name is Jehovah ALoah Va Daath, the archangel is Raphael, and the angelic order is the Malachim or Kings. Its correspondence in man is the breast. It is also identified with the sun.

In Tiphareth we see that by the union of Mercy and Justice (Chesed and Geburah) we obtain Beauty or Clemency, which completes the second triad of the Tree of Life.

Tiphareth is the center of equilibrium of the Tree of Life. As such it is seen as a link, a point of transition. The four sephiroth represent the Higher Self, while Kether is the Divine spark in which is the seed of manifestation. The four lower sephiroth are representative of the personality or lower self.

Two of the symbols ascribed to Tiphareth are a child and a sacrificed god, in which may be seen both the Christ and the Egyptian god, Osiris. In the child we see a beginning that ends in the sacrificed god for the purpose of transformation of the material into the Divine. This aspect of Tiphareth is "the point of transmutation between the planes of force and the planes of form."

Another symbol of this sephira is the sun, the giver of life, which may also be found in the gold of the alchemists.

7. Netzach—Victory:

The numeral ascribed to this sephira is 7. Netzach is a male potency, emanated from Tiphareth.

The title given to Netzach is Firmness. The God name is Jehovah Tzabaoth, the archangel is Haniel, and the angelic order is the Elohim or gods. Its correspondence in man is the hips and legs. It is identified with the planet Venus.

Netzach represents the instincts and the emotions. It is a sphere densely populated with the thought forms of the group mind. Thus it is essentially an illusory plane, where the archetypal ideas have not yet been expressed as forms.

The planet Venus, which is ascribed to Netzach, is also a symbol of the Roman goddess of love. Venus is not a fertility goddess like Ceres or Persephone. She is pure emotion. And the essence of this emotion is never crystallized into form. This may be seen clearly from the fact that the hips and legs which are assigned to this sephira are the seat of the generative organs, but not the generative organs themselves. Netzach, then, represents the instinctive, emotional side of our nature.

8. Hod—Glory:

To this sephira is assigned the number 8. Hod is a feminine potency, emanated from Netzach. The God name of this sephira is Elohim Tzabaoth, the archangel is Michael, and the angelic order is the Ben Elohim or Sons of God. Its correspondence in man is the loins and the legs. It is identified with the planet Mercury.

Hod is the seat of the intellectual powers in man. It is the sphere where the emotions and instincts of Netzach finally take form and come into action. Hod and Netzach must always function together for just as the instinct or emotion cannot be manifested without the creative power of the intellect, the intellect cannot manifest itself without the thought forms that arise out of instinct and emotion.

In the Practical Kabbalah, Hod is the sphere of magic because it is the sephira where forms are created. The practicing Kabbalist uses this sephira to formulate with his mind images of things he wants to attain in the material plane. Since Hod is the seat of the intellect or human mind, any thought forms projected from Netzach into it may be impressed upon the higher consciousness, which will then bring the images thus formed into realization.

9. Yesod—Foundation:

The number ascribed to this sephira is 9. It is located in the Middle Pillar and is a result of the union between

Netzach and Hod. The God name of Yesod is Shaddai El Chai, the Almighty Living God. The archangel is Gabriel and the angelic order is the Kerubim or the Strong. Its correspondence is the reproductive organs. It is identified with the Moon.

Yesod is the seat of intuition in man. It is the sphere of the Astral Light and the receptacle of the emanations of the other sephiroth. According to the Kabbalah the function of Yesod is to purify and "correct" the emanations. Yesod, which is essentially the sphere of the moon, reflects the light of Tiphareth, which is the sphere of the sun. Therefore the light of Yesod-Moon is always in a state of flux and reflux because the amount of sunlight received waxes and wanes in a twenty-eight day cycle.

Since Yesod is the sphere of the moon, it is ruled by the moon goddess, which is seen in her various aspects of Diana, the virgin goddess of the Greeks; Isis, the fertile moon goddess of the Egyptians; and Hecate, the goddess of witchcraft and of childbirth. The reason why the mystical moon is sometimes seen as a virgin and other times as a fertile mother may be found in the rhythmical nature of the moon and of the sex life of the female. The magnetism of all living creatures is affected by these lunar tides. To Yesod is also assigned the element of water. The lunar tides also affect the oceans and the body fluids in man. The magnetic influence of the moon can only operate through the sphere of Yesod.

10. **Malkuth—Kingdom:**
To this sephira is ascribed the number 10. Malkuth is an emanation of Yesod and represents the material world. It is also known as the Queen, the Inferior Mother, the Bride of Macroprosopos and the Shekinah. It is the last of the sephiroth and it is placed in the

Middle Pillar.

Some of the titles given to Malkuth are the Gate of Death, the Gate of the Garden of Eden, the Virgin. The God name is Adonai Ha Aretz, the Archangel is Sandalphon, and the angelic order is the Ashim or Souls of Fire. Its correspondence in man is the feet and the anus. It is also identified with the planet earth and with the four elements.

Malkuth is essentially the sphere of man, of sensation. It is also the only sephira that does not form part of a triad. It is therefore seen by the Kabbalists as a container for the emanations of the other nine sephiroth.

Malkuth is the seat of matter and also of fire, water, air, and earth, the four elements of the ancients. The physicist recognizes three states of matter—solid, liquid, and gas. These three modes of matter correspond to the elements of earth, air, and water, while electricity corresponds to the element of fire. The esotericist classifies all physical phenomena under these four elements in order to understand their nature.

The intrinsic quality of Malkuth is stability, the inertia of matter that is like the sway of a pendulum rhythmically oscillating throughout eternity.

The *Zohar* describes the Infinite Light as a

very expansive sea, for the waters of the sea are themselves without limit or form. It is only when they spread themselves upon the earth that they assume a form. Following is the order of the development of the sephiroth: the source of the sea's water and the water stream that comes therefrom are the first two sephiroth, Crown and Wisdom; a great reservoir is then formed just as if a huge hollow had been dug, and this is called a sea. It is the sephira

Understanding, which is called Marah, the Great Sea. This reservoir is an unfathomable deep which issues seven streams, which are the seven channels or sephiroth: Mercy, Judgment, Beauty, Victory, Glory, Foundation, and Kingdom. The source, the water stream, the sea, and the seven streams make up the ten sephiroth.

The ten sephiroth are classified in five stages or phases, which are known as "worlds." In the beginning, the first ten sephiroth that emanated from the Infinite Light were too powerful and man could not receive illumination from them. It was then necessary for these initial sephiroth to be extended further, veiling their light so that man could receive it. The process had to be repeated four times until the light was sufficiently diffuse for man to partake of the Infinite Light. This resulted in the Four Worlds of the Kabbalists, which we have already discussed. The first world that emanated from the Infinite Light in the form of the Primordial Point was that of Adam Kadmon. The next world that emanated from Adam Kadmon was the World of Emanation of Atziluth, also composed of ten sephiroth, but with dimmer lights. Then came the ten sephiroth that made the World of Formation, Yetzirah, and lastly, the World of Action, Assiah, which is also the world of man.

The distance in degree between the worlds of the sephiroth is carefully stipulated according to Divine decree, by which this order was arranged for the purpose of creation. It is interesting to note that the famous Bode-Titius rule of planetary system, the "distance of each world from the sun is approximately twice the distance of the previous one," almost as if it had been stipulated according to Divine decree.

In each of the five worlds, the World of Adam Kadmon

and the Four Kabbalistic Worlds, the ten sephiroth are divided into three triads, composed of the first nine sephiroth, and the last sephira, Malkuth.

The first triad is formed by the three "Supernals," Kether, Chokmah, and Binah. The Kabbalistic books give many "strange" names to the sephiroth, but each of these titles has a distinct reason for being, for they are in fact precise metaphysical terms of almost scientific accuracy. The actual meaning of Kether in the Hebrew language is Crown. Chokmah means Wisdom and Binah means Understanding. A "crown" is a kingly attribute that is placed on top of the head. The "magical" image associated with Kether is that of a Bearded King seen in profile. This sephira is also known as The Head Which Is Not. In all this symbolism we see distinct correspondences with the human head, which in the world of archetypal ideas represents the highest level of consciousness. Indeed, The Head Which Is Not is a clear image of a superconsciousness that lies outside the realm of human experience and thus cannot be encompassed within the limits of the human brain. It is the Crown that adorns the brow of the Bearded King seen in profile, which is none other than Adam Kadmon, the first manifestation of the Divine Light.

The first outpouring from the Crown, which is Kether, is Wisdom, the absolute, perfect knowledge that is an attribute of this higher consciousness. Chokmah, which is Wisdom, is also the Supernal Father.

From Wisdom springs forth Understanding, which is Binah, the Supernal Mother, the Great Sea. From this symbolism we conceive the idea of the vast waters of interstellar space where worlds were created. We are also reminded that the first manifestation of primordial life, in the form of the first unicellular organism, arose from the waters.

Binah is also known as Ama, the Dark Sterile Mother, and as Aima, the Bright Fertile Mother. As we have already stated, she is also Marah, the Great Sea. Marah is the root of Mary. Thus we have a concept of a virgin (Ama) which becomes a mother (Aima) by the power of the Holy Spirit.

The secret of the transition of Binah from the Dark Sterile Mother (Ama) is in another sephira that lies concealed midway between the sphere of Chokmah and that of Binah. This "hidden" sephira is called Daath, and its meaning is Knowledge. When we refer to the Bible and find that sexual encounters between a man and a woman are described as a man *knowing* a woman, we have a clear "Understanding" of the properties of Daath. An example of this is found in Genesis 4:1, "And Adam knew Eve his wife; and she conceived, and bare Cain, and said, I have gotten a man from the Lord." The position of Daath between the two spheres of Chokmah and Binah, the Supernal Father and the Supernal Mother, makes it obvious that the Kabbalistic "secret" of their union is sex. This Knowledge that is Daath, conceived in the material plane as the sexual union between a male and a female, is what made possible the transition of Binah from virgin (Dark Sterile Mother) to mother (Bright Fertile Mother).

In the archetypal world to which the three Supernals belong, the concept of Daath is not one of sex in the physical sense of the word, but of realization and illumination. It is the union of cosmic opposites for the purpose of manifestation. In the words of modern Kabbalist Dion Fortune, "Daath is the secret of both generation and regeneration, the key to the manifestation of all things through the differentiation into pairs of Opposites and their union in a Third." In the Supernal Triad, Kether, Chokmah, and Binah, we have the key to our cosmogony.

The second Triad is formed by the fourth, fifth, and sixth sephiroth: Chesed (Mercy), Geburah (Judgment), and Tiphareth (Beauty). The union between the Supernal Mother and the Supernal Father by means of Daath gave birth to Mercy, which is also called Love. Thus we see how on the archetypal planes the union of the male and female principles gives rise to that which on the material plane is the most sublime feeling man can experience. Mercy emanates Judgment, which is also known as Strength. Chesed or Mercy is, as we have seen, also a Father image, while Geburah is a Mother image, strong and severe. From this "Strong Love" that is the union of Chesed and Geburah is born Tiphareth or Beauty, the sixth sephira, which is also known as The Son, and has the image of a child as one of its symbols. Tiphareth is situated in the Middle Pillar, directly underneath the sphere of Daath. We see therefore how through the realization that is Daath, the Supernal Mother, Binah, "gave birth" to Chesed, Mercy or Love, which then united with Geburah, Strength, to "give birth" to Tiphareth, The Son. This triad symbolizes the evolution of ideas conceived in the archetypal matrix of the Three Supernals.

The third triad is composed of the seventh, eighth, and ninth sephiroth: Netzach (Victory), Hod (Glory), and Yesod (Foundation). Netzach is a male potency that reflects the pure love of Mercy on a lower plane, that of emotions and instincts. Thus the Divine love that was emitted from Binah into Chesed becomes sexual desire in Netzach. The emotions that are the essence of this sephira have not yet been manifested into action; that may be likened to the instinctual drives in man, before they are channeled into form. In Netzach we find all the basic instincts and emotions latent in man, from the instinct of preservation to ambition and raw passion. But before there tenuous thought forms may find expression, Netzach must emanate and then fuse with Hod (Glory), which is the seat of intellectual endeavor and the will of man. The union of the will of Hod and the emotions of Netzach give rise to the next sephira, Yesod, which is represented by the sexual organs in man. Through Hod, therefore, the sexual desires latent in Netzach find actual expression and form in a physical vehicle. They are then "realized." And since Yesod is also placed in the Middle Pillar, the same as Daath, we see how the sephira of Foundation is really the realization of Daath on a lower plane. But Yesod is also seen as the sphere of the Moon and of intuition. Therefore it is still not realization on a physical plane, but on a mental level. This triad is seen by Kabbalists as the Astral World, where all forms are composed of a plastic, etheric substance, which acts like a matrix to the physical world. All the actions that take place in the material world must first be "shaped" and actualized in the Astral World. This is the action of the union of Hod and Netzach.

Below the third and last triad is the lone sphere of Malkuth, which represents the material world. The restriction of the Infinite Light being completed, the nether world of form and action comes into manifestation. Here is the seat of the four elements of the alchemists—fire, water, air, and earth—which must not be conceived as their material counterparts, but rather as cosmic essence brought into differentiation. It was to the "qualities" of the elements that the ancients referred and not to the elements themselves. Thus we see in the element of fire the quality of expansion, and also of heat, which is evident in the material world in the physical phenomena of combustion, digestion, and oxidation. The quality of the element of water is contraction, which is seen in muscular action and in the solidification of water into ice. The quality of the element of air is locomotion, movability, which does not need to be exemplified. And lastly, the quality of the element of earth is inertia, cohesion, which are qualities of solid matter.

The qualities of expansion, concentration, locomotion, or movement and cohesion (union) are all external manifestations of the World of Action, Malkuth. They can be seen not just in physical phenomena but also in human relations and in international affairs. The interplay of the

Fig 4 Kabbalistic Square

The square connotes the four sides of the world. The upper side is "East," the lower side is "West," the right side is "South" and the left side is "North." The four diagonal lines causes the admixture of the diverse climates to each side of the world. These are the four basic elements: Air is East, earth is West, fire is South and water is North. Warmth and dryness is the nature of the fire element. Moisture and coldness is the nature of the water element. Because the East and West sides are connected with the South and North sides, it follows that East and West partake of a double climate due to being linked to the South and the North sides of the world. East, which is air, has the warmth of the South and moisture of the North, therefore its climate is warm and moist. The warmth is derived from the fire element of the South and its moisture from the water element of the North. The West side, which is earth, gets its dryness from the fire—South, and its coldness from the water—North. Therefore, the nature of the earth is cold and dry.

Fig 5 The Star of David

forces of expansion and contraction (fire and water) can be seen in the two triangles that form the Star of David. The upward-pointing triangle symbolizes fire, while the downward-pointing triangle represents water. Tradition teaches that King David was a master Kabbalist, and this symbol is strongly indicative that indeed he was. For by means of the proper interaction of strength (Fire) and restraint (Water), so visually expressed in the Star of David, he was able to unify Israel after generations of strife and dissolution.

In Malkuth, then, we see the materialization of the intangible and abstract concepts that originate in the higher spheres. It is in this last sephira, also known as Kingdom, that the Bearded King of Kether reigns in all His Glory. It was to this Kingdom (Malkuth) that Jesus referred in the last part of the Lord's Prayer (Matthew 6:13), "For thine is the Kingdom (Malkuth), and the Power (Netzach), and the Glory (Hod), forever, Amen." It is obvious that only a consummate Kabbalist could have composed this prayer.

The ten sephiroth are also divided by Kabbalists into Arik Anpin (the Vast Countenance), Zaur Anpin (the Lesser Countenance), and the Bride of Microprosopos. Arik Anpin, which is also known as Macroprosopos, is formed by the Three Supernals, Kether, Chokmah, and Binah. Zaur Anpin, or Microprosopos, is composed of Chesed, Geburah, Tiphareth, Netzach, Hod, and Yesod. The Bride of Microprosopos is the sephira Malkuth, which is sometimes referred to as the Queen, or the Inferior Mother. Microprosopos is called also Melech, or the King.

The Tree of Life in the Four Worlds

As we have already discussed, the ten sephiroth that form the Tree of Life were emanated from the Infinite Light into the Primordial World of Adam Kadmon and thence to the Four Worlds of the Kabbalists. The sephira Kingdom (Malkuth), which is the densest of the sephiroth, and in

TABLE 3
The Divine Names and the Tree of Life

Sephira	God Name	Archangel	Order of Angels
1. Kether	Eheieh	Metatron	Chaioth ha Qadesh
2. Chokmah	Jehovah	Ratziel	Auphanim
3. Binah	Jehovah Elohim	Tzaphkiel	Aralim
4. Chesed	El	Tzadkiel	Chasmalim
5. Geburah	Elohim Gebor	Khamael	Seraphim
6. Tiphareth	Jehovah Aloah va Daath	Raphael	Malachim
7. Netzach	Jehovah Tzabaoth	Haniel	Elohim
8. Hod	Elohim Tzabaoth	Michael	Beni Elohim
9. Yesod	Shaddai el Chai	Gabriel	Kerubim
10. Malkuth	Adonai Ha Aretz	Sandalphon	Ashim

which the Divine Light is more restricted, is the source for each of the next worlds. Thus we see that the sephira Kingdom of Adam Kadmon emanated the ten sephiroth of the World of Emanation, and the sephira Kingdom of the World of Emanation issued the ten sephiroth of the World of Creation, and so on, until the world of Action was emanated. In the World of Emanation God acts directly; in the World of Creation He acts through the archangels, in the World of Formation He acts through the angels, and in the World of Action He acts through the elemental forces of Nature.

The Four Worlds, therefore, form a vast system of classification that expresses all the aspects of the Cosmic

Essence at any level. (See Table 3.)

The most important divisions that are classified within the Four Worlds are the four elements of the alchemists, the four seasons, and the four astrological triplicities. There is also a color scale (see Table 4) assigned to each sephira in each of the Four Worlds, which is of great significance in the practical Kabbalah. Each of the worlds falls under the supervision of one of the letters of the Tetragrammaton, IHVH, as follows: The first letter, I, is the World of Emanation; the second letter, H, is the World of Creation; V stands for the World of Formation; and the last letter, H, is the World of Action.

The Tetragrammaton, also known as Jehovah, is the God name assigned to the second sephira, Chokmah. The first sephira, Kether, is under the presidency of another four-letter name: Eheieh (AHIH). Through the symbolism of the names we see how AHIH, which is that aspect of God that is latent force, as yet unmanifested, transmutes Itself into IHVH by changing Its first and third letters from A (Aleph) to I (Yod) and from I(Yod) to V (Vau). As we have seen in the analysis of the twenty-two letters of the Hebrew alphabet, Aleph is the dual principle that represents life and death, existence; and indeed, existence is the meaning of the name AHIH. Yod, on the other hand, is the opposite of Aleph; it is continuity, the manifestation of existence. Thus in the first transmutation, the Cosmic Energy is transformed from pure existence into continuous existence, steady-state. The second transmutation involves the exchange of a Yod (I) to a Vau (V). As we have seen, Vau is the archetype of all fertilizing substances, it is the plastic substance whence the universe sprang. Through this transmutation, AHIH, pure being, is transformed into IHVH, which is the vehicle of existence. In this transformation lies the essence of the Kabbalistic teaching.

Tetragrammaton, then, is the continuous (I) pulsation

of cosmic energy (H) evolving (V) into the created universe (H). According to astrophysics, these were the conditions existing at the time of the "big-bang theory."

The Tetragrammaton and the Four Worlds are also associated with the four kerubim of Ezekiel's vision and the biblical revelation of St. John the Divine. Again, there is a correlation with the four elements and the astrological triplicities, as follows:

Letter	Kerubim	Element	Zodiacal Sign	World
I	Man Image	Air	Aquarius	Emanation
H	Lion	Fire	Leo	Creation
V	Eagle	Water	Scorpio	Formation
H	Bull	Earth	Taurus	Action

From the preceding we see that in order to know the qualities of any of the sephiroth of the Tree of Life, it is necessary to know its correspondences in all the Four Worlds. This is no mean task when we consider the vastness of the classification system that is the Kabbalah.

The Paths

According to the *Sepher Yetzirah* there are thirty-two Paths of Wisdom, but in reality, there are only twenty-two paths. The other ten are ascribed to the ten sephiroth for reasons best known to the ancient Kabbalists.

The twenty-two Paths correspond to the twenty-two letters of the Hebrew alphabet, but according to the Practical Kabbalah they are also assigned to the twelve signs of the Zodiac, the seven planets, and the four elements. The element of earth, however, is usually assigned to the sephira Malkuth, so that the remaining twenty-two symbols correspond exactly to the twenty-two Paths. These subtle discrepancies in Kabbalistic symbolism are seen by many as intended "blinds" designed by the ancient Kabbalists to misguide the profane.

As we have already seen, the Paths are connecting lines between the various sephiroth. The best description of the Paths, in the opinion of this writer, is that of Johannes Stephanus Rittangelius (1642), translated from its original Hebrew by W. Wynn Westcott. We can do no better than cite it here. We will omit the first ten paths, since, as we have stated, they are assigned to the ten sephiroth. Following, then, are the descriptions of the twenty-two Paths, from eleven to thirty-two, according to Rittangelius:

11th Path—(connecting Kether and Chokmah)
"The Eleventh Path is the Scintillating Intelligence, because it is the essence of that curtain which is placed close to the order of the disposition, and this is a special dignity given to it that it may be able to stand before the Face of the Cause of Causes."

12th Path—(connecting Kether and Binah)
"The Twelfth Path is the Intelligence of Transparency because it is that species of Magnificence called *Chazchazit* (vision), which is named the place whence issues those seeing in apparitions. (That is, the prophecies by seers in a vision.)"

13th Path—(connecting Kether and Tiphareth)
"The Thirteenth Path is named the Uniting Intelligence, and is so called because it is itself the Essence of Glory. It is the consummation of the Truth of individual spiritual things."

14th Path—(connecting Binah and Chokmah)
"The Fourteenth Path is the Illuminating Intelligence, and is so called because it is that *Chasmal* (scintillating flame) which is the founder of the concealed and fundamental ideas of holiness and of their stages of preparation."

15th Path—(connecting Chokmah and Tiphareth)
"The Fifteenth Path is the Constituting Intelligence, so

called because it constitutes the substance of creation in pure darkness, and men have spoken of these contemplations; it is that darkness spoken of in Scripture, Job 38:9, 'and thick darkness a swaddling band for it.' "

16th Path—(connecting Chokmah and Chesed)
"The Sixteenth Path is the Triumphal or Eternal Intelligence, so called because it is the pleasure of the Glory, beyond which is no Glory like to it, and it is called also the Paradise prepared for the Righteous."

17th Path—(connecting Binah and Tiphareth)
"The Seventeenth Path is the Disposing Intelligence, which provides faith to the righteous, and they are clothed with the Holy Spirit by it, and it is called the Foundation of Excellence in the state of higher things."

18th Path—(connecting Binah and Geburah)
"The Eighteenth Path is called the House of Influence (by the greatness of whose abundance the influx of good things upon created beings is increased), and from the midst of the investigation the arcana and hidden senses are drawn forth, which dwell in its shade and which cling to it, from the cause of all causes."

19th Path—(connecting Chesed and Geburah)
"The Nineteenth Path is the Intelligence of all the activities of the spiritual beings, and is so called because of the affluence diffused by it from the most high blessing and most exalted sublime glory."

20th Path—(connecting Chesed and Tiphareth)
"The Twentieth Path is the Intelligence of Will, and is so called because it is the means of preparation of all and each created being, and by this intelligence the existence of the Primordial Wisdom becomes known."

21st Path—(connecting Chesed and Netzach)
"The Twenty-first Path is the Intelligence of Conciliation, and is so called because it receives the divine

influence which flows into it from its benediction upon all and each existence."

22nd Path—(connecting Geburah and Tiphareth)

"The Twenty-second Path is the Faithful Intelligence and is so called because by it spiritual virtues are increased, and all dwellers on earth are nearly under its shadow."

23rd Path—(connecting Geburah and Hod)

"The Twenty-third Path is the Stable Intelligence, and it is so called because it has the virtue of consistency among all numerations."

24th Path—(connecting Tiphareth and Netzach)

"The Twenty-fourth Path is the Imaginative Intelligence and it is so called because it gives a likeness to all the similitudes which are created in like manner similar to its harmonius elegancies."

25th Path—(Connecting Tiphareth and Yesod)

"The Twenty-fifth Path is the Intelligence of Probation, or is Tentative, and is so called because it is the primary temptation, by which the Creator trieth all righteous persons."

26th Path—(connecting Tiphareth and Hod)

"The Twenty-sixth Path is called the Renovating Intelligence because the Holy God renews it by all the changing things which are renewed by the creation of the world."

27th Path—(connecting Netzach and Hod)

"The Twenty-seventh Path is the Exciting Intelligence and it is so called because through it is consummated the nature of every existent being under the orb of the Sun, in perfection."

28th Path—(connecting Netzach and Yesod)

The Twenty-eighth Path is not described in this translation.

29th Path—(connecting Netzach and Malkuth)

"The Twenty-ninth Path is the Corporeal Intelligence, so called because it forms every body which is formed beneath the whole set of worlds and the increment of them."

30th Path—(connecting Hod and Yesod)

"The Thirtieth Path is the Collecting Intelligence, and is so called because Astrologers deduce from it the judgement of the stars, and of the celestial signs, and the perfections of their science, according to the rules of their resolutions."

31st Path—(connecting Hod and Malkuth)

"The Thirty-first Path is the Perpetual Intelligence: but why is it so called? Because it regulates the motions of the Sun and Moon in their proper order, each in an orbit convenient for it."

32nd Path—(connecting Yesod and Malkuth)

"The Thirty-second Path is the Administrative Intelligence and it is so called because it directs and associates in all their operations the seven planets, even all of them in their own due course."

The Qliphoth

According to Kabbalistic tradition, when the cosmic energy was overflowing from Kether (the first sephira) to form Chokmah, its force was not fully stabilized, for it still lacked form and direction. From this surplus of excess energy, the adverse sephiroth or Qliphoth were evolved. (Qliphah is the singular form of the noun, and it means a woman of easy virtue, a harlot.)

The Qliphoth, then, are a group of ten sephiroth, unbalanced and chaotic, that are the complete opposites of the harmonious forces that form the Tree of Life. As such, they are termed evil, and are the infernal regions mentioned in the Bible. They are not independent principles in the cosmic scale, but the "unbalanced and destructive aspects" of the spheres of the Tree of Life. Therefore, there are two Trees, and they both must be taken into consideration for the proper understanding of the Kabbalistic doctrine. For wherever there is a virtue or positive sephira, there is a corresponding vice, which is symbolized by the adverse Qliphath.

The two Trees, Sephirotic and Qliphotic, are often represented as if the infernal spheres, which are on the reverse side of the Divine ones, like the opposite side of a coin, were a reflection of the Tree of Life, from a mirror placed at its base. In this concept, the Qliphoth seem to extend downward from the sphere of Malkuth, where they abut. Malkuth, according to tradition, is a "fallen sephira," for it was separated from the rest of the Tree by Adam's Fall. Thus the material world rests upon the top of the infernal world of "shells." That is the reason why their influence is felt so strongly in human affairs.

The demons of the Qliphoth are the most unbalanced and chaotic of all principles. The first two spheres of the Qliphotic Tree, corresponding inversely to Kether and Chokmah, are void and disorganized, while the third sphere is known as "the abode of darkness." The reigning prince of the Qliphoth is Samael, "the angel of poison and death." He corresponds to the sphere of Crown, Kether, and also answers by the name of Satan. His wife, Isheh Zenunim, is the harlot, and corresponds to the sphere of Chokmah. From their union springs the Beast, Chiva, often represented by Satanists as a goat with female breasts. Together, they form the infernal trinity in direct opposition to the Three Supernals. Below the first demonic triad are the seven hells, which are occupied by cohorts of devils who represent all the vices and crimes of humanity, and whose infernal duties are to torture and inflict punishment on those who abandon themselves to those vices.

The pentagram, or five-pointed star, is one of the symbols used to indicate the harmonious (Sephiroth) or chaotic (Qliphoth) forces of the Cosmos. The five points of the pentagram symbolize the four elements of the ancients, plus a fifth element, which is known as "akasha" or ether.

Fig 6 The Pentagrams

This fifth element is not to be confused with the material concept of ether. It is a very tenuous "substance" which is found only in the abstract worlds. Just as the four elements are assigned to the Four Worlds of the Kabbalists, this fifth element is ascribed to the archetypal world of Adam Kadmon. When the pentagram is used to symbolize the harmonizing forces of the elements in the Tree of Life, the glyph is presented with one point uppermost and two points extending on either side, like a man standing with open arms, absorbing into his soul the bounties of the Divine Light. The two lower points represent the figure's spread legs. The Tetragrammation, or IHVH, is also hidden in the pentagram, as follows: the upper point of the Yod (I) corresponds to the upper point of the pentagram, or the World of Adam Kadmon; the body of the Yod corresponds to the right point of the star and the World of Emanation; the letter He (H) corresponds to the right-hand "Leg" of the pentagram and to the World of Creation; the letter Vau (V) corresponds to the left-hand "leg" and to the World of Formation, while the last letter He (H) corresponds to the left point of the pentagram and to the World of Action.

When the position of the pentagram is reversed, the two lower points, which form the "legs" of the glyph, are placed uppermost. The pentagram then resembles the head of a goat, where the two points form the horns, the points protruding on the sides are the ears and the lower point forms a beard. This is a common symbol among Satanists, by means of which they contact the adverse Qliphoth, the infernal habitations of the demonic hordes.

From the preceding discussion we see that the Qliphoth are the result of the unbalanced surplus of energy that gave rise to the sephiroth of the Tree of Life. This unbalanced force forms the center around which revolve all the evil thought forms of mankind. It is therefore the source as well as the consequence of all man's evil thoughts and actions. Because the Qliphoth were evolved from an overflow of cosmic energy, their influence is directly related to excess in any form. Thus, an excess of love gives rise to jealousy, an excess in sexual desire gives rise to lust, an excess of worldly ambition leads to avarice, until all the gamut of human qualities and inspirations are debased and vilified.

The infernal Qliphoth is seen by Kabbalists as the monster Leviathan, the serpent that rears its ugly head behind the shoulders of the Bride of Microprosopos, the Queen, Malkuth, also known as the World of Men.

The Practical Kabbalah

The Practical Kabbalah, with its array of rituals and magical ceremonies, will be discussed in some detail in Part II of this book. In that section we will attempt to elucidate the intricacies of the magical realms of the Kabbalah. Here we will confine ourselves to a general discussion of the magical aspects of the Kabbalistic doctrine, and how they are applied by the Kabbalists in order to achieve results on the material planes.

Something must be said at this juncture about the "ascent" or "descent" or power through the various spheres of the Tree of Life. As we have already seen, the Tree of Life is the essence of the Kabbalah. It is also the working tool of the practicing Kabbalist. To elucidate this point further, let us look into the two methods that are used by the Kabbalists to "draw power" from the Tree.

The first method that we will discuss is used only by mystics, or by those who wish to acquire illumination, or, which is the same thing, to establish a perfect equilibrium within their personalities and a total harmony with the soul of the universe. This method is known as "the Path of the Arrow, which is shot from the Bow of Promise, Quesheth, the rainbow of astral colors that spreads like a halo behind Yesod."* This system does not confer any magical powers, and is used by the mystic to rise from the material world to the higher planes of exalted consciousness. It is called the Path of the Arrow because it moves in a straight line from Malkuth, through Yesod and Tiphareth, traversing Daath and the Abyss, directly into Kether. The process is conducted chiefly through meditation upon the various symbols associated with the sephiroth just mentioned, which are all placed upon the Middle Pillar. There are no worldly ambitions in the hearts of the mystics who follow this Path, only the desire to unite with their Higher Selves and to blend with the soul of Nature. The rewards of this Path are, as we have said, illumination, and the perfect equilibrium of the personality.

The second method is used by practicing Kabbalists as

---

*See Dion Fortune. *The Mystical Qabalah*. London, 1935.

a magical system. It is known as the Flash of Lightning, and it is also likened to the coils of a serpent that extend in zig zag throughout the tree, traversing its whole length, sephira by sephira. Contrary to the Path of the Arrow, which is an ascending Path, the Flash of Lightning is mostly for the "descent of power." In order to bring down power the practicing Kabbalist, or magician, must have a perfect knowledge of the Tree of Life and of the correspondences of the various sephiroth. This means he must know the God name assigned to each sephira, as well as the archangels and the angelic orders. He must also be familiar with the various color scales of the Tree, as each of the Four Kabbalistic Worlds has a color scheme assigned to it. For the purpose of magical work, the color scale used is that of the World of Creation, which is known as the "Queen Scale" (see Table 4). The practicing Kabbalist must also know by heart the various magical images and the symbols ascribed to each sephira, because it is by means of these images and symbols that he will attempt to contact the forces represented by the spheres of the Tree. Once he is equipped with this formidable array of magical symbolism, the Kabbalist proceeds to invoke the force that he wants to contact in the tree (see Table 5). The forces in the tree are elemental in nature, they may be likened to a plastic substance with which one can shape and mold different forms. It is the etheric substance known as the akasha. Once the Kabbalist has contacted the sphere he is working with, he proceeds to mold, by means of powerful visualization, the images of the things he wishes to acquire in the material plane. When he has finished doing this, he brings down the force from its place in the Tree to his material level. This last part is the most difficult to accomplish, and is known by occultists as "earthing" the force. If the magician fails to "earth" the force he has contacted, the purpose of the ceremony is nullified and the power invoked is dispersed and returns whence it

TABLE 4 The Color Scales and the Tree of Life in the Four Worlds

Sephiroth	Atziluth (King Scale)	Briah* (Queen Scale)	Yetzirah (Emperor Scale)	Assiah (Empress Scale)
1. Kether	Brilliance	White brilliance	White brilliance	White, flecked gold
2. Chokmah	Light blue	Gray	Iridescent gray	White, flecked with red, blue, yellow
3. Binah	Crimson	Black	Dark brown	Gray, flecked with pink
4. Chesed	Violet	Blue	Purple	Azure, flecked with yellow
5. Geburah	Orange	Red	Scarlet	Red, flecked with black
6. Tiphareth	Rose pink	Yellow	Salmon pink	Amber
7. Netzach	Amber	Green	Yellow green	Olive flecked with gold
8. Hod	Violet	Orange	Brick red	Yellowish black, flecked with white
9. Yesod	Indigo	Violet	Dark purple	Citrine, flecked with azure
10. Malkuth	Yellow	Citrine, olive, russet, black	Citrine, olive, russet, black, flecked with gold	Black, rayed with yellow

*The Briatic or Queen Scale is used by Kabbalists in their magic rituals. For example, if the magician is doing a ritual for love he has to work with the sphere of Netzach, whose color is green in the Briatic scale. That means that the magician should surround himself with the color green during the ritual, and visualize this color vibration around him as he works.

TABLE 5 Correspondences in the Tree of Life

Sephiroth	Planet	Physical Correspondence	Symbols	Magical Image	Virtue	Vice
1. Kether	First swirlings	Cranium	Point, Swastika	Bearded king in profile	Attainment	—
2. Chokmah	Zodiac	Left side of face	Phallus, straight line	Bearded male	Devotion	—
3. Binah	Saturn	Right side of face	Cup, Female Sex Organs	A matron	Silence	Avarice
4. Chesed	Jupiter	Left arm	Orb, Tetrahedron	Crowned and Throned King	Obedience	Tyranny
5. Geburah	Mars	Right arm	Pentagon, Sword	Warrior in his chariot	Courage	Destruction
6. Tiphareth	Sun	Breast	Cube	Majestic King, a Child	Devotion to the Great work	Pride
7. Netzach	Venus	Loins, Hips, Legs	Rose, Lamp and Girdle	Lovely naked woman	Unselfishness	Lust
8. Hod	Mercury	Loins, Legs	Names, Versicles and Apron	Hermaphrodite	Truthfulness	Dishonesty
9. Yesod	Moon	Reproductive	Perfumes, Sandals	Beautiful naked man	Independence	Idleness
10. Malkuth	Earth, 4 elements	Feet, Anus	Equal-armed Cross	Young Woman, crowned and throned	Discrimination	Inertia

came. If the Kabbalist is working with a positive force for a noble purpose, or if the ritual is intended to benefit him or someone else, without harming anyone, there is nothing to fear, for the force invoked is a pure, Divine Essence. If, however, he is laboring for the purpose to harm someone or to cause any form of destruction, the force that he has failed to "earth," which is Qliphotic in principle, can spread its evil tentacles around him and can easily destroy him.

One of the things that the practicing Kabbalist must bear in mind when he is doing practical work on the Tree is that the sephiroth work in pairs. Thus if he wishes to contact the sphere of Netzach on the right-hand pillar, he must remember to establish a link with the sphere of Hod, on the left-hand pillar. This way he is working with a pair of oposities, which is, as we have seen, the principle upon which the universe was created. If he fails to do this, he throws the entire Tree out of balance, giving rise to the chaotic forces of the Qliphoth, which are always lurking in the background of every magical ceremony.

The reason why the magical system of the Practical Kabbalah is known as the "Flash of Lightning" is that the Sephiroth emanate from each other in a zig-zag form (see Fig 3, p. 75).

Another system that uses the Flash of Lightning as a working method is that known by occultists as "rising on the planes." By means of this system the Kabbalist elevates his consciousness by contacting the various sephiroth. For this purpose he "travels astrally" over the different Paths that connect the sephiroth.

As a practical system the Tree of Life is of immense value, not only to the magician, but also to anyone who desires to harmonize the cosmic forces that form the structure of his soul. For we must remember that each sephira represents the purest essence of a human quality or virtue. If we absorb the Tree into our souls, we are harmonizing ourselves with the Divine aspects of these qualities and virtues. This is the highest and purest aim of practical work on the Tree of Life.

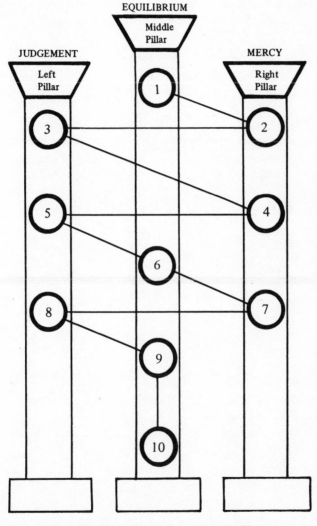

Fig. 7   The Flash of Lightning or Descent of Power

8 The Nature of the Soul

The Soul of Man

Before man's soul was manifested in the World of Action, it was in a state of nonexistence ("oyin"). That is, it was blended with the Infinite Light. After the Light became "restricted," and issued the World of Emanation, the soul assumed the form of "yesh meoyim," which is existence from nonexistence. This means that the soul is in reality a part of God, for it originates in the Infinite Light.

According to the Kabbalistic doctrine, the nature of the soul is fivefold. The first two divisions are archetypal in essence and thus transcend man's ability to understand or even to conceive of them. They are called Yechida and Chaya and correspond respectively to the World of Adam Kadmon and the World of Emanation. The next three divisions are the three "elements" of the soul. The first of these is called Neshamah (the Higher Self), and comprises the first sephiroth of the Tree of Life—Crown, Wisdom, and Understanding. It resides in the brain. The second is known as Ruach (Spirit), which comprises the next six sephiroth of the Tree, from Mercy to Foundation. Its seat is in the heart. The last one is Nephesch (Lower Nature), to which is assigned the last sephira, Kingdom. It resides in the liver.

Neshamah is the source, the intelligence or knowledge; Ruach is the incentive to action; and Nephesch is the power of life that gives movement to the members of the body. Thus every act must start in the brain (Neshamah), be transmitted to the heart (Ruach), and finally to the organs that bring the act to completion (Nephesch) because the body by itself has no volition or power to move. Ruach or the "heart" in this Kabbalistic concept is the power of the will. Because the soul is an "offspring of the Heavenly Man (Adam Kadmon)" it is also called Adam or "man," while the body is called the "flesh of man." Therefore the *real man* is the soul and not the body.

The three degrees of the soul are also assigned by the Kabbalists to the three pillars of the Tree of Life, where Neshamah represents the Pillar of Mercy, Ruach corresponds to the Pillar of Judgment, and Nephesch is the Middle Pillar. Neshamah is also seen as the representation of Kether, the first sephira of the Tree, which is the "highest state of being." Ruach is then seen as Tiphareth, which is placed in the center of the Middle Pillar and corresponds to the heart in the human body, or the moral world. Lastly, Nephesch is assigned to Malkuth, the seat of the animal instincts and desires, known as the material or sensuous world.

Interestingly enough these three divisions of the "soul" according to the Kabbalistic doctrine can be equated with the Jungian concepts of the *Self*, the *Psyche*, and the *Shadow*. The reason for the distinct correspondences between these Jungian concepts and the Kabbalistic degrees of the soul may be found in Jung's lifetime interest in occult matters, notably the alchemical sciences. It is a well-known fact that Alchemy bears a strong correlation with the Kabbalah, and one of the most significant works on the Kabbalistic concepts is the *Aesch Metzareph*, which is a "chymico-Kabbalistic" treatise almost entirely alchemical in its teachings. The principal aim of the *Aesch Metzareph* is to assign the various sephiroth of the Tree of Life to the alchemical principles and metals. Since Jung is known to have read practically every alchemical treatise in existence, it is reasonable to assume that he was acquainted with the *Aesch Metzareph,* and thus with the Kabbalistic doctrines.

The first degree of the soul, according to the Kabbalah, is Neshamah, the highest state of consciousness, also identified with Kether, the first emanation of the Infinite Light. It is comparable with Jung's concept of the Self. But the term "Self" is not used by Jung in the ordinary sense of the word, but rather in the Eastern manner, where the Self is conceived of as the "Supreme Being," the sum and total of all things, the "substance" of being. To Jung this concept of the Self is not universal consciousness, which is also known as the "unconscious." It is rather "an awareness on one hand of our unique natures, and on the other of our intimate relationship with all life, not only human, but animal and plant, and even that of inorganic matter and the cosmos itself." The Self, says Jung, "is not only the centre but also the whole circumference which embraces both conscious and unconscious." In Kabbalistic terms, it is the point within a circle and the circle itself. It is All that man may be and the totality of all possible knowledge, both conscious and unconscious. It is Neshamah.

The second degree of the soul, in Kabbalistic terms, is Ruach, equated with the heart or the "will." It is the centre of outward consciousness, where man becomes aware of thought forms and is able to mold thoughts into action. It is vastly similar to the Jungian concept of the *Psyche,* which is the mind and all mental activity on a conscious as well as on an unconscious level. According to Jung, the conscious mind "grows out of an unconscious psyche which is older than it, and which goes on functioning together with it or even in spite of it." Everything made by man had its beginnings in the Psyche; it was something he "thought about" and thus molded into action. The mental energy that gives rise to thoughts that are then brought into action was called *Libido* by Jung, and it does not have an exclusively sexual meaning as in Freudian psychology, but has the "general sense of desire, longing, urge." It may be comparable to the "etheric" substance of Yesod, the lunar sephira that is the last component of the Ruach, and in which, according to Kabbalists, thoughts are molded before they become actualized in the World of Action. To Jung, the Psyche is a system that is dynamic, constantly moving and self-regulating. It is interesting to note that in this Jungian concept of the Psyche, the natural movement of the libido, or psychic energy, is forward and backward like the "movement of the tides." This is a clear correspondence with the lunar forces of Yesod, which is in the Ruach. To Jung, all human experience is psychic in principle. In *The Basic Postulates of Analytical Psychology*, he stated:

> All that I experience is psychic. Even physical pain is a psychic image which I experience; my sense-impressions—for all that they force upon me a world of impenetrable objects occupying space—are psychic images, and these alone constitute my immediate experience, for they alone are the immediate objects of my consciousness. My own psyche even transforms and falsifies reality, and it does this to such a degree that I must resort to artificial means to determine what things are like apart from myself. Then I discover that a sound is a vibration of air of such and such a frequency, or that a color is a wave of light of such and such a length. We are in truth so wrapped about by psychic images that we cannot penetrate at all to the essence of things external to ourselves. All our knowledge consists of the stuff of the psyche which, because

it alone is immediate, is superlatively real. Here, then, is a reality to which the psychologist can appeal— namely, psychic reality.

If the Ruach is "psychic reality," the Nephesch or Lower Nature is the Jungian concept of the *Shadow*. This term is used by Jung to define what he called "the personal unconscious," that is, those instincts and desires that are against society and our "ideal personality." But, as he also pointed out, there is no shadow without the sun, or some form of light. Thus the shadow may be seen as the dark side of the consciousness that resides in the "sun center of Tiphareth," in the Ruach, or human mind. The Shadow may be also equated with the dark forces of the Qliphoth, which are forever lurking in the background of every human action.

According to the Kabbalah, souls are androgynous in their original state; that is, they are bisexual in nature. When they descend to the material world, they separate into male and female and inhabit different bodies. If, during their mortal lives, the two halves of the soul meet, a great attachment develops between them, and thus it is said that through their marriage, or union, they become again conjoined. This is the source of the term "soul mates." This concept also finds a correspondence in the Jungian school, in the dual idea of "animus and anima." The "anima" is the unconscious of a man, containing a complementary feminine counterpart, while the "animus" is the woman's unconscious, with masculine characteristics. Jung stated that "an inherited collective image of woman exists in a man's unconscious, with the help of which he apprehends the nature of a woman." The same is true of a woman in relation to a man's nature. That is the reason why it is so common to find both masculine and feminine characteristics in one person.

The Evil Spirit

According to the Kabbalah, when They created the Qliphoth, or evil beings, the Creators intended that in the material world there would be a power of evil that would necessitate choice on the part of man in order that he might be again united with the Infinite Light. It is almost as if there was a dual quality to God's nature, half of which is good and half of which is "evil." It may then be conceived that the Deity, by manifesting Themselves through man, intended, not to annihilate this "evil" or negative aspect, but rather to harmonize it and equilibrate it with the positive or "good" aspect. This is the eternal struggle in man's soul over "good" and "evil." For in man the consciousness of the atom becomes manifest. Man is "aware." He *knows* he is. To use Rene Descartes famous statement, *Cogito, ergo sum* ("I think, therefore I am"). For man is not just a part of God, he *is* God on a lower, material level. Just as a photon is a unit of light, not a "part" of light, but light itself with all of light's qualities and attributes. The Kabbalah states that "all multiplicity, all defects and all judgements arise from the Ain Soph." The question of how could multiplicity and defects be derived from the Ain Soph, which is both Unity and Perfect Purity, is answered by the Kabbalists with the concept of "yesh me-oyin," that is, existence from nonexistence. The Infinite Light, since It has within Itself the hidden seed of all future manifestations, has also the latent power to create "evil" as well as "good."

The ten sephiroth of the Tree of Life, as we have already seen, have four stages of "light differentiation," which are called the Four Worlds of the Kabbalists, and which correspond to the four elements of the alchemists. The ten adverse sephiroth, or Qliphoth, have also four divisions, which correspond to four "negative" elements. These four Qliphotic elements are present in man as follows:

1. Negative fire—arrogance
2. Negative air—superfluous talk
3. Negative water—cupidity
4. Negative earth—melancholy

According to Rabbi L. I. Krakovsky,

> the element of water in the world of shell (Qliphoth) is called 'proud waters.' In man this is the white fluid or lymph which is the source of his phlegmatic states. This power seduces man to iniquity. In the source it is called the great cloud. The second element is the element of fire which burns the world in its flame and from it is also derived the fire of hell. In man it is the gall which embitters the world with its bitterness. In the origin it is called a flashing fire. The third element is air, or wind. It is a whirlwind from out of the north which stirs up the entire world. The fourth element is that of earth, the black earth, the dry, the empty.

The dual concept of "good" and "evil," which is represented so vividly by the Kabbalah in the glyphs of the Tree of Life and the Qliphoth, can be seen in the worlds of matter and "antimatter." As early as 1930, physicists had postulated that for each atomic particle an "antiparticle" ought to exist. That meant that the negatively charged electron should have as equivalent an antielectron with similar properties, except for the possession of a positive charge of the same size as the electron's negative charge. The same would be true of a negatively charged proton, in contrast with the actual proton, which is positively charged. The neutron, which is uncharged, would have its equivalent in an "antineutron" with a magnetic field oriented in the opposite direction to that of the regular neutron. Although this theory seemed farfetched at first, in 1932, the American physicist Carl D. Anderson discovered the "antielectron," which we know today familiarly as the positron. The "anti-proton" and the "antineutron" were discovered in 1956. These discoveries led to further speculations among physicists and astrophysicists who argued that at the time of the explosion of the "cosmic egg" a particle and an antiparticle must have been formed. This theory was finally actualized by Austrian-American physicist Maurice Goldhaber, who has suggested the possibility of the existence of a Universe of matter and an Anti-Universe of anti-matter, which he calls "cosmon" and "anticosmon," respectively.

This duality of nature, so evident throughout the created universe, has been termed by Jung "the opposites." The action of these "opposites" is linked by the Jungian school to the positive and negative poles of an electric circuit, or to the diastole and systole movement of the heart. The greater the tension between two opposites, the greater the energy that will be derived. According to Jung, "without opposition there is no manifestation of energy." The list of opposites that can be cited is endless. Among them, there are progression and regression, extraversion and introversion, thinking and feeling, and so on, ad infinitum.

The cosmic energy in man, what Jung called psychic energy and which manifests itself perennially in the form of two diametrically opposed principles, has its seat in the "libido." Since the libido is natural energy, its principal purpose is to serve the principles that govern life and the creation, but because of its "plastic" quality it can be used also for creative purposes. According to the Jungian school, "this direction of energy becomes initially possible by transferring it to something similar in nature to the object of instinctive interest." This is what is called "magic" in the practical Kabbalah. But it is in itself a completely natural act because all it necessitates is the strong will of man and his vehement desire to bring his thought forms into actual realization. In this sense man is simply using the divine spark that is in him to bring about an Act of Creation.

Throughout our discussion of the Kabbalistic doctrine, we have seen how it is permeated with the concept of two opposites united for the purpose of manifestation. From proton and electron to man and woman, all the mysteries of creation are explained by the Kabbalah with this intensely sexual philosophy. To the Kabbalist, all the various degrees of manifestation are reduced to the essential Kabbalistic equation: "The pulsation of life-death which is Aleph, latent existence, personified in the name AHIH (Eheieh), perennially emanates IHVH (Jehovah), with whom It unites for the purpose of creation." Thus, in the Kabbalistic view, the Act of Creation was essentially an Act of Love. And, since according to the established laws of physics, the Universe renews itself continuously throughout eternity, we can say with reasonable certainty that God *ARE* well, and alive and forever loving.

Part
II

THE PRACTICAL
KABBALAH

How Man May Gain
Material Prosperity and
Attain Spiritual Evolution

9 Torah

The practical kabbalah has been often defined as a magical system based on the esoteric doctrine of the Jews. The intricate rituals of the kabbalists and the laws of correspondences embodied in the Tree of Life are to many students the entire edifice of the practical kabbalah. Accordingly, they set out to familiarize themselves with the spheres and the paths of the Tree, the Divine and angelic names of evocation, and the various correspondences. Armed with this scant knowledge and with a few rituals, such as those of the Invoking and Banishing Pentagrams, and others made popular by the Hermetic Order of the Golden Dawn and other magical groups, they stand at the door of the mysteries to bring down power, often for mundane reasons. Most of the time these efforts fail. Sometimes, when the individual has the capacity to build up large quantities of energy, he may see results, but seldom of a lasting nature. Worse yet, if he is unable to direct the energies he has unleashed along constructive channels, he may find himself in the grip of a devastating cosmic backlash. The experience can be terrifying, as I know from personal experience.

How do we avoid these mistakes? Is there a safe way to

practice kabbalistic magic? The answer to both questions is: we must go down to basics. And basics in Kabbalah means the Torah. To attempt a kabbalistic ritual without a thorough understanding of the Torah is the same as a small child attempting to solve a differential equation when he does not yet know how to add and subtract.

Many esoteric schools and mystical orders have been created for the purpose of instructing people in the mysteries of the kabbalah. Most of these groups include rituals in their teachings, but very few stress the importance of observing the Torah as an intrinsic part of the Kabbalistic training. Neither do they stress the vital role that the Hebrew alphabet plays in the practice of kabbalah. The emphasis is invariably on ceremonial magic, with its attending array of vestments, magical implements, colors, perfumes and assorted correspondences. Also heavily underlined are the magical initiations with the various grades of attainment.

Ritual is of great importance in the "practical kabbalah." In fact, ritual is an important part of our everyday life. Getting up in the morning is a ritual we perform every day. We arise from our beds, wash our teeth, take a shower, dress, have breakfast, then go to work. It is a ritual because we conduct it every day, using the same motions and the same tools for the same purpose. Getting married is a ritual, and so, for that matter, is getting a divorce. A graduation ceremony, the swearing in of a president and the coronation of a king are far more grandiose rituals, but rituals nonetheless. In the practice of kabbalah, ritual is very heavily emphasized. Every prayer and invocation is uttered in a specific way at a specific time. This can be traced back to biblical times. In chapters 25-27 of the book of Exodus God gives detailed instructions to Moses on the construction of the ark of the covenant, the tabernacle, the candlestick, the altar, the priests' garments, the anointing oil and incense to be used in the various sacrificial ceremonies. Every ritual act was carefully delineated, and so was the behavior of the priest before, during and after the ceremony.

Ritual to the kabbalist is therefore vital and God-given. It is in fact a *mitzvah* or command that must be observed in the worship of the Godhead. But ritual should be the last of the endeavors to be considered by anyone seriously interested in understanding and practicing the kabbalah. Only after a rigorous basic training where the individual has learned to control his baser instincts, and to embrace the Torah with his whole being, can he dare to consider an actual rite.

The various orders and schools of mysticism serve a useful purpose in introducing their members to the mysteries of kabbalah, but they often fail in their lofty goals by ignoring the most basic tenets of the kababalistic doctrine. The most important of these tenets is the total surrender to God's will. This is followed in importance by a thorough understanding of the Torah. Without those two precepts there can be no kabbalah.

The various grades of initiation used in the magical orders are necessary to ascertain the degree of advancement reached by each individual. But in truth there are no magical orders, no adepts, no hierarchies in the true kabbalah. There is only perfect love and perfect trust between the kabbalist and the Godhead. Every kabbalistic rite is an act of love in God's honor. The vestments, the flashing colors, the magical implements are all secondary to this essential truth. When the will is surrendered to God and becomes one with His, each of our acts becomes Divine in essence. What we will comes to pass because it is what God wills Himself.

When the individual has reached the state of willful surrender to God, he begins to receive instructions on the kabbalah through "inner levels." That is, he suddenly "knows" intuitively what rites to perform and when and for what purpose. He often finds that certain things of a material nature are forbidden to him. This is not always easy to accept, but submission is necessary so that spiritual evolution may continue. After a while it seems as if a definite path had been blazed in front of him, a path from which he cannot deviate even when he tries. Eventually he learns to accept that this guidance comes from within, and then he simply leans back and enjoys the experience.

Sometimes an individual is led to a material teacher who has received the kabbalah through "inner levels." The teacher then provides the initial training the person needs before he himself is ready to receive inner guidance.

One of the central teachings of kabbalah is the unity of all things, and the interrelationship of all worlds and all levels of being. Everything is connected with everything else and governed by exact, unfathomable laws. This is best expressed in the *Shema* or daily prayer that devout Jews recite daily,

Shema Israel! Adonai Eloheinu, Adonai Echad!

(Hear O Israel! The Lord Our God is the Eternal.

The Eternal is *One!*)

This unity of God, of which we are a part, is the key to all kabbalistic thought. That is why God, speaking through the prophet Isaiah to a rebellious Israel, said, "I *am* the first, and I *am* the last; and besides me, *there is* no God . . . yea, *there is* no God. I know not *any.*" (Isa.24). This Being that encompasses a million universes in a single point of light is aware of every single human thought and every movement of every atom in everything that exists. It does not matter if you worship him in a Hindu shrine, in a Muslim mosque, in a Jewish temple, in a Christian church or a forest glade. It matters little whether you call him Jehovah, Brahman, Allah, Olofi, Isis and Osiris, Habondia and Cernunnos. What matters is that you recognize that *He is all there is and*

and that there is no one else but He. That is why all magical systems interrelate and why there is such a thing in magic as the law of correspondences. *It is all one and the same thing.*

It has been said that in kabbalah the law of the Torah became a symbol of cosmic law, and the history of the Jewish people a symbol of the cosmic process.* This is so because in Kabbalah, Israel is a symbol of mankind. According to Kabbalistic lore, when Moses received the Law on Mount Sinai, he received it in the 70 languages representing the 70 nations of the earth. But then the knowledge was concentrated in one single process and one set of symbols, which are the 22 letters of the Hebrew alphabet. This then symbolized the entire human race.

In Hebrew, Torah means the Law, and it is the esoteric name given to the first five books of the Old Testament, also known as the Pentateuch, which according to Jewish tradition were written by Moses. The Torah begins with the Book of Genesis and ends with Deuteronomy. Within the text comprised in between are not only the commandments, the statutes and the judgments, but also the history of creation and the mysteries of the Godhead. Kabbalists point out that it is no coincidence that Genesis begins with the word "Berashith" (In the beginning) and that Deuteronomy ends with the word Israel. For the entire Torah can be concentrated in a simple phrase, "In the beginning . . . Israel." That is, Israel and therefore mankind was pre-existent in God's mind before creation. From this thesis there is only one step to the concept of an identification between God and man. For while the first two words of Genesis are *Berashith Elohim* (In the beginning God . . .), this is only the first seed of the Torah. The complete Torah starts *Berashith* and ends *Israel.* Thus the Torah starts with *In the beginning God* and ends with *In the beginning Israel.* The substitution of Elohim's name for that of Israel emphasizes the divinity of man.

---

*See Gershom G. Scholem, *On the Kabbalah and Its Symbolism,* Schoken, 1965.

According to the *Zohar*, the Torah has a body, which consists of the commandments and the ordinances which are the Law. These are known as *gufe torah*, bodies of the Torah. This body is cloaked in garments which consists of worldly stories, the narrative part of the Scriptures. The uninitiated see only this garment, but fail to comprehend what lies underneath. Those who know more see not only the garment, but the body that is inside it. But the truly wise look only upon the soul, which is the true foundation of the Torah. It is only when we can discern the soul of the Torah underneath its outer "body" that we will possess the secrets of the kabbalah. And the keys to this knowledge are the 22 letters of the Hebrew alphabet in which the Torah was written.

Kabbalah uses two sets of symbols to convey knowledge. One is the Tree of Life and the ten sephiroth that form it. The other are the 22 letters of the Hebrew alphabet. The sephiroth describe the divine attributes and the hidden world of the Godhead under ten different aspects. The 22 letters are the matrix of the Torah and the divine names. But as we have seen, they are more, for they are concentrations of energy upon which an entire universe was built. It is therefore of vital importance for the would-be kabbalist to familiarize himself with the 22 letters and with the Hebrew language. Otherwise all the subtleties of the divine and angelic names and the hidden meanings of the Torah will be a closed book to him. He can still acquire some of the knowledge, but only through outside sources and through other people, never through himself. We can express this better by the well-known analogy between Creation and Revelation. The process of creation is unfolded in the ten sephiroth of the Tree of Life, which are not only representations of the Godhead, but also of man and nature. The act of Revelation is only possible through the illumination received by means of the understanding of the divine language as expressed in the Torah. Through Revelation, the purposes of Creation and its intrinsic meaning are clear to the kabbalist. With this Understanding, symbolized by the third sephira, Binah, the kabbalist can be one with the godhead and be also a creator in his own microcospic world.

According to the kabbalah, the world of the Godhead is a world of language, of sound. The universe was created through God's spoken word. This divine language as expressed in the Torah is intensely magical in nature. All the early kabbalists agreed on the belief that the various sections of the Torah were not given by God in their correct order, for if it had been so, anyone who read them would be able to perform extraordinary miracles. This thesis is largely based on a verse in Job 28:13 that says that "No man knoweth its order." The implication is that originally the writing of the Torah was continuous, without any division into actual words. For that reason the scrolls of the Torah kept in the synagogues are written without punctuation or without the points underneath the letters that denote vowel sounds. The Hebrew alphabet lends itself to incredible configurations of letters that can form words with many different meanings, all of which depend upon the points underneath the letters. Thus one group of letters can mean many different things. If all the words in the Torah were run together without separation and without points, the possible meanings would reach infinity. The kabbalistic belief is that the entire Torah, seen in this way, consists of the various names of God, and certain esoteric names that can be used as magical formulas of extraordinary power. The Spanish kabbalists took this thesis one step further, and avowed that the Torah is not only made of the names of God, but that in its entirety is the one great name of the Deity.

We can see from the preceding that the Torah is intrinsically woven with God's divine essence, and that its order (which only He knows) is the order of creation. This occult form of the Torah is often called *torah kedumah*, the primordial Torah, often identified with God's infinite Wisdom, embodied in the sephira Chokmah.

Tradition says that there are two Torahs, the Written Torah and the Oral Torah. The Written Torah is the text of the Pentateuch, from Genesis to Deuteronomy. The Oral Torah is the entire body of esoteric knowledge that has been passed by "word of mouth" from teacher to pupil. Moses is said to have received both Torahs in Mount Sinai, the Oral Torah being the unpunctuated and continuous body of knowledge which is God's greatest mystery. In kabbalah the Written Torah is identified with the sephira Tiphareth, which is the "giving sphere," while the Oral Torah is associated with Malkuth, the sphere of the Shekinah and the Congregation of Israel (mankind). Both Torahs are known as black fire on white fire, the black fire being the knowledge of the Oral Torah which conferred upon the Written Torah the separation of the divine letters into words.

In the *Zohar*, the Torah is seen as the outer garment of the Shekinah which she must wear because of man's fall. This created Torah is known as *torah de-beriah* and includes the actual Laws given to man by Moses. Here we have both negative and positive precepts, and not only the Ten Commandments, but also the huge body of the Statutes and Judgements as given in the Books of Leviticus and Deuteronomy. These garments of the Shekinah are black as a symbol of her mourning because of man's sin, and also of her exile from her Divine Bridegroom. Through his good actions man can "strip the Matrona of her somber garments and adorn her with radiant garments which are the mysteries of the Torah."

Long before the *Zohar*, the Tree of Life had been identified with the Written Torah, while the Tree of the Knowledge of Good and Evil was identified with the Oral Torah. Here we see once more that in order to comprehend the mysteries of the Tree of Life, the oral and therefore deeper knowledge is necessary.

According to kabbalah when God manifests Himself, He does so through the creative power of the sephiroth. But these manifestations take place in different stages through the four kabbalistic worlds. In Atziluth, or World of Emanation, the Torah is first manifested as the different combinations of consonants that can be created from the 22 letters. This was the first linguistic movement of the Godhead. In Beriah, or World of Creation, the Torah is manifested as a sequence of the names of God, formed by the combinations present in Atziluth. In Yetzirah, or World of Formation, the angelic names were formed, while in Assiah, or the World of Action, the Torah took the form that is familiar to us.

I have delved for some time in the mysteries of Torah because it is the richest source of kabbalistic knowledge and the starting point of every kabbalist. The term *devekkut*, which means cleaving on to God, defines best of all the attitude of the true kabbalist. This devekkut is only possible through the strict observance of the Law as given in the first five books of the Old Testament. This Law is not confined to the observance of the Ten Commandments, but also to the obedience of all the Statutes and Judgments, as given by the books of Leviticus and Deuteronomy. Accordingly, the first rule that must be observed by anyone who wishes to practice kabbalah with any degree of success is to read the Pentateuch from Genesis to Deuteronomy, and make a list of all the Ordinances, both negative and positive, which were given by God through Moses. These precepts must then be strictly obeyed as they apply to us in our modern times, for there are laws, such as the laws of bondage, which no longer apply. But whenever a Commandment, a Statute or a Judgment commands us or forbids us to do or not to do something, we must comply without hesitation.

When the kabbalist obeys the Law willingly and totally, he is perceiving the body of the Torah, stripped of its outer garment of Biblical narrative. To perceive the soul of the Torah, he must go one step further and learn the symbols and the meanings of the 22 letters, and if possible, learn the Hebrew language. This is not as difficult as it may seem, as there are many excellent self-taught methods to learn Hebrew. The time and effort will not be lost, and what will be gained in exchange will be a Revelation.

10 The Importance of Ritual

In kabbalah, all ritualistic actions are a representation of the divine life in specific symbols. This life or cosmic energy is called forth through the various steps of the ceremony. God therefore is brought into human action through the kabbalistic ritual which gathers its power of transformation from the dynamic forces of the sephiroth.

The kabbalists believe that every human action finds an echo in the divine realm. Man is indeed the master of his own destiny, and he alone decides what is going to happen to him and to his kind. God has given man that freedom of choice. Whichever action man takes is followed by a reaction from the Upper Worlds, and whether it is positive or negative depends on man's initial action. This is true of any action, be it magical or natural, and entails a tremendous responsibility: *not only are we responsible for our own lives and those around us, but also for the balance of the cosmic order.* Those who are unaware of this responsibility will still be called to answer for their wrongdoings; those who, like the kabbalist, know their own power, face severe consequences for their negative acts. That is why the principal aim of the kabbalist in conducting a ritual is to preserve the cosmic order and be one with the will of God.

Isaac Luria, also known as the Ari, who, as we discussed earlier, was one of the greatest kabbalists of all times, placed a great deal of emphasis on ritual as a means of restoring the cosmic order. In the Ari's system, there were three great symbols. The first was *tsimtsum,* or God's self-limitation; the second was *shevirah,* or the breaking of the vessels; and the third was *tikkun,* or the restoration of the cosmic order of things.

The concept of *tsimtsum* was not Luria's original idea, as it appears in several older treatises, but it was only in his system that its complexities became lucid and understandable. According to the theory of the *tsimtsum,* God's creation is not the result of His emanation, but of His withdrawal into Himself. This withdrawal created a primordial space, or pleroma, in which God's powers of judgment were concentrated. Prior to the *tsimtsum* the powers of judgment were in perfect harmony with the powers of mercy, but at the withdrawal they separated and were deposited in the pleroma. Because these powers of judgment include certain evil tendencies, some kabbalists see the *tsimtsum* as a form of purification of the Godhead from the elements of evil. Others see it as a free act of love, in which God gives of His essence for the purpose of creation. And indeed, it would seem that the purpose of releasing the powers of judgment separated from the powers of mercy would be a purely creative act, for creation would necessitate perfect judgment, untouched by the softening influence of the powers of mercy. If God had created the world through the combined powers of judgment and mercy, it would not have been the world as we know it. The lion would not hunt the deer out of compassion, and in so doing would die of starvation and condemn to extinction all the other predators who depend on his hunting skills for survival. We would not eat other forms of life, and would probably deny ourselves the eating of an apple out of compassion for the tree. As it is, the interaction of life forms on the planet creates a perfect balance in nature. The lion only kills when he's hungry.

Only man kills for pleasure. The lion, in accordance to immutable cosmic laws, is exercising perfect judgment. Man is not.

After the *tsimtsum*, the powers of judgment released into the pleroma joined with the remnants of God's infinite light. They were galvanized into action by a divine ray from God's essence that broke through space into the pleroma. This ray of divine light is the Ain Soph Aur of kabbalistic tradition. The combination of the three elements were in the Lurianic thought, the one living God: not the totality of God's essence, His immanence, which will forever remain unknown to us, but His willful manifestation in the created world.

This one living God is the Adam Kadmon, formed by the ten sephiroth of the Tree of Life. All the archetypes of being were formed in the confines of this divine body. But the tension exerted by the perpetual withdrawal of *tsimtsum* and the equally eternal influx of the Ain Soph Aur into the pleroma affected all the various stages of being. As the light broke through the pleroma and went downwards, it was divided into vessels of lesser concentrations of the divine essence. At this point, great fountains of light poured forth from the eyes of Adam Kadmon. This was the element of creation which was to be contained in the lower vessels. But the force of the light from Adam Kadmon's eyes was too powerful and the vessels shattered under its impact. This is the concept of *shevirah,* the breaking of the vessels.

Two hundred and eighty-eight sparks from the powers of judgment which were the heaviest, mingled with the fragments of the broken vessels and precipitated downwards where they became the powers of evil known as the Qlipoth. All the other light rebounded from the vessels and returned to the eyes of Adam Kadmon. Since that primordial happening, everything that exists is in a state of exile, and must be returned to its initial state. The part of God that separated from the initial source through the *shevirah* is known as the Matrona, the Shekinah, and that is why it is said that She is in exile from Her divine bridegroom. The reason for this cataclysm is seen by many kabbalists as a necessary expulsion of the demonic powers in the original powers of judgment, necessary for creation and for a perfect balance in God's divine essence.

The fallen sparks must now be purified and returned to the divine Source. This act of restoration is the concept of *tikkun*. For this purpose new, healing lights issued from the forehead of Adam Kadmon and renewed configurations of the sephiroth came into being. To aid in restoration, five faces of the Adam Kadmon, known as the *partsufim*, were created. The first is the *arik*, or long suffering; the second is that of the Father; the third that of the Mother; the fourth that of the *zeir anpin*, or the impatient; and the fifth is *zeir anpin's* complement, the Shekinah. The relationship between these last two *partsufim* is the union between the male and the female aspects of the Godhead described in the *Zohar*.

Whatever happens in the world of the *partsufim* is repeated with greater intensity in the four worlds that are formed below them. Their interrelationship and influence speeds up the process of *tikkun*. But the light lessens as it goes downward, and in the last world of Assiah, it mixes with the Qlipothic powers. To free the remnants of the divine light from this demonic entanglement, and to purify the Qlipoth itself, thus releasing the Shekinah from her enforced exile, man was created. It was up to him through perfect actions to release the sparks of light and complete the work of the *tikkun*. But Adam, the first man, failed at his task. And his sin drove the sparks even deeper into the Qlipoth, re-enforcing the Shekinah's exile. That is why in Genesis, Adam himself is sent into exile, away from Paradise. His divine soul is also shattered by the greatness of his failure, and its sparks join those imprisoned in the Qlipoth. The world we live in, and the natural laws that sustain it are the scene of the exile of Adam's soul. In this kabbalistic concept, our world is the world of the Qlipoth. Each evil action perpetrated by man enforces the exile of the Shekinah and the divine light, while each good action helps to the release of some of the sparks and restores them to their initial source. For that reason the Torah was given to man, to help him in the process of restoration known as *tikkun*. This is the aim of redemption. Every human being must participate in the process of *tikkun*, which is not only a restoration of creation, but its eventual fulfillment.

Once man knows the meaning and importance of *tikkun*, every one of his actions should be directed towards this purpose. This is particularly true of rituals, whose mystical intention or meditation is known by the kabbalists as *kavvanah*. To perform a ritual without *kavvanah* is like having a body without a soul; the intention is perverted, the results not of a divine origin.

Kavvanah may be seen as a mystical instrument by means of which each ritual action is transformed into a mystery rite. In meditation, *kavvanah* is used to transform the human will and make it one with God's. In ritual prayer, a group of steps are often follwed that ensure the ascent of *kavvanah* from the lowest to the highest realms.

Through *kavvanah*, the unity of things and the restoration of the cosmic order is accomplished. But the elimination of the evil forces concentrated in the Qlipoth is also important, and can also be accomplished by means of ritual. This concept, which the Ari called *berur*, implies that the Torah also aims at the repression and the control of the shells, extricating them from the sparks of the divine light. This does not imply a destruction of the Qlipoth, which can only be accomplished in the Messianic Age.

In kabbalah therefore the purpose of ritual is fourfold.

First it must accomplish a harmonious balance between the powers of judgment and those of mercy; second, it must propitiate a union between the male and the female aspects of the Godhead; third, it must attempt the redemption of the Shekinah from her exile; and fourth, it must provide a defense or dominion over the Qlipothic powers.

To the kabbalist, every human action should attempt all of the above, either magically or through everyday behavior. Even eating and sexual intercourse are used by the kabbalists to achieve *tikkun*. The Torah itself urges man to take his meals facing God's altar, which immediately transforms this natural act into a ritualistic action. And the sexual act is performed by Orthodox Jews every Sabbath eve as a mystical union with the Shekinah.

Kabbalah even urges meditation on the Godhead or one of His aspects during the performance of our daily work. The patriarch Enoch is said to have meditated on the union of the lower and the higher realms as he stitched the leather of a shoe to its sole. Being a cobbler by trade, he repeated this action through many years of labor. Eventually he was transformed into the archangel Metraton who was one of the subjects of his meditation.

On the other hand, the act of ritual prayer brings a man into total union with the Godhead. In the Lurianic system of prayer, the kabbalist concludes his morning prayer by throwing himself on the floor and surrendering himself to God's will. Through this *kavvanah* a high initiate has the power to go into the depths of the Qlipoth in order to rescue some of the sparks imprisoned within. But kabbalists warn against this practice which only should be undertaken by perfectly developed initiates or *zaddiks*, as an inexperienced practitioner may be unable to return from the Qlipoth and remain there until the Messianic redemption. Therefore, in the light of this concept, prayer is an act through which man offers himself as a sacrifice to God.

We can see from the preceding that the Kabbalistic ritual is never conducted for personal gratification. The intention is to accomplish a total identification with God's will and to surrender to His divine wisdom. The reason for this *kavvanah* is *tikkun*, the ultimate restoration of the cosmic order. But in identifying with the Godhead and surrendering to Him, the kabbalist also accomplishes his wishes because since his will is one with God's, what he wants is also what God wants. To perform a kabbalistic ritual without these intentions is a perversion of the soul's energies. For this reason kabbalists warn against the use of kabbalistic knowledge for selfish reasons. The proper observance of the Torah and the use of ritual for the purpose of a unification with the Godhead can accomplish far more things for the initiate and with more safety.

The main source of power in kabbalah for ritual purposes is the Tree of Life. As we have seen, balancing the Tree is of great importance to maintain inner harmony and the cosmic order. This balance is accomplished through the perfect equilibrium of the Pillar of Mercy and the Pillar of Judgment. These pillars are equated by kabbalists with the pillars of the Temple of Solomon, which were built according to Divine specifications. Each pillar was 18 cubits high (approximately 27 feet) and four fingers wide, and both were overlaid with brass. The right-hand pillar was called Jachin and the left, Boaz (1 Kgs. 7:21). The prophet Jeremiah (Jer. 52:21) stresses the fact that they were *hollow*, a significance that cannot be overlooked kabbalistically, for through them flowed the Divine energy which was the building block of Solomon's power.

The Scriptures do not mention the Middle Pillar—the Pillar of Mildness and Equilibrium—because it has no counterpart in the physical world. Its significance is *consciousness* and its structure lies within the Kabbalist's own psyche. When Jachin and Boaz (Mercy and Judgment) are balanced in the kabbalist, he *becomes* the Middle Pillar. That is why all work in the Tree must be done by pairing opposite spheres, thus balancing their respective pillars.

Successful work in the Tree requires that vast amounts of energy be raised by the practitioner. There are several methods to accomplish this. Relaxation, meditation, and breathing techniques can be used quite successfully for this purpose, especially if they are used together. Concentration and ritualistic dancing can also be used to release energy from the psyche, and many modern rhythms can be very effective in achieving this aim. The intention is to enervate and overexcite the mind and the nervous system in order to release the necessary forces. This means that soft romantic music is not suitable for this work. The music must be vibrant and alive with sound and power. Interestingly enough, some rock music is ideal for the building up of energy because of its exhilarating beat. This is probably because this beat is created by different drum rhythms, which tend to be repetitive and hypnotic in quality. They are also a primeval call to the most basic instincts in the human soul, and the resulting excitement is very erotic in essence. That is because sexuality is at the core of every human being, and this sexuality is simply a desire for unification with the All. Any type of music that has a steady drum beat in the background is apt to create this state of nervous excitement, with the resulting flow of psychic energies.

As the energies build and gather strength, the kabbalist concentrates on their release and "sees" them emerge from within and surround him in vortices of fire. It is at this time, when the energies have been raised and concentrated, that the kabbalist begins to do his work in the Tree. He may do this simply by willing and visualizing his desire on the sphere that controls it, while carefully balancing the opposite sphere; or he may devise a more complex ritual, using thought forms or the forces traditionally associated with the spheres.

The building of thought forms utilizes visualization techniques and great concentration power. Some of the uses of thought forms in Kabbalah are closely linked to the concept of the Golem, a magical being well-known in Jewish lore. The Golem, which is a symbol of the unredeemed soul of Israel, is built of clay—very much like Adam, who is, according to kabbalistic sources, the first Golem. This clay figure is then infused with life through words of power, which are the 231 combinations of the Hebrew alphabet derived from the Yetzirah. There are various treatises that give specific instructions on the creation of a Golem, but the experiment is said to be both delicate and dangerous, as it presumes to imitate God's creation of Adam.

Thought forms do not require clay for their creation, but they are astral versions of the Golem. That is, the kabbalist concentrates his energies into a definite form and consciously gives it life. This creation is generally used to carry out the will of the kabbalist. There are several methods for the building of thought forms along kabbalistic lines, but as I said before, the concept is too dangerous to be used lightly and therefore should be avoided.

The forces of the spheres of the Tree are invoked by the enunciation of the Divine Names associated with each sphere. These names include the God Names, the Archangels and the Orders of Angels (see Table 3 of Part I). The kabbalist pronounces the Names only after fasting and purification, and the raising of adequate amounts of energy. In most kabbalistic rituals, the uttering of the Names is the culminating point of the ceremony, for it is through their power that the will of the kabbalist is realized. The Names should be pronounced with great force and authority, while concentrating firmly on the aspired goal.

Much has been written about the importance of "vibrating" the Divine Names, and this importance cannot be minimized. For the sake of simplicity, however, "vibrating" the Names can be equated with the careful and slow pronunciation of each Name in a loud, sonorous voice. This is best accomplished by dividing the Name in syllables and uttering each one individually in a resonant tone of voice, stressing the consonants and accenting the vowels. For example, the Name of the archangel Raphael, who presides over Tiphareth, should be enunciated as RRRAAH-PHAAH-EELLL. While his Name is pronounced, the kabbalist should visualize the great archangel in yellow robes (the color of Tiphareth in Briah), with violet facings, violet being the complementary color of yellow. Likewise, the Name of the archangel Haniel, who presides over Netzach, should be pronounced HAAAH-NNEEH-EELLL, and he should be visualized dressed in green robes with red facings. The color scale of Briah is used because this is the World where most kabbalistic work is done (See Table 4 of Part I).

The order of the Divine Names should be as follows. First the God Name should be pronounced, followed by the archangel and the Order of Angels. The Archangel's Name and the Order of Angels are pronounced last because they are the ones in charge of carrying out the mandates of the God force ruling that particular sphere.

It should always be remembered that all kabbalistic work takes place in the Astral World, which is the realm of imagination. The Astral World is formed of the Astral Light which is the malleable energy used by the kabbalist to build his images. Everything that happens in the material world is first formed on the Astral. That is why a careful hold should be kept at all times on the imagination, because every stray thought is building-material in the Astral World, and we can unknowingly surround ourselves with a slew of potentially destructive vibrations if we do not take proper precautions.

The work that the kabbalist does in the Astral Light is the seed from which will grow the realization of his hopes in the physical world. It is a blueprint of the events that will later on take place to consolidate the work he did on the Tree. This means that creation takes place on two different levels. First on the world of imagination and then on the world of matter. When God created the universe he also used these two levels. The Creation that takes place in the first chapter of the Book of Genesis is taking place in the Mind of God. The second version of the Creation, as given in Chapter 2 of Genesis, is taking place in the world of matter. Therefore, God first "imagined" the creation of the universe, then proceeded to realize it on the physical level.

Because the Astral Light is malleable and in constant motion, what happens in the material world as the result of work on the Tree does not always happen exactly as the kabbalist visualized it. This is the result of energy changes in the light after the work is completed. For this reason, it is very important that the visualization of the event desired be very firm in the mind of the practitioner. This will give it stronger consistency and make its physical counterpart easier to materialize. The ritual should also be "earthed" by a physical action, such as eating a piece of bread, consecrated during the ceremony, or drinking a cup of wine, also consecrated.

There are many rituals on the practice of kabbalistic magic, but the experienced kabbalist knows that the simpler the ritual, the more effective the results are likely to be. This is because an abundance of ritual forms deplete the energies raised by the kabbalist, thus weakening his power to create in the Astral Light. For that reason, rituals should be designed with a minimum of complexity and with careful attention to purification as the strongest protective measure to be taken prior to the ceremony. Protective measures are necessary because the energies released during ritual work inevitably attract a host of negative entities that seek to feed upon them. The best way to keep these negative forces at bay is by fasting and purification. This includes refraining from impure or destructive thoughts, avoiding contact with any dead matter and refraining from sexual activities for at least 24 hours before the ceremony. Yoga exercises are very helpful in inducing the state of asceticism and religious fervor which is so central to the practice of kabbalistic magic. Contrary to popular belief, Yoga is not an alien concept to kabbalistic thought, as it was introduced to the Kabbalah as far back as the thirteenth century, chiefly by the kabbalistic master, Abraham Abulafia.

Another common protective measure used by the kabbalist is a circle of light that is visualized around him and his place of work. The four great archangels that stand at the four cardinal points are also visualized immediately outside the circle. The Archangel Raphael (yellow robes with violet facings) stands in the East quarter; the Archangel Michael (green robes with red facings) stands in the South; the Archangel Gabriel (blue robes with orange facings) stands in the West; and the Archangel Uriel (robes of citrine, olive, brown and black) stands in the North. Both the circle and the Archangelic forces should be visualized as fading slowly after the work is completed. But these are secondary protective measures. The most important are, as I have said before, fast and purification. Only these will ensure safety during the ritual and the successful outcome of the magical work.

11 The Tree

The first major class of manifested reality is the Noumenal or Spiritual plane. This is the *Shamaym* or Heaven, a plane of pure thought and the basis of the various kinds of phenomenal energies. The second class of manifested reality is the Phenomenal plane of the objective realm. It is called *Aretz* or Earth, and represents the entire material plane.

Shamaym is composed of the first three worlds of the Kabbalists: Atziluth, Briah and Yetzirah. The first triad of the Tree, Kether, Chokmah and Binah, are known collectively as the *Neshamah*, or World Soul, a vehicle of Self-Realization where the experience of Oneness with the Godhead is realized. Kether furthermore corresponds to *Yechida*, which is undifferentiated energy, pure thought, and is ascribed to the plane of Atziluth.

Chokmah, the second sphere, corresponds to *Chaya*, which represents the Self's Will or potential of activity. Binah, the third sphere, corresponds to *Neshamah* itself, and embodies the attributes of the Self's Soul and its capacities for action and realization. Chaya and Neshamah belong to the plane of Briah.

Spheres 4-9 belong to the plane of Yetzirah and are divided into the Upper and Lower *Ruachs*, or soul categories. Chesed (the fourth sphere), Geburah (the fifth sphere), and Tiphareth (the sixth sphere) compose the Upper Ruach, the vehicle of rational, moral and intuitive faculties. Chesed represents the unity of all things via Synthesis; Geburah represents the differentiation of all things via Analysis; and Tiphareth, which corresponds to the Self's faculty of "Seeing," is the principle which balances all opposing forces.

The Lower Ruach is composed of Netzach (the seventh sphere), Hod (the eighth sphere) and Yesod (the ninth sphere), and is the vehicle of the intellectual and artistic faculties. Netzach represents the harmonious interrelations of forms; Hod represents the segregation of the outer forms; and Yesod represents the sphere of awareness affecting duality.

Aretz corresponds to the plane of Assiah or fourth world of the Kabbalists and to Malkuth (the tenth sphere). This plane is divided into the *Nephesch*, which is the electromagnetic vehicle of physical vitality, the emotions and sensations; and the *Guph*, which is the gross, physical body.

All the various differentiations and manifestations that take place in Shamaym through the progressive actions of the first three worlds are eventually materialized in Aretz, the Earth; in the fourth and last world of Assiah. This world coincides with the sphere of Malkuth, which is divided into the Nephesch and the Guph. As we have seen, the Guph is identified with the material body. The Nephesch, on the other hand, is the vehicle through which we experience emotions and sensations. This is a subtler "body" organized on a sub-atomic region of electromagnetic forces whose energy animates the "baser" physical body, or Guph. One may think of the Nephesch as the Astral Body or the vehicle of perception and awareness.

The Lower Ruach is motivated through sensual and emotional attachments. Its reactions and relations to morality are affected and influenced by external stimuli and conditioning. As much as 95% of the average person's mental activities are conditioned reflexes, which explains the irrational and illogical behavior of many people. This falls within the realm of Yesod, which corresponds to indiscriminate imitation and automatic thought reflexes. Traditional values and customs are all part of Yesod's conditioned reflexes. Hod, on the other hand, tends to segregate things on the basis of their outer form. This includes race, religion, sex, and other material considerations. In may ways Hod is responsible for the fragmentation of the various areas of knowledge into artificial components. Netzach corresponds to the harmonzing of forms and to the emotional nature of man. On their positive aspects, Yesod represents imagination, Hod represents intelligence and Netzach represents feelings and sensations.

The Upper Ruach acts out of Reason and Logic. The individual who functions on this level is motivated by his insight into Life's individuality, as well as by its essential unity with the All. The initiation into the Upper Ruach has been called the "rending of the Veil Parakeeth," which is the external aspect of things. These Initiates are more concerned with the inner significance of things and with spiritual values than with material considerations. The emotions exemplified by Chesed are devoid of selfish interests, and are motivated by pure love. Geburah, on the other hand, is intellect free from discrimination; that is why it is pure judgment. Tiphareth, the harmonious interaction of Chesed and Geburah, is a symbol of the unity of all things.

The High Initiates of the Upper Ruach are the prophets and sages of the world who are able to perceive the knowledge of the universe and are no longer interested in material things. When they reach this point, they are ready for the ultimate initiation, that of the "Crossing of the Abyss," when they attain to the Understanding of the sphere of Binah and reach the "deconditioning" of the soul. This is the level of Self-Realization, the Nirvana of the Vedantas.

Part of the kabbalistic Self-Realization is the identification with the Ain Sup or Ain Soph, which is equated with the Self. This Self is not the conscious part of the personality (the familiar, everyday ego), but a divine spark of the Infinite Light, full of infinite potential and the power of being. The Self—emanated from the Ain Soph—is man's personal God and the true essence of his being. When we reach within for strength and fortitude, it is to the Self to whom we are appealing, for the Self is our direct link with the Godhead. It is to the Self to whom we pray, it is the Self whom we invoke and to whom we direct our thoughts in times of need. Every kabbalist rite is directed to this inner Self in a search for unification with God. That is why, in order to achieve this synthesis, the first kabbalist act must be an act of surrender to the Divine Will and the acceptance of all the changes it may demand in our lives, regardless of how they may affect our human expectations. Only then can we dare to attempt to make changes of our own, secure in the knowledge that our changes are also part of the Divine Plan.

The most immutable of the universal laws is the Law of Change. Everything is in constant motion, and motion is change. From the motion of the atomic particles to the motion of the tides, all that *is* must constantly be changing for creation to continue. That is why life must give way to death, and death must be reborn again. This is a very important consideration in the Practical Kabbalah. That is why one must build in the higher worlds what one wishes to realize in the world of matter. Everything that exists in the material world first began as a seed-thought. Thought, therefore, is the matrix of all created things.

The first and most vital of all the works in the Tree is that of Self-Evaluation and Self-Understanding. This is best accomplished through meditation on the sphere of Tiphareth, the equilibrating principle between the Synthesis of Chesed and the Analysis of Geburah. A simple ritual for this purpose will be given in Chapter 14.

Before we can discuss the practical work on the Tree we must become very familiar with the Tree and its correspondences. It has been said that The Tree of Life is a gigantic filing system where everything that exists can be found. It is good to bear this in mind while working with the Tree. Tables 3–5 in Part I give some of the correspondences, including the color scales, the Angelic names, the symbols, magical images, planets, virtues and vices associated with the various sephiroth. Tables 6 and 7 give other correspondences which are important for the implementation of rituals.

Table 6

Other Correspondences of the Tree

Sphere	Plant	Animal	Incense	Stone
1. Kether	Almond flower	--	Ambergris	Diamond
2. Chokmah	Amaranth	Man	Musk	Ruby, Turquoise
3. Binah	Cypress, Poppy	Woman	Myrrh, Civet	Sapphire
4. Chesed	Olive, Shamrock	Unicorn	Cedar	Amethyst
5. Geburah	Oak	Basilisk	Tobacco	Ruby
6. Tiphareth	Acacia, Bay, Vine	Lion	Olibanum	Topaz
7. Netzach	Rose	Lynx	Benzoin, Rose	Emerald
8. Hod	Moly	Hermaphrodite	Storax	Opal
9. Yesod	Mandrake, Damiana	Elephant	Jasmine	Quartz
10. Malkuth	Lily, Ivy	Sphinx	Dittany of Crete	Crystal (Rock)

Table 7

Elements and Metals in the Tree

Sphere	Element	Metal
1. Kether	Root of Air	--
2. Chokmah	Root of Fire	--
3. Binah	Root of Water	Lead
4. Chesed	Water	Tin
5. Geburah	Fire	Iron
6. Tiphareth	Air	Gold
7. Netzach	Fire	Copper
8. Hod	Water	Quicksilver
9. Yesod	Air	Silver
10. Malkuth	Earth	Rock, Mica

The four elements (air, fire, water and earth) are linked with the four cardinal points and the four great archangels (see Table 8).

Table 8

The Elements and Cardinal Points

Air	East	Raphael	Yellow and Purple
Fire	South	Michael	Green and Red
Water	West	Gabriel	Blue and Orange
Earth	North	Uriel	Citrine, Olive, Brown and Black

Before a ritual can be planned by the kabbalist, he must first decide which of the spheres he will be working with (always keeping in mind that they must be worked in pairs). He then ascertains through a compass the cardinal point to which the sphere belongs (see Tables 7 and 8) and places his altar on that quarter. He then proceeds with his ritual.

The importance of the Tree and its correspondences cannot be overemphasized. Equally important is the full understanding of the various components of the Tree, the

Neshamah, the Ruachs and the Nephesch and Guph. This helps put into proper perspective the work that is planned and how it can best be accomplished.

As I already mentioned in Part I, the Tree has a mirror image where the forces of the Qlipoth are gathered. These "shells" are the depositories of every negative or destructive action, and are forever lurking in the background of all magic rituals. Any mistake or miscalculation on the part of the Kabbalist results in the outpouring of negative energies which often nullify any protective devices used in the preparation of the ritual. The Qliphotic forces are waiting to "pounce" on the halpless magician who commits an error, and the results of such careless actions can be sometimes terrifying. This is true of any ritual, regardless of how simple or pure in intention it may be. For this reason it is very important to plan each ceremony with the greatest of care, paying special attention to such things as correspondences, planetary hours, the cardinal points and lunar cycles.

It is important to remember that Kabbalistic magic should always be practiced for positive reasons. Any negative intentions fall within the realm of "black magic" and can be very dangerous for the would-be Kabbalist, particularly if a mistake is made during the ritual. As I mentioned earlier, even simple and positive rituals can result in disaster if an error is made. A negative ritual badly conducted can result in tragedy and physical death.

Kabbalistic rites are generally conducted in the sphere of Briah, where the seed of formation first comes into being. All the things visualized in this sphere through proper meditation will be manifested in the material world, if the ritual is done correctly. The sphere of Briah uses the Queen Scale of colors as given in Table 4.

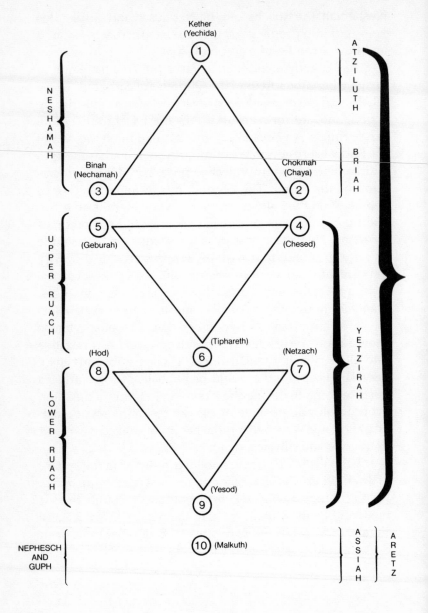

Figure 8.

12 Invocation and Evocation

Invocation and evocation are often confused in the practice of magic, but in reality one is quite different from the other. Invocation can be a prayer or supplication to a specific deity, and it can also be the calling down of power or of protective forces. Evocation goes one step further and *summons* these forces to appear in front of the magician, in a material form. Invocation just calls the force and the energy it embodies to aid us in our magical endeavors. Evocation commands the force to make itself visible.

Both invocation and evocation are used in the practice of kabbalistic magic, but only an experienced kabbalist should undertake evocation. The reason for this precaution is that materialized forces are more difficult to handle and can result in an overflow of energy with dangerous consequences.

Invocation

The most common form of invocation is prayer. To the kabbalist prayer is the simplest and most direct way to reach the Godhead. *But prayer without emotion is useless.* That is why the kabbalists insist that a person must inflame himself with the most powerful feelings before praying. "Your word is fire" is what you must remember during your prayers. The Hassidim, who are a Jewish sect well-versed in kabbalistic practices, use not only great feeling in their prayers but also motion. Quiet, static prayer is not very successful. The Hassidim sway as they pray and cry out their love and devotion to the Deity with great passion. This fiery emotion, coupled with constant movement, activates the energies they release during prayer and catapults them towards their intended goal. There are times when a person's body may remain completely still while his soul serves his Creator in silent prayer. But only those who are already at one with the Godhead may attain this prayer of inner flame and outer stillness.

The union which is attained with the Diety in prayer is very similar to sexual union, for as we have seen, kabbalah has deep sexual undertones. The master kabbalists explain that prayer is union with the Divine Presence, the Shekinah, and that just as two people will move their bodies back and forth as they begin the act of love, so must a person accompany the beginning of prayer with the rhythmic swaying of his body. But as he reaches the heights of union with the Presence, the movement of his body should cease.

Prayer should always be joyful. One should never pray in tears of sadness, which reflect doubt and lack of faith. Negative or distracting thoughts are not to be allowed to disturb one's concentration in prayer. On the contrary, they are to be seen as sparks of light trapped by the shells of the Qlipoth and should be offered to the Shekinah with deep devotion so that she may bring them to her divine spouse and thus redeem them from darkness.

As you stand before the Creator in prayer you should feel that you stand alone. In all the world only God and you exist. Then there can be no distractions. Nothing can disturb such prayer.

There are two types of prayer-states generally described by the Hassidic kabbalists: *Qatnut,* which is the "lower" or ordinary state in which one generally begins his prayers, and *gadlut,* the "greater" or expanded state of mystical consciousness. The state of qatnut may contain within it great devotion, but it is usually a simple prayer where one gives himself to God and accepts his will. In gadlut one transcends time and space and reaches a state where life itself has lost all meaning.

The first step in the attainment of gadlut is the involvement of the entire self in the act of worship, without any reservations. The body must become involved along with the soul in the act of prayer: the rhythmic movement of the body, the sometimes loud outcry of the voice, the concentration on the spoken or written words of prayer, are all aids in the total involvement of the conscious personality in the act of worship. The prayer furthermore must always be accompanied by the love and fear of God, which are the "wings" that allow it to ascend to the Deity. As love and fear lift the words upward, the letters become liberated from their verbal patterns and lead the soul from the "World of Speech" to the "World of Thought." First the energies are concentrated on the words, then the words are released and nothing remains within but an empty vessel, ready to receive the light from above. The "World of Speech" is identified with the Shekinah, the Presence, to be found in Malkuth, and which represents the indwelling glory of God that fills all creation. The "World of Thought" is identified with Chokmah. Therefore the ascent of the worshipper from speech to abstract thought is a journey which reaches from the lower to the higher realms of divine light.

In kabbalistic thought the best prayer is that said in the Hebrew language. Even if one does not know how to pronounce the words properly, or is not thoroughly aware of their actual meaning, the power of the words is such that they inevitably will reach the higher realm, if they are uttered with true love and devotion. The master kabbalists say that one who reads the words of prayer with great devotion may come to see the light within the letters, even though he does not understand the meaning of the words he speaks. Such prayer has great power. It is similar to a father who has a young child whom he greatly loves. Though the child has hardly learned to speak, his father takes great pleasure in listening to his words, which he fully understands although mispronounced. The Hassidic masters tell a story about a simple man who used to speak to God and say: "Lord of the World! You know that I have not studied, that I cannot even read the words of your holy books. All I remember and know is the alphabet itself. So I will give you the letters of the alphabet, and you can form the words of my prayer yourself." And he then proceeded to recite the letters of the alphabet: "Aleph, Beth, Gimel . . ." This story underlines the virtues of simplicity and the creative powers of the letters which are, as we have seen, the building blocks of all that is.

The most important and dynamic of all prayers to the Deity is taken from Psalm 51:15:

"O Lord, Open thou my lips
and my mouth shall declare thy praise . . ."

So powerful is this prayer that when it is uttered the kabbalists say that the Presence of God comes unto the worshipper. Then it is the Presence herself who commands his voice. It is she who speaks the words through him. This, therefore, is the opening prayer which should be said before all others. It should be followed by other verses from the same Psalm, combined with other sources:

"Purge me with hyssop and I shall be clean,
wash me and I will be whiter than snow . . .
Thou art holy and thy name is holy

and all who are holy shall praise thee daily,
　　Selah.
Holy, Holy, Holy is the Lord of Hosts,
　　replete is all the world with his glory . . ."

This is the most powerful of all the prayers to the Godhead and it should precede all other prayers. Ideally, it should be said in Hebrew, and those interested in the Hebrew version will find it in any of the common Jewish books of prayer. These books usually have traditional prayers on the left page and their Hebrew versions on the right page. It is not necessary to speak or read Hebrew fluently or even poorly. It will suffice to recognize the various letters and pronounce them individually. If that is also difficult, then saying the prayer in English and concentrating on the form of the Hebrew version without pronouncing the letters will suffice. Kabbalists claim that saying this prayer devoutly every day immediately upon awakening, before showering or even brushing the teeth, brings the individual close to the Godhead and grants him many blessings. The prayer should be uttered standing up, then the individual should kneel down and kiss the ground.

Ideally, one should never petition God for specific favors. Prayer is an act of love. One thanks God in prayer for all the benefits He has conferred upon us, asks His forgiveness for our faults and weaknesses, and asks for the strength to overcome them and the wisdom to understand and obey the Law, the Torah. If something specific is desired one then adds, "I would be immensely happy and grateful if You would illuminate me and show me how I may acquire this which I desire." The only way we can ask God to do for us and give us something is by first surrendering our will to Him in its entirety. This is important because God created man free and therefore will not interfere in worldly matters. To do so He would have to overcome man's freedom of choice and man would then be forced to do God's will. But man has been made free, and all of his decisions are his and his alone. To surrender one's will and freedom to the Creator is the greatest act of love, but one which must not be undertaken lightly. One must first be ready to accept all of God's decisions and be one with His will at all times without questioning. This is a total surrender of both soul and will, and must be understood perfectly and adhered to at all times. Until this decision is made, the ideal act of prayer should be conducted along the lines previously described.

Prayer is only the simplest of many forms of invocation. Practically all magical acts are invocations of one type or another. But while in prayer we petition God, we are also aware that our prayer may not be answered. Sometimes what we want is not possible or not readily available to us. What we must remember in prayer is that the laws of the universe must always be observed. Even when "miracles" seemingly happen it is because their occurrence will not disturb the perfect structure of the universe. Under a different set of circumstances, the same "miracle" could not have possibly happened. I remember meeting a man once who told me he did not believe in God because He allowed this man's mother to die at a very early age. The man had prayed to God to save his mother, who was dying of a very unusual form of brain cancer, and had promised God he would be faithful and good always if only his mother would live. When his mother died, he became enraged with God and cried out: "You don't exist! I don't believe in you. If you were really God you would have listened to my prayer and saved my mother." It never occurred to this man that by his very words he was proclaiming a very strong belief in God's existence. What he did was rebel against God because of his mother's death, something which due to the nature of her illness was inevitable if natural law was to be preserved. His rage and pain were understandable, and also part of a natural reaction. When we pray therefore we should remember the laws of probablility and possibility, and ask not for that which is clearly impossible or against natural laws.

In magic we are no longer placing our fate in God's hands. We are taking matters in our hands and stressing our own wills. We are still using the same energies we use in prayer, but this time we are channeling the energies ourselves. This is within man's right, for again, he was created free, with his own individual will. The advantage of prayer is that when we pray we are not breaking any laws, something which can happen in the practice of magic, and which is the reason magic so often fails. Personally, I believe that the first act of magic is the proper observance of the Law, and this includes the Torah as embodied in the Ten Commandments, and the laws of nature. I would therefore recommend to anyone who intends to practice kabbalistic magic to become familiar with physical laws. For this purpose, he should buy a small volume describing in simple language the most basic of natural laws, such as the law of gravitation, the laws of momentum, inertia, cohesion and adhesion, and so on. A good understanding of the basis of nuclear physics, including atomic particles and electromagnetism, is quite desirable. The first part of this book speaks of the parallels between the creation of the universe according to both physicists and kabbalists. When one attempts to alter the course of natural things, one should know the nature of the things one is attempting to change. Then he will know what he can and cannot do successfully *and* safely.

The foregoing admonition may seem unnecessary to some, but in reality it is good, sound advice. Magic, after all, deals with changes in the material world. There is nothing "supernatural" about it. On the contrary, all the forces we work with in magic are very real and very natural. It is important therefore for us to understand what we are doing. And because the changes we hope to create first take place in the realm of the mind, we should also try to understand the basis of our mental makeup. A small manual on general psychology should provide that factual information.

Once we know the basic nature of the universe and the essential components of our minds, we are ready to tackle magic. The first thing we must remember is that all the forces we will deal with, angelic or otherwise, are an intrinsic part of our own minds. Whatever energies we release through ritual come from ourselves. We are the central channel through which these universal forces are manifested. As the energies pour out we then direct them in the direction we want them to take. All of this takes place in the realm of Mind, which is where all magic takes place.

Much has been written about the importance of fasting and purification before a magic ritual. This importance cannot be overemphasized. During any ceremony vast amounts of energies are released by the practitioner, and there are always clusters of negative forces gathering around him at this time hoping to tap in on these energies on which they feed. It is therefore very important for the would-be magician to strengthen himself with the proper methods of self-purification. Fasting for at least 24 hours before any major operation is highly advisable, and so is the refraining from sexual activity, anger or any other powerful emotion. Meditation and controlled breathing prior to the ceremony is also helpful. Chapters 11 and 12 give examples of kabbalistic rites of invocation with specific instructions as to how they should be performed.

Evocation

The practice of magical evocation deals, as I mentioned earlier, with the actual summoning of "spirits" or concentrations of energies for the purpose of materialization. There are innumerable treatises that give instructions for the summoning of spirits, most of them dating from the Middle Ages. Among them are the famous or infamous Grimoires and the various "Goetic" books. Chief among these are the *Greater* and *Lesser Keys of Solomon,* the *Grimorium Verum,* the *Grand Grimoire,* the *Grimoire of Honorius,* the *Almadel,* and the *Sacred Magic of Abramelin the Mage.* More recently, German kabbalist Franz Bardon wrote several books on the practice of magic, one of which deals specifically with evocation and is entitled, *The Practice of Magical Evocation.*

Many of the treatises above-mentioned deal specifically with the summoning of evil spirits, which for some obscure reason seem to have appealed more to the writers of the Middle Ages. The instructions included the preparation of the robes and magical apparel, the inks and pens and parchments to be used in pacts, the best times for invocation and the names and seals of the spirits, among other things. They are for the most part quaint and fascinating, but have come down to us badly diluted with many gross inaccuracies and misspellings of the "barbarous names of evocation." For that reason the efficacy of the various formulae is believed to have been lost in most cases.

Many people doubt that rites of evocation can be successful, as they find it impossible to believe that spiritual forces may take material form. This is not true, as I know from personal experience. Matter, as we know from the study of physics, is made of energy. It is perfectly possible and quite within the realm of natural things for energy to be materialized quite suddenly in front of our eyes. During a winter day we can see our breath, which is usually invisible, become condensed into visibility. If it is extremely cold, the breath can actually solidify into ice in a matter of seconds. This is a simple physical change of matter from gas to solid, something which we studied in grammar school. The "spiritual forces" invoked and evoked in magic are also concentrations of energy and are therefore a form of matter.

Because they are invisible we can assume they may be gaseous in nature. But as we well know gas can be solidified into a visible form, therefore it is within the realms of possibility for a spiritual force to be solidified as well. The form and shape it takes has already been established through countless centuries of visualization by long-gone magicians. The power of the human mind is awesome, and causing a mental force to materialize is only one of its great powers. Several years ago, while I was still living in Vienna during a two-year tenure with the United Nations, I had the opportunity to prove this. At the time I had been experimenting with various magical systems. I was particularly interested in ritual magic, and I had been quite successful in my magical work. One day I came upon a ritual of evocation entitled The Rite of Queen Hagiel. It gave detailed instructions on the summoning of Hagiel, who is the Intelligence of Venus (Netzach), when the planet enters the signs of Taurus and Libra. The instructions called for a robe made of blue satin worn with a green or rose-colored girdle, a lamp made of copper and seven pieces of green glass (all Venus attributes), and cinnamon as incense. The square of Venus with its traditional 49 squares was to be made on a piece of parchment, and Hagiel's seal and sigil were to be drawn on another piece of parchment cut in the shape of a heptagon. A triangle was to be drawn on the floor outside the magic circle, and Hagiel's seal was to be placed therein. All in all, it was a simple rite of great beauty and I was captivated by the idea of attempting to contact the spirit, which is said to be very kind and beneficent. I was able to prepare most of the things required by the rite, but I was unable to find in Vienna seven pieces of green glass shaped like heptagons for the lamp; the copper was just as hard to locate. Virgin parchment was also an impossibility, so I decided to improvise. I used seven green candles instead of the lamp and regular paper in place of parchment.

The rite called for the invocation of Hagiel seven times and for walking around the circle the same number of times. As I started the invocation, I had the distinct feeling that I was not alone. The room seemed to fill with an indescribable presence, and I kept watching the outer triangle expecting a materialization at any moment. Suddenly, on the floor above the triangle someone began to throw what sounded like heavy stones. As these weights crashed down on the floor, the ceiling above the triangle began to warp and weave. I was sure it would cave in at any second. But just as suddenly as it started, the noise stopped. It was immediately replaced by an eerie melody which someone was whistling on the floor above. The whistling moved twice along the perimeter of the circle and also stopped. What made the entire episode uncanny was the fact that I lived on the building's top floor and that above me was an empty attic which had been padlocked for years. No one could possibly enter that attic except the owner of the house who was not in Vienna at the time. In spite of the terrifying impression I received, I managed to finish the rite without further mishaps. As soon as it was all over, I ran outside and climbed up to the attic to check the door; but the padlock was not only secure, but covered with spider webs. No one had entered through that door. When I returned to the room where I had conducted the ritual I found that the ceiling which had I seen weave and nearly collapse was perfectly intact. To complete the experience, that night I dreamt of Hagiel. I saw her exactly the same way she had been described in the ritual, a beautiful, fair-skinned redhead with blue eyes, naked from the waist up, wearing a blue satin skirt and a rose-colored girdle. She was quite pleasant and amiable and told me that she had been unable to come to me during the day because the rite was incomplete. She could only materialize in a green haze, which was the purpose of the green lamp. But she answered all my questions quite willingly and gave me other instructions I had not asked for.

My experience with Hagiel has only been one of many encounters with materialized forces. I therefore know through experience that evocation rituals can be successful if properly conducted. But I still must caution beginners against its practice. Any mistake or omission in a rite can be the cause of some very frightening phenomena, as my experience with Hagiel shows. The rites of evocation should only be undertaken by experienced magicians, and then, with the utmost caution.

13 Rites of the Kabbalists

The Kabbalists have always stressed the interrelation of all worlds and all levels of being. Everything is connected, and this interpenetration of all things is governed by exact and unfathomable laws. Furthermore, all created beings exist according to the archetypes (*dugma*) of the ten sephiroth. This world of the archetypes is often called the *merkabah*, or Chariot of God, and every detail in the ritual of the Torah is connected with a particular part of the merkabah. Every commandment (*mitzvah*) of the Torah has a high principle and a secret foundation. And just as God is One, so all the commandments together form one power, that of infinite divine life. The Torah as the totality of the commandments is anchored in this divine world, which is the pleroma of the ten sephiroth. More important still, God does not transcend the Torah, nor is Torah outside God, for He Himself *is* the Torah. That is why observing the Law is so vital in kabbalistic thought.

The early Rabbinical rites were intrinsically linked with this observance of Divine Law and revealed an intimate bond with nature. The first of the six parts of the *Mishnah*, which is a codification of Jewish religious law and ritual, deals with the commandments as applicable to an agrarian society. These mitzvoth, as stipulated in the Old Testament, describe the regulations concerning harvesting and gleaning, the first fruits and the sabbatical year, and the sowing of plants of different species. According to these Laws, the fruits of a first harvest could not be gathered and had to be allowed to rot on the trees and the vines. Strangers could eat of them, but not their owners, for these first fruits belonged to God. The same applied to the first-born of all the animals in a herd, which were to be sacrificed to God after a suitable period. In fact, all first borns, human beings included, belong to God according to the Torah, for everything that "opens the womb" is sacred unto Him.

Another part of the mitzvoh concerned itself with the sabbatical year. According to this Law all debts were to be forgiven and slaves were to go free every seven years. This part of the Torah is observed even in our modern societies. Outstanding bank loans and debts of all types are automatically cleared at the end of seven years, whether or not they have been paid.

During the early Middle Ages, the contact with nature was gradually lost. Because the ordinances of the Torah were valid only in the Holy Land, where they concerned agriculture, the Jews in exile abandoned them. They were replaced with historical rituals of remembrance centering around the various festivals on the Jewish calendar.

It has been said that the rituals of Rabbinical Judaism make nothing happen and transform nothing. It is not the same with kabbalistic rituals which are mainly concerned with change. Some of these are very old and go back to the mystics who preceded the thirteenth-century kabbalists. Chief among these are special rites of initiation.

A rite of initiation in kabbalistic tradition is generally concerned with the transmission of God's name from master to pupil. According to Eleazar of Worms, a famous kabbalist of the 13th century, the Name is transmitted only to those specially chosen who are not prone to anger, who are humble and God-fearing, and who carry out the commandments of their Creator. And it is transmitted only over water. Before the Master teaches it to the pupil, they must both bathe in 40 measures of flowing water, then put on white garments and fast on the day of instruction. Then both must stand up to their ankles in the water and the master must say a prayer, ending as follows: "The voice of God is over the waters! Praised be Thou, O Lord, who revealest Thy secret to those who fear Thee, He who knoweth the mysteries." Then both must turn their eyes toward the water and recite verses from the Psalms, praising God over the waters. The master then reveals the pronunciation of one of the Names of God that the disciple is allowed to hear. They both return to the Master's house where they say a prayer of thanksgiving over a vessel full of water.

The correct pronunciation of God's Names is of great importance in kabbalistic magic. But the ancient kabbalists were careful to stress that the invocation of God's Name does not oblige Him to do the will of the invoker or that He is coerced by the recital of His Name. It is simply that the Name itself is invested with the power to fulfill the desires of he who utters it. As far back as the seventh century, the ten most powerful of God's Names were El, Eloe, Zelioz or Ramathel, Eyel, Adonai, Jah, Tetragrammaton, Saddai, and Elohim. But of course, the most powerful of the Names was and is the Tetragrammaton, YHVH. As we saw in Part I the Name has twelve forms which it can assume by the transposition of its letters. Although the letters form the "body" of the name, its proper pronunciation can only be ascertained through the correct placement of the vowel points under the right consonant. The Name can be pronounced in myriad ways, and among some of the versions offered by kabbalists are Jehovah, Yaweh, Yahavha, Yavah, and Yeheveh. The uncertainty that prevails concerning the vocalization of these

Names and the varying traditions about their pronunciation make it impossible to know for certain which is the correct way to utter the Name. This knowledge can only be imparted orally, from Master to pupil, and there are very few kabbalists in the world today who have attained the knowledge of the Name.

There are other Names of God which are more readily accessible, as their pronunciation is known by kabbalists. Among these are the Name of 22 letters and the Name of 42 letters. The pronunciation of the first of these is *Anaktam Pastam Paspasim Dionsim.* This Name first appeared in Sepher Raziel, attributed to Eleazar of Worms, and soon became very popular in incantations, as it was believed to be extremely potent. In the 17th century it was introduced into the ritual of the synagogue in a prayer attached to the Priestly Benediction. The pronunciation of the second Name has been shortened to *Abgitaz Shakvazit,* which comprises the first and the last parts of the Name. This Name is supposedly very powerful for the healing of the sick, for the destruction of enemies and the acquisition of power over others. But the kabbalists caution against its usage in an unclean state as it would then cause the death of the invoker.

The pronunciation of the various Names over water is part of the rites of purification which are so persistently stressed by the kabbalists. Uncleanliness is equal with ungodliness in their view, and water is the supreme cleanser of evil. The rite of baptism initiated by John the Baptist was based on this same kabbalistic belief.

Another rite that concerns itself with the Name of God is the one called, "Putting on the Name." For this ritual the kabbalist needs a piece of pure deerskin parchment from which he cuts a sleeveless garment, modeled after the High Priest's ephod. This tunic covers the shoulders and chest down to the navel and falls down the sides to the loins. A hat is connected to the garment. On this magic tunic some of the secret Names of God are inscribed. Then the adept must fast for seven days, eating nothing of animal origin, including milk, eggs or fish. He also must abstain from touching anything unclean and refrain from sexual activity. At the end of seven days he must go at night to the water and call out the Name or Names written on the garment. If he perceives a green form in the air above the water, it is a sign that he is still unclean and he must repeat the same preparations for another seven days, accompanied by acts of charity. If the form over the water is red, then he is deserving to put on the Name. At this time he must go into the water up to his loins and put on the garment with God's Name. This ritual is said to give the adept irresistible strength.

Other kabbalistic rites of great importance are based on the sacred "marriage" between the spheres of Tiphareth and Malkuth, which represent the male and female aspects of the Godhead. The Shekinah, or female aspect of God, is identified with Israel. The Feast of Weeks, which takes place on the 50th day after Passover, is in reality a sacred marriage feast where the covenant between God and Israel is again commemorated. From the beginning of the 16th century a set ritual was established based on a passage from the *Zohar* on the marriage between the male and female aspects of God. The whole night before this holy marriage took place the kabbalists meditated, sang songs and read specific selections from all the books of the Bible, from all the treatises of the Mishnah and from the parts of the *Zohar* dealing with the ceremony. This rite became very popular and it is still practiced today. The concept of an actual marriage was carried so far that some kabbalists read a formal contract stating the terms of marriage between the "Bridegroom God" and the "Virgin Israel."

The Sabbath eve itself is considered the night of sexual union between the Shekinah and Her spouse and many scholars consider this Sabbath eve *the* day of Kabbalah. At this time the light of the upper world bursts into the material world and endures into the following week growing gradually dimmer until the rising light of the next Sabbath. Kabbalists believe the Sabbath eve is the perfect night for sexual union between a man and his wife which is blessed by the union of the Shekinah and Her spouse. On Friday afternoon the Song of Songs, which is traditionally identified with the indissoluble bond between God and Israel, is often said with great devotion. The Song of Songs is extremely powerful in love rituals. A popular rite using the 8 verses of the Song calls for reciting each verse on succeeding Fridays at midnight while standing up to the ankles in water. The person must have fasted 24 hours prior to the ritual and must be crowned with a wreath of myrtle and roses intertwined. He should hold a lit white candle in his right hand while uttering the prayer.

The separation of the Shekinah from Her Lord and Her anguish in exile are the basis of another famous kabbalist ritual. The evening hours up to midnight are, according to kabbalists, ruled by the powers of stern judgment. From midnight onwards these powers are broken, and hope and peace can once more rule the world. But the hour of midnight itself is the time of greatest sorrow for the Shekinah because then the powers of darkness are at their peak. Accordingly, a rite devised to relieve some of Her sorrow was created by the kabbalists of the Middle Ages. In this ritual, the kabbalist rises and dresses at midnight and stands near the doorpost of his house. He then removes his shoes and covers his head with a veil. Weeping, he covers his forehead with ashes, and lying on the ground, he rubs his eyes with the dust he finds there. He then recites a set liturgy composed of Psalms 137 and 79 and the last chapter of Lamentations. Even noninitiates should perform this rite, according to kabbalists, because the time of midnight onwards is a time of grace, and a ray of this grace will fall upon him through his identification with the Shekinah's sorrow.

The day before the New Moon, when the moon is at its darkest, is also observed by kabbalists in still another ritual to honor the Shekinah. On this day, called *Yom Kippur Katan* or Lesser Day of Atonement, kabbalists recommend fasting and praying in repentance of all sins. The Shekinah, who is also known as the "holy moon," has been robbed of Her light by the sins of mankind. This is exemplified by the lessening of the moon's powers during its waning period. By fasting and repenting at this time, some of the Shekinah's light is restored unto Her. The following day, which is the beginning of the New Moon, is a day of special celebration and the *Hallel* or praises to God are sung by the kabbalists and in all synagogues. No fasting is allowed on this day. A ritual of great beauty and simplicity for the New Moon calls for the lighting of seven candles representing the seven animal offerings made to God on this day in ancient times. A glass of clear water should be placed on the altar, and Psalms 113 and 118 should be said over the water. A small glass of wine should be drunk in God's name after the conclusion of the ritual, praising Him for the Creation of the Universe and thanking Him for all His blessings. Incense and music pertaining to the moon, such as Debussy's Claire de Lune and Beethoven's Moonlight Sonata, are not traditional but are lovely offerings to God.

I must stress here that the use of Psalms in kabbalistic rituals is of immense power, particularly Psalms 22, 23, 8, 51, 45 and 91. Each Psalm has a specific use according to tradition, and reading them through should make it clear what Psalm is good for what purpose. As I mentioned earlier, a good understanding and observance of the Torah is absolutely vital in the practice of kabbalah. I would also like to add that there is great power in all the books of the Old Testament, particularly the Prophets, the Psalms, the

Song of Songs, Ecclesiastes and Proverbs. The prophet Isaiah is very powerful in works of love and positive action. The prophet Jeremiah is excellent in works of dominion and in overcoming difficulties. But it is important that you find out for yourselves where the power lies and how to use it. Searching for this power is in itself a kabbalistic exercise for spiritual attainment.

14 Kabbalistic Magic

There have been many books written on the "Western Tradition" of kabbalistic magic. Among them are the works of modern magicians like Aleister Crowley, Dion Fortune, Israel Regardie and a host of others, most of them members of the Order of the Golden Dawn. Their works were largely influenced by the kabbalists of the turn of the century, among whom were Eliphas Levi, Stanislas de Guaita, Gerard Encausse (Papus), Wynn Wescott, MacGregor Mathers and last but not least, Arthur Edward Waite, who was undoubtedly the most scholarly of the lot. Although bombastic and pretentious to the extreme, Waite's erudition in kabbalistic matters can hardly be denied. While Waite decried Ceremonial Magic as "puerile and imbecilic," he recognized the magical potential of the Divine Names and their numerical permutations. In spite of his antagonism to magical practices, Waite's *Holy Kabbalah* remains one of the most thorough and comprehensive ever written by a Christian kabbalist. It should be read by anyone interested in the history and traditions of the kabbalah.

Waite is important specifically in that he points out quite correctly that modern Ceremonial Magic is not pure kabbalah, but rather a mixture of several systems, among which are gnosticism, astrology, alchemy, Indian and Egyptian mysticism, *and* kabbalah. And although kabbalistic elements are of great importance in the so-called Western Tradition of magic, there would still be a Western Tradition if there were no kabbalah.

It is therefore very important to understand that beneath the glorious effulgence of kabbalistic thought lies the simple uncluttered truth of its intrinsic Jewishness. If we are to understand kabbalah and practice its magic, we first must come to terms with the fact that here we are dealing with esoteric Judaism. Pure kabbalistic magic uses some of the elements of modern Ceremonial Magic, but only some. Most of its practical aspects come from Biblical and Talmudic sources, and its rites are always concerned with the love of God and the observance of His Law. The most powerful of kabbalistic grimoires is undoubtedly the *Siddur* or *Jewish Prayerbook*. The *Siddur* is prayer constructed along kabbalistic lines, and one does not have to be Jewish to use it successfully. Israel is after all a symbol of mankind, and we are the strangers at her gate, the strangers who, according to God Himself, would one day inherit the Torah. Those who are Christians among us should find our roots in Judaism because Jesus was a Jew, and to judge by his works, someone quite familiar with kabbalistic thought.

The truth of the matter is we cannot divorce Judaism from kabbalah, nor kabbalah from Judaism. The two are intrinsically linked, and although we do not have to be Jewish to practice kabbalah, we would do well to remember that link.

The *Siddur* is a vehicle of kabbalah because kabbalah is essentially prayer, an act of love and devotion to God's will. The highest kabbalistic magic is the surrender to God's will, because at this point man achieves his most cherished aims. Because his will is one with God's will what he wants is also what God wants. Nothing can be denied to him. But for this fusion between human and Divine wills to take place, the surrender has to be selfless, with no desires for worldly ambitions. The intention must be for God to do with our wills what He wants and to work His will through us. Only when the intention is pure and the love absolute is the fusion complete. This is not easy, and requires much prayer and purification, but it is the highest aim of the kabbalist. This is known magically as the completion of the Great Work and the Conversation with the Holy Guardian Angel.

In the long climb on the Ladder of Lights which is the kabbalah, perhaps the first rung is an identification with nature in general. Because nature is in Malkuth and Malkuth is the sphere of the Shekinah, to love nature is to love Her. Here we should begin our magical work. The kabbalist always seeks to merge with nature, to understand its myriad voices. In the sea, the wind, the birds, the forests, the mountains, and every creature that walks on earth, in the lava of the volcano and the foam of the waterfall, he seeks and finds the Divine. Through love and understanding he merges with the soul of the flowers and merges with nature. Through quiet contemplation he enters into the temple of nature and it surrenders its mysteries to him. Malkuth is the first step in magic, and perhaps the most important one. If that basis is well-established, the rest of the work will be much easier.

Here then are the elements of the practical kabbalah or kabbalistic magic. First, there should be an attempt to identify with nature. There are various ways to do this. Whenever you are in a park or a forest, stop for a moment and let your love flow out to the trees and the plants therein. As you walk, brush lightly with your fingers every shrub or tree in your path. If you see or hear any birds, stop for a moment and try to reach them and caress them with your mind. If you see a flower, stop and smell its fragrance, marvel at its beauty and the creative genius that made it possible. Stop by the largest and strongest tree that you can find and lean on it, embrace it and ask it silently to give you some of its strength. If you are near the sea, visit it one day at a time when there is no one around. Sit facing the waves, a short distance away from the surf and let your mind flow out to the sea with great love. Because the sea is the most responsive of all of nature's forces, if you concentrate deeply, you will see how the water will climb slowly until it reaches you. As soon as the water wets your feet, stand up, open your arms as if to embrace the sea and give it your love. Then leave right away. Also very powerful as a form of identification with nature is meditating alone on top of a hill. Because kabbalists believe God is in all "High Places," you should fast for 24 hours before the meditation, abstain from sexual activity, be scrupulously clean and preferably dress in white. Once on top of the hill, sit on the highest point and start your meditation. This should begin by quieting your mind, and breathing rhythmically for a few minutes. This you do by breathing deeply through the nose in a slow count of four, holding the breath in for a count of four, and exhaling in a count of four. You should sit in a relaxed yoga position, back straight and eyes closed. When your mind has relaxed, let yourself flow out to the universe, embracing with your love all that exists. Feel grateful for the air that you breathe, for the beauties of the earth, and for the life around you. Feel also pain for the polluted waters, for the ravished forests, for the endangered species, for the miseries of mankind. After a while you will feel as if you were beating along with the pulse of nature, as if you were one with the All.

The foregoing are only a few examples of the ways you can merge with nature. You can of course devise your own methods, and perhaps those will work best for you. Also remember to try to establish contact with animal life. When you do this remember never to touch an animal unless it wishes you to do so. You must respect its privacy, as you wish your privacy to be respected. The best way to contact an animal is with your mind. Let your mind flow out to the animal in love and friendship, ask it mentally to come to you quietly, peacefully. At first you will not succeed, but in time you will notice the animal will turn to look at you and then it will approach you. Don't attempt to touch it until you can see it feels comfortable in your presence and wishes to be your friend. Then put out your hand and if it wants your contact, it will establish it first. Only then should you touch or pet it. Be very relaxed and calm when you touch or contact an animal because they can sense your every emotion.

The second element in kabbalistic magic is purification. Before any ritual, however simple, you should bathe thoroughly and dress in clean clothes, preferably white. A simple tunic can be made of a length of cloth in which you have cut a hole for your head. This makeshift tunic hangs loose and open at the sides. You can tie it around your waist with a plain ribbon, either white or of the color of the sephirah you will be working with. After you have dressed you should anoint your temples, your forehead and the back of your neck with holy oil. This you can prepare by mixing in a small clay vessel half a cup of pure olive oil with a pinch of salt and a handful of powdered myrrh and cinnamon. When the mixture is ready, pass it through incense, also of myrrh and frankincense, and recite the 23rd Psalm over it. The oil is now purified. Use a small amount for the anointing, and store the rest for future use. Also part of the purification is abstaining from sexual activity and animal products, including milk and eggs, for three days before the ritual, and total fasting, except water and juices, for 24 hours. If you choose to wear a tunic remember not to mix materials. That is, if the tunic is made of cotton, the ribbon should also be made of cotton or one of its derivatives. If the tunic is made out of nylon or satin, so should the ribbon. Never should you mix cotton and silk or satin and wool or any two types of material. These are all Torah ordinances.

The third element we must consider is time, which is known in magic as the course of the Tides. In the Western Tradition various Tides are taken into consideration in preparing for a ritual. Among them are the Seasonal Tides, which divide the year into four sections; to wit, the Winter Solstice, the Autumnal Equinox, the Summer Solstice and the Vernal (Spring) Equinox. Then there are the Tattvic Tides which concern the five elements of Akasha (Ether), Vayu (Air), Tejas or Agni (Fire), Apas (Water) and Prithivi (Earth). Each Tattvic period lasts approximately 24 minutes. Third come the Lunar Tides composed of the Waxing (New Moon to Full Moon) and Waning (Full Moon to New Moon) periods of the Moon. Each lasts about 14 days. Last of the Tides to be considered are the Planetary Hours, which concern the seven planets and their constant rotation. The order of the planets never varies. They are Sun, Venus, Mercury, Moon, Saturn, Jupiter and Mars. Table 9 shows the days and the hours ruled by the planets.

Of the four Seasonal Tides, the Winter Solstice should be avoided for magical purposes according to the Western Tradition. This does not apply to kabbalah which is an eternal concept of union with the All. Therefore, the Seasonal Tides do not have to be considered in kabbalistic magic. The Tattvic Tides, on the other hand, with their 24-minute span, are too short for ritual purposes. This leaves us with the Lunar Tides and the Planetary Hours. Because Astrology is an ancient Chaldean science, it must have been known to the first kabbalists. Moon observances, like the Rites of the New Moon already described, are common in kabbalah, as are the planets. Therefore in kabbalistic magic we should always determine which Moon aspect and which Planetary Hour we will use for a given ritual. Because kabbalistic rites are rites of a positive or creative nature, only the Waxing Period of the Moon should be used, from New Moon to Full Moon included. Which Planetary Hour and which day we

Table 9

THE PLANETARY HOURS

PLANETARY HOURS COMPUTED FROM MIDNIGHT TO MIDNIGHT

HOURS OF THE DAY

	Sunday	Monday	Tuesday	Wednesday	Thursday	Friday	Saturday
1.	Sun	Moon	Mars	Merc.	Jup.	Venus	Sat.
2.	Venus	Sat.	Sun	Moon	Mars	Mrc.	Jup.
3.	Merc.	Jup.	Venus	Sat.	Sun	Moon	Mars
4.	Moon	Mars	Merc.	Jup.	Venus	Sat.	Sun
5.	Sat.	Sun	Moon	Mars	Merc.	Jup.	Venus
6.	Jup.	Venus	Sat.	Sun	Moon	Mars	Merc.
7.	Mars	Merc.	Jup.	Venus	Sat.	Sun	Moon
8.	Sun	Moon	Mars	Mrc.	Jup.	Venus	Sat.
9.	Venus	Sat.	Sun	Moon	Mars	Merc.	Jup.
10.	Merc.	Jup.	Venus	Sat.	Sun	Moon	Mars
11.	Moon	Mars	Merc.	Jup.	Venus	Sat.	Sun
12.	Sat.	Sun	Moon	Mars	Merc.	Jup.	Venus

HOURS OF THE NIGHT

	Sunday	Monday	Tuesday	Wednesday	Thursday	Friday	Saturday
1.	Jup.	Venus	Sat.	Sun	Moon	Mars	Merc.
2.	Mars	Merc.	Jup.	Venus	Sat.	Sun	Moon
3.	Sun	Moon	Mars	Merc.	Jup.	Venus	Sat.
4.	Venus	Sat.	Sun	Moon	Mars	Merc.	Jup.
5.	Merc.	Jup.	Venus	Sat.	Sun	Moon	Mars
6.	Moon	Mars	Merc.	Jup.	Venus	Sat.	Sun
7.	Sat.	Sun	Moon	Mars	Merc.	Jup.	Venus
8.	Jup.	Venus	Sat.	Sun	Moon	Mars	Merc.
9.	Mars	Merc.	Jup.	Venus	Sat.	Sun	Moon
10.	Sun	Moon	Mars	Merc.	Jup.	Venus	Sat.
11.	Venus	Sat.	Sun	Moon	Mars	Merc.	Jup.
12.	Merc.	Jup.	Venus	Sat.	Sun	Moon	Mars

Table 10

The Tree and Human Endeavors

Sphere	Planet	Endeavor
1. Kether	—	—
2. Chokmah	Zodiac	—
3. Binah	Saturn	—
4. Chesed	Jupiter	Superiors, achievement, career
5. Geburah	Mars	War, enemies, court cases, control over others
6. Tiphareth	Sun	Unity of Self, Money, success in all things
7. Netzach	Venus	Love, art, pleasure, music, theater
8. Hod	Mercury	Papers, writing, books, contracts, business
9. Yesod	Moon	Letters, trips, women
10. Malkuth	Earth	—

should use depend on the sphere of the Tree we will be working on and what we hope to accomplish with the ritual. Table 10 gives the planet associated with each sphere and the human endeavors they control.

The first three spheres are not used for magical purposes, other than spiritual attainment. The last sphere represents the magician and is used only as his starting point in his magical work.

The fourth element to consider concerns the altar and the magical implements to be used. Ideally, the altar should be made to specifications, 5 feet in length, 5 feet in width and 3 feet in height of any light wood. It should have a small enclosure where the magician may keep his implements when not in use. But if this altar cannot be constructed, then any new table will do which will only be used for that purpose. As far as the implements are concerned, they include a brass censer, a brass goblet, a small brass dish and a brass concave dish. Ten small candlesticks complete the implements. Only those things which are needed for each ritual should be on the altar, which should be set facing the East, where the sun rises. The altar should be covered with a white cloth.

The brass goblet is for wine, the small brass dish is for the bread offering, and the brass concave dish is for water. All three vessels must be kept on the altar, together with the censer and two of the candlesticks for all rituals that do not use the Tree of Life. (See Figure 2).

The Rituals

There are two types of rituals in kabbalistic magic. Those which concern prayer and invocation and those which concern the spheres of the Tree of Life. For both types of rituals, the magician should have purified himself and should be anointed. If possible, he should be dressed in

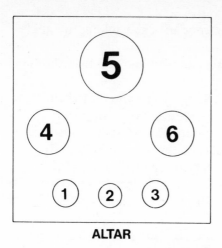

1. Candlestick
2. Goblet
3. Candlestick
4. Small Brass Dish
5. Censer
6. Concave Brass Dish

ALTAR

Figure 9.

hite robes. He should have carefully observed the Lunar period and the Planetary Hour governing his specific aim.

Before starting the ritual he should fill the concave dish with water and sprinkle it with salt for purification. He should have filled the censer with the incense belonging to the sphere and planetary force ruling his aim. He should then sprinkle the salt water in a circle, starting in the east and moving clockwise, making sure the altar lies within the center of the circle. He should then repeat this action with the censer. He's now ready to begin his work.

Rite of Prayer and Invocation

For this type of ritual, the altar should be set as in Figure 9. The goblet should be half full with a rich, sweet red wine. The small dish should have a small bread roll placed on it. Preferably the roll should be made of Challah, easily available in any Kosher bakery. If Challah is not available, a plain roll can be substituted. The incense to be used in this rite is a mixture of myrrh and frankincense. Two white candles should be placed on the candlesticks flanking the goblet, but not lit.

The magician then faces the altar and says the following:

"Oh Adonai, open thou my lips and they shall declare thy praise. Purge me with hyssop and I shall be clean, wash me and I shall be whiter than snow. Thou art holy and thy name is holy, and they who are holy shall praise thee daily, Selah. Holy, holy, holy is the Lord of Hosts, replete is all the world with His glory. Hallellujah."

He kisses the altar and continues, this time with the Shema:

"Hear O Israel, The Lord our God is the Eternal. The Eternal is One. Blessed be the glory of His sovereignty forevermore."

He then lights the candles and says:

"As I light these candles may they shine upon me in love and in peace."

He places a hand lightly upon the goblet and says:

"Thank you, God, for the grapes that grow from which wine is made for our celebrations."

He places a hand lightly upon the bread and says:

"Thank you, God, for the blessing of bread, the staff of life.
"Bless, Oh Father, these humble offerings with your bountiful blessings that I may rejoice in

your glory. And bless this moment that I may
prosper and be joyful as you intended me to
be from the moment of my creation."

Now he says the prayers or invocations that he had
previously chosen for the specific achievement of his goals.
Then he eats the bread slowly, asking for special blessings
and desires with each morsel of bread. He then drinks the
wine in a spirit of joy, certain that his desires will be granted.
The candles are left to burn out, but the rest of the
implements are cleaned and put away.

Special Prayers and Invocations

There are many special prayers that can be said for
specific purposes. Among them are the Psalms, the Song of
Songs and various other parts of the scriptures. Following
are some examples of these Biblical excerpts and their
traditional uses:

1. To win favor—Genesis 46:17 and Numbers 26:46; Also
   Canticles (Song of Songs) 6:4-9
2. To arouse love—Canticles 1:3
3. For sucess—Genesis 39:2 and Exodus 15:11
4. For success in business—Genesis 31:42 and 44:12
5. In times of trouble—Canticles 2:14 and 5:2
6. Against an enemy—Exodus 15:5; 15:6; 15:9; 15:19; and
   Isaiah 10:14
7. To cure sterility—Deuteronomy 7:12
8. To counteract magic—Exodus 22:17; Isaiah 41:24 and
   Leviticus 1:1
9. To maintain peace between lovers—Canticles 8:5
10. On entering a new home—Genesis 37:1 and 47:27

The words of these prayers are said over the goblet of

wine together with the intention attached to them. When the wine is drunk at the end of the ritual, the power of the words is absorbed by the body which then projects the desire outwardly, making it come true.

Other rites that can be used at this time are the Ritual of the New Moon, which is carefully delineated in the Siddur, and the use of Psalms 45 and 46 for marriage purposes. This latter rite calls for the uttering of the two Psalms over a clay vessel with anointing oil and over a small cake. After the end of the ritual a bit of the oil is dabbed on the temples and the various pulse points and then the cake is offered as part of other refreshments to the one desired as a marriage partner.

Perhaps one of the most extraordinary of the kabbalistic rites is the one concerning the Archangel Michael and which can only be done once a year on one's birthday. The rite calls for a strip of red towel which is soaked in the salt water and placed upon the eyes. This action is repeated until all the water has been taken from the water dish.

While this is being done Michael is invoked in the name of Elohim Tzabaoth to be propitious to the intention of the magician. After the water is evaporated, the strip of towel is placed inside an envelope with a letter to Michael delineating the magician's desires. This letter is then addressed to *Michael Arch* and sent to any fictitious address in the country which lies exactly opposite in longitude and latitude from those where the magician was born. The letter is sent certified to ensure its return. The moment the letter reaches its point of destination Michael receives the message which is immediately carried out. But not until the letter is returned to the magician will he see the successful outcome of the ritual. Every person I know who has conducted this ritual properly has succeeded in his wishes. When I did it several years ago I wasn't as successful because I sent the letter to Karachi, Pakistan by mistake. Because the latitude and longitude opposite Puerto Rico, where I was born, was smack in the middle of the Indian Ocean, I though that Karachi was the closest city where I could send the letter. I forgot that there are clusters of small islands in the middle of the Indian Ocean and that the closest place where I should have sent the letter was Mauritius. Michael did not get the letter, but he sent me a message anyway. The message was a post card from Mauritius from the person I wanted to influence and who still doesn't know what made him leave his native Norway to go by boat to the Indian Ocean. My wish was not totally fulfilled because of that one error, but at least I know where I have to send the next letter.

The Rites in the Tree

Undoubtedly, the best ritual to be conducted through the spheres of the Tree of Life are those devised by each individual kabbalist. For this type of ritual only the censer should be on the altar with incense belonging to the particular sphere to be used. Some of the symbols attributed to the sphere according to the various Tables of correspondences should also be present on the altar. My personal rite in the tree is simple, but I have always found it extremely successful.

The first thing one must remember in Tree work is that the spheres or sephiroth must be worked in pairs. To work with Netzach means that Hod must also be part of the ritual. If the work is on Geburah, Chesed must also be involved. Only the sephiroth of the Middle Pillar can be worked singly. That is because they are depositories of the energies of the spheres next to and above them, which makes them perfectly balanced within themselves.

In the special rite I use I form a schema of the Tree on the altar using nine of the ten candlesticks that form part of the magical implements. The candlesticks are placed in the positions of the sephiroth and the candles they hold are in the correct colors of each sephira, according to the Briatic color scale. After all the preliminary preparations, large quantities of energy should be built through rhythmic breathing and intense concentration, or any method that the magician finds successful.

The nine candlesticks occupy the positions of sephiroth one through nine, Kether through Yesod. In place of Malkuth I use a goblet of wine. As the energy begins to build, the names of God, the Archangels and the Angelic Orders can be vibrated, starting with Kether. That candle is then lit. As the flame in Kether gathers strength, its energies are absorbed in a deep sucking breath. The breath is held and its energy poured on to the next sephira to be used whose candle is then lit. If the rite is to be worked on the sphere of Chesed, the outpouring of energies are concentrated there and the intention of the ritual is uttered with the breath. Then the energy is quickly passed on to Geburah with another breath, and from that sphere to Tiphareth, and from Tiphareth to Yesod. In Yesod the intention is uttered *and* visualized. Then the energies are gathered in another great breath and brought down into the wine which represents Malkuth. As soon as the energies are poured into Malkuth the wine is drunk with the forceful will that what is aimed will be realized. As the energy is brought down from sphere to sphere, the corresponding candle is lit. After the wine has been drunk the candles are allowed to burn themselves out.

The Names vibrated in this rite are those corresponding to the spheres used. The Names of each sphere are uttered as the energy is poured into the candle representing that sphere.

The rite of Self-Evaluation and Self-Understanding that I mentioned in Chapter 3 as the first and most vital work in the Tree can be done by using the aforementioned schema. In this ritual the kabbalist seeks to balance the Synthesis of

Chesed with the Analysis of Geburah. This is done by meditating on the sphere of Tiphareth, which is the equilibrating principle between Chesed and Geburah.

The ritual begins by concentrating the raised energies on the sphere of Kether, enunciating the Names and lighting the corresponding candle. The energies are then brought down to Tiphareth, again using the Names and the candle of that sephira. The kabbalist then proceeds to project himself into Tiphareth, while meditating on the qualities of the sphere. As he does so, he should feel himself vibrating with the radiant peace and splendorous beauty of this sephira. At the same time, he should draw equal power from both Geburah and Chesed, acting as the willing recipient of the energies of both sephiroth. He should endeavor to maintain this attitude of receptivity, feeling the mercy and love of Chesed blend and fuse with the stern judgment of Geburah until he achieves the perfect understanding of both sephiroth, which is the Self-Understanding that he seeks. The end result of this ritual should be great stability and a sense of compassion for others, tempered by righteousness and fairness. When the energies in Tiphareth begin to dissipate, they are brought down to Yesod, uttering the Names and lighting the candle of the sephira. Then they are earthed in the wine cup that represents Malkuth and the wine is drunk, thus taking the released energies back within the Self.

This same ritual can be used for many purposes, varying the spheres of work according to the end desired. Table 11 gives the spheres to be used for specific work on the tree.

There are an infinity of rituals which can be created using the various Tables of Correspondences and some kabbalistic know-how. The more personal the rite, the better its chances of success. Try to avoid at all costs complicated rituals with special calls and orations and a non-ending stream of knives, swords, wands, lamens, pentacles and hexagrams, flashing tablets and other paraphernalia. Complex

Table 11

The Sephiroth and Work On the Tree

Selhira	Attributions	Briatic Color
Kether		
Chockmah	No material work is done on these spheres	
Binah		
Chesed (with Geburah)	Growth, journeys, banks, debts, gambling, abundance	Blue
Geburah (with Chesed)	Dangers, surgery, construction, destruction, war	Red
Tiphareth (alone)	Success, money, power, superiors, mental power	Yellow
Netzach (with Hod)	Love, passion, women, arts, music, enjoyment, pleasure	Emerald green
Hod (with Netzach)	Papers, business matters, contracts	Orange
Yesod (alone)	Affairs of women, the mother, changes, moves, short trips	Violet
Malkuth	Where energies are gathered.	

rituals do not generate more energy, they deplete it. A simple ritual, using the proper correspondences, and above all, a strong will and determination and unwavering faith in God will seldom fail.

The best advice I can give to anyone interested in practicing the kabbalah is to observe the Law, the Torah, and try to identify with natural forces before attempting to achieve anything lasting with kabbalah. Observing the Law does not mean only observing the Ten Commandments, but also all the negative and positive precepts as outlined in the first five Books of the Bible or Pentateuch, and applicable to our modern times. For example, there are certain meats which are forbidden. Among them are pork and its derivatives; clams, lobster, shrimp and all shell fish, rabbit and so on. It is part of observing Torah not to eat these meats. If you own a fruit tree, don't eat of its first fruits. If someone owes you money for more than seven years, forgive the debt. Don't work on Saturdays if you are Jewish or on Sundays if you are Christian. These are all ordinances that must be observed if you wish to have God's blessings. Observing these regulations does not make you impervious to unhappiness nor a sure candidate to the state lottery. What it does is widen your spiritual awareness and bring you close to the God within. Eventually the distance between you and Him will lessen, and one day you will be face to face with your Creator. And that is what kabbalah really is, synthesis, union, and above all, an act of love.

Part
III

A KABBALAH OF UNDERSTANDING

God and Sex, the Structure of
the Psyche, Correspondences,
and the Oneness of All Things

15 Sex and the Divine

The sexual impulse in human beings is not simply an act of procreation for the preservation of the human race. Neither is sexual pleasure just a "clever" incentive created through natural evolution to entice humans to mate. All animal life on this planet mates for procreation purposes, but only mankind mates at will. All the lower animals, including the apes, have mating seasons or periods when the female of the species is receptive to the male's sexual advances. If the female is not in *oestrus*, that is, biologically ready to be fertilized, she will not be interested in mating and neither will the male. But human females, although being more sexually receptive during their fertile cycles, are still interested in sexual encounters, even when they are not in their *oestrus* periods and cannot be fertilized. Human males, on the other hand, show an interest in sex, whether or not the female is in her fertile cycle. Sexual pleasure is also a permanent feature in the life of human beings, whether or not the individual is able to produce offspring.

Biologists are baffled by mankind's ability to enjoy sexual activity even when there are no natural advantages, such as procreation, involved. Everything nature does has a reason for its existence. The songs of birds, which are so delightful to the ear, are in reality warning signals to other birds not to tresspass into the singer's territory. The brilliant colors and fragrance of flowers are designed to attract the birds and insects which are responsible for their pollination. There is a reason why elephants have tusks and why lions have manes. There is a reason why the grass is green and why the oceans have tides. But there is no reason—at least apparent—why, of all creatures on this planet, man should mate at will. At least there is no evolutionary reason why he should.

All creatures, even those of the lower species, show a tendency to fondle or caress their prospective mates. Fish, birds, insects and mammals often engage in very complex courtship rituals before mating. Some species of apes groom each other affectionately, before and after mating. This primordial urge, which biologists explain as a necessary precursor of the mating event, becomes in mankind the overwhelming feeling we know as love. It is present in the lower forms of life as a faint breath of divinity, which expresses itself throughout creation in the union between the male and the female of the various species. Because mankind was created in God's image, the sexual urge in human beings becomes more than a procreative urge. It is a divine attribute that shows a direct link to the Godhead.

To kabbalists God is both male and female. As we saw in our earlier discussion of these two divine aspects of the Godhead, the union between the male and the female manifestations resulted in the creation of the universe. But although there are two aspects in God, the unity between them is so everlasting that the kabbalist still refers to Them as One. That is why the Shema emphasizes:

> Hear, O Israel, the Lord, Our God is the
> Eternal
> The Eternal is ONE.

As a result of Adam's fall, the female aspect of God,

the Shekinah, went into exile, away from Her Divine Bridegroom. The place of her exile is our material world, and it is up to us, through our good actions, to hasten Her return to Her Lord. Once a week, during the time of the Sabbath, a new union between the Shekinah and Her Bridegroom takes place. This sacred marriage, or *conjunctio,* is consummated on Friday evening at midnight. That is why many devout Jews and practicing kabbalists engage in the marital act at this time, believing that such unions are blessed by the Shekinah in her rejoicing over her own union with Her Lord. This *hieros gamos* or *zivvuga kadisha,* as the Zohar calls it, is consummated in the union between Tiphareth (the Holy Bridegroom) and Malkuth (the Shekinah). Tiphareth is the sphere that represents the male aspect of God because it is directly below Kether on the Middle Pillar and is a recipient of the forces of the first five sephiroth. Tiphareth is also known as Zoar Anpin, the Lesser countenance, and as Meleth the king. It is the supreme balancing force of the Tree of Life and its energies pervade all the other spheres of the Tree. It is the only sephira that has connecting paths to all the other sephiroth except Malkuth, which is a symbol of the material world and the embodiment of the Shekinah.

Tiphareth's energy flow is cut off from Malkuth by the ninth sephira, Yesod, which intercepts the divine flow, depriving Malkuth of its life-giving rays. This causes an eclipse of Tiphareth's light which throws Malkuth into darkness and confusion. That is why Tiphareth is associated astrologically with the Sun, Yesod with the Moon and Malkuth with the Earth (see Table 5). Whenever the Moon comes between the Earth and the Sun a solar eclipse takes place. In the Tree of Life, and therefore both in the world and in the universe, Tiphareth's light, which is the energy of God's male aspect, is always in eclipse. That is why Malkuth, the Shekinah, is in exile, and why our world is in turmoil.

Yesod, the intercepting sephira, is the sphere of mind

and of the Astral World. It is in Yesod that the kabbalist works to make changes in the material world. But Yesod's light is not pure light. Its light is reflected from Tiphareth and tempered by the forces of Netzach and Hod. Netzach is known as Firmness, but although its virtue is unselfishness, its vice is lust. Its qualities hover between illusion and reality. Hod, on the other hand, has truth as its virtue and dishonesty as its vice. It symbolizes caution but also pessimism; swiftness but also weakness. The combined forces of Netzach and Hod, not as pure or strong as Tiphareth, further weaken its light as it comes through Yesod.

Netzach's correspondences are the loins, hips and legs. Hod's correspondences are the sexual organs. Netzach and Hod are therefore the seeds, the precursors of the vital sexual instinct. Yesod, on the other hand, is the actuating principle between Tiphareth and Malkuth, but because of its sexual qualities, the union is far from perfect because it is facilitated through Yesod, who is the receptacle of the Hod and Netzach elements, and the resultant light is not the pure cosmic light of Tiphareth. Therefore the light received by the Shekinah is reflected light, the Moon's light, rather than the Sun's. That is why She is in constant sorrow. Only in the Messianic Age, when all the sparks of light imprisoned in the Qlipoth are finally released, and God's true and perfect light illuminates with equal power all of the sephiroth, will the Shekinah achieve total union with Her Divine Spouse. In the meantime she effects a union with Him during the Sabbath.

In the middle of the 16th century, the Safed kabbalists developed a very impressive ritual, these central theme of which was the sacred marriage or *zivvuga kadisha*. In this ritual the Shekinah was identified with every Jewish wife who celebrated the Sabbath. The ceremony began on Friday afternoon, sometime before the Sabbath. The kabbalists of Safed and Jerusalem dressed for the rite in white or light colors, never in red or black, as those are the colors of Geburah and Binah, representing the powers of severe judgment and limitation. Thus attired, they went to the open fields to meet the Divine Bride. The fields became holy apple orchards in Her honor, apples being sacred to Her. On the way to the field they sang hymns and psalms of joy, such as Psalms 92 and 95 through 99. One of the hymns sung during these festivities is still sung to this day in the synagogues during the Sabbath. It begins:

> Beloved, come and meet the Bride
> Bid welcome to the Sabbath tide . . .

Eventually the processions to the fields stopped, and the meetings took place in the synagogues. It then became customary to turn to the west at the last verse of the hymn and bow to the coming Bride. This custom is still observed in modern synagogues. In ancient times the psalms were sung with closed eyes because, according to the Zohar, the Shekinah is a beautiful virgin who has no eyes, as She lost them through weeping in exile.

The Song of Songs, which is a symbol of the union between the Holy Bridegroom and His Shekinah, as well as that of the Godhead with the Virgin Israel, was also sung at this time. Then all the Sabbath prayers were uttered.

The ritual in the fields was continued at home, where the entire family greeted the Bridegroom and His Bride with two bundles of myrtle and more prayers, particularly a recitation of Chapter 31 of Proverbs. Before the meal was eaten, the master of the house invited the divine spouses to partake of it and then uttered the mystery of the meal, stating in explicit terms the meaning of the "secret action" between the Zoar Anpin—the Bridegroom—and the Shekinah. Isaac Luria, who was undoubtedly the greatest of the Safed kabbalists, wrote a famous hymn that describes this secret action.

I sing in hymns
to enter the gates
of the field of apples
of holy ones.

A new table
we lay for Her,
a beautiful candelabrum
sheds its light upon us.

Between right and left
the Bride approaches
in holy jewels
and festive garments

Her husband embraces Her
in Her foundation,
gives Her fulfillment
and squeezes out His strength.

Torment and cries
are past.
Now there are new faces
and souls and spirits.

He gives Her joy
in twofold measure.
Lights shine
and streams of blessing.

Bridesmen, go forth
and prepare the Bride,
victuals of many kinds
and all manner of fish.

To beget souls
and new spirits
on the thirty-two paths
and three branches.

She has seventy crowns
but above Her the King,
that all may be crowned
in the Holy of Holies.

All worlds are formed
and sealed within Her,
but all shine forth
from the Old of Days.

to Southward I set
the mystical candelabrum,
I make room in the north
for the table with the loaves.

With wine in beakers
and boughs of myrtle
to fortify the Betrothed,
for They are feeble.

We plait Them wreaths
of precious words
for the coronation of the seventy
in fifty gates.

Let the Shekinah be surrounded
by six Sabbath loaves
connected on every side
with the Heavenly Sanctuary.

Weakened and cast out
the impure powers,
the menacing demons
are now in fetters.*

To the discerning kabbalist the entire hymn is rich
in kabbalistic symbology. The holy jewels and festive

See Gershom G. Scholem, *On the Kabbalah and Its Symbolism*, New York, 1965.

garments of the Shekinah are the prayers of the elect. The "foundation" alluded to in the hymn is Yesod, which is, as we have seen, the sphere associated with sex and the sexual organs. Fish are served to the Shekinah because they are symbols of fertility. The thirty-two paths and the three branches are the twenty-two paths connecting the sephiroth and the ten sephiroth themselves, as well as the three columns of the Tree of Life. The worlds formed and sealed within Her are the four worlds of Creation. The table with the loaves is set on the north because that is the quarter of the earth, where all material things are realized. The Betrothed are feeble as all lovers are after their lovemaking. The Shekinah is surrounded by six loaves in the hopes that there will be food and prosperity in the home during the following six days. Finally, Luria alludes to the menacing demons now in fetters which are the Qliphotic powers held at bay by the renewed stream of Creation.

It is clear that the secret action between the Holy Bridegroom and His Shekinah is the sexual act, albeit on a cosmic level. From this divine union are born new, perfect "souls and spirits," and undoubtedly new stars and solar systems, and entire universes. Thus Creation continues, although not as before. For while In the Beginning, God created the universe in six days and rested on the seventh, according to this kabbalistic concept, He (They) now create on the seventh day and rest on the following six days.

The importance of the Sabbath—both to the Jew and to the kabbalist—is twofold. On this day we commemorate the day of rest of the original Creation, as well as the renewed union of the Godhead which results in a continuous stream of Creation. During the Sabbath the Shekinah is fortified with the light from Her spouse, and the entire world is in a state of blessing through their union. This light diminishes throughout the following week until it is once more replenished in the next Sabbath. Such is the love of God for

His Shekinah and the world She encompasses that He has instituted the Sabbath as a time of hope and renewal for Her sake and ours. That is why the observation of the Sabbath is so important to the kabbalist. In fact, it has been called by many the day of the kabbalah.

Next in importance to the Sabbath as a sacred marriage feast is the Feast of Weeks which takes place on the 50th day after Passover. This day commemorates Moses' revelation on Mount Sinai when he received the Ten Commandments. According to the Torah, this happened 50 days after the Exodus from Egypt. It celebrates the covenant between God and Israel, which is a symbolic marriage between the Godhead and the Virgin Israel. On the eve of the Feast of Weeks, kabbalists and students of the Torah "dress" the Shekinah in the bridal garments she will wear next day when She meets Her spouse. These "holy jewels" which Luria mentioned in his hymn, are composed of 24 items (Isa. 3). These, according to the Torah, are the 24 books of the Old Testament. Anyone who recites verses from all 24 books and adds his own interpretations of their secret meanings helps dress Her in Her bridal robes and "holy jewels" and rejoices with Her throughout the night, becoming her "best man" in Her marriage. Next day, when Her divine Bridegroom asks Her who dressed Her so magnificently, She points to the adept and calls him to Her presence. This rite, which was initiated in the 16th century, is still very popular today and is commonly practiced in the sephardic synagogues of Jerusalem.

The day before the New Moon—Lesser Day of Atonement—kabbalists fast the whole day, meditating on the Shekinah's exile and eventual redemption. At this time the days of the preceding month are purified as the New Moon (the forces of Yesod) replenishes Her strength and Her waning light. The Jewish Book of Prayers has many prayers for this festival which is observed with its own rites. An ancient prayer for this day starts: "I am the Moon, you are my Sun." Several years ago, perhaps inspired by these words, Neil Diamond wrote a song using this same stanza, but with a variation: "You are the sun, I am the moon; You are the words, I am the tune, play me . . ."

The sacred marriage of the Shekinah and Her spouse is a ritual in which the hope of redemption is anticipated. At this time Her exile is at least temporarily suspended, and She enjoys once more, however briefly, the divine embrace of Her spouse.

Sexual union to the kabbalist is a divine act during which a man and a woman play the parts of the Shekinah and Her spouse on a material level. For this reason, great care should be taken in the choice of a mate and promiscuity of any type is forbidden. That is why one of the commandments prohibits adultery. A man should only have one woman and a woman should only have one man. If their union becomes unsatisfactory, they should separate, but never, under any circumstances, should they be unfaithful to each other. In kabbalah this is more than a moral standard. It is an observance of a divine law serenely rooted in the eternal love that flows between the male and the female aspects of the Godhead.

Not only infidelity, but all types of unorthodox sexual practices are forbidden by the kabbalah, including the practice of onanism which is seen as demonic in nature. The kabbalist believes in the sanctity of the human seed, and when it is poured outside the vessel of the woman's body it is said to become prey to the Qliphotic demons. Lilith, who is the she-demon that heads the Qliphoth, and her demonic hordes, are constantly trying to incite men to engage in sexual acts without the benefit of a woman so they can make themselves bodies of the lost seed. Such demonic offspring are known as the *Shovanim* (the ill bred). The ancient kabbalists used to practice a ritual called *tikkumn shovanim*.

During this rite, which was conducted specially on leap years, they fasted on Mondays and Thursdays on certain weeks of the winter season in order to atone for the seed lost in nocturnal emissions and onanism.

Sex should be cherished as a perfect vessel of divine power and should be kept pure and undefiled. This is accomplished by practicing it with only one individual with whom a great deal of love is shared. Sex during the Sabbath is commended as an act of worship to the Godhead, and if it is conducted as a ritual of deep spiritual significance, the resulting pleasure can be overwhelming in its power and beauty. To the kabbalist, orgasmic ecstasy is the closest contact which man and woman can achieve with God. It is also an infinitesimal taste of the eternal *extasis* that He (They) enjoy through their union. If you can conceive a never-ending, eternal *extasis*, you can begin to comprehend the nature of God. That is why sex is sacred and must be kept holy. That is why only human beings mate at will. It is so that they eventually understand the meaning of pleasure and of God's true essence, and what they can achieve if they can purify themselves and become one with God.

Adepts in kabbalah sometimes use sex in their rituals to achieve their material goals. After fasting and purification and ritualistic preparation, the two partners, both of whom must be well versed in the true kabbalah, engage in the sexual act holding firmly in mind their collective goal. At the moment of orgasm, which should be mutual, they release their aim while calling one of the holy names of God, usually Shaddai El Chai because it is connected with the sphere of Yesod. The resulting energies are so powerful that the kabbalist's aims are invariably accomplished. This rite, however, because of its great power, should not be used for material endeavors and should be used instead for spiritual advancement.

The sexual rites of the kabbalists find echoes in the

rites of Sartori, Alchemy, Tantric yoga and those used to awaken kundalini. Tantric yoga is used by many kabbalists in their rites because, as I said earlier, yoga elements have been incorporated into the kabbalah for many centuries. Tantric yoga or Tantra is amenable to kabbalists because of its great mystical beauty and power. In the Tantric ritual the intention of both partners is the union with the Godhead for purely mystical reasons. The rite begins with both the man and the woman dressed in colorful robes, preferably decked with jewels and flowers. There should be plenty of incense in the room and soft mood music. The partners eat sweets and drink sweet wine and chat pleasantly before their union, prefacing the sexual act with great gentleness and delicacy. After a prolonged foreplay, they engage in the sexual act using any of a number of Tantra positions. There are many variations to this rite, but ideally neither partner moves during the act. Neither does either one attempt to achieve physical orgasm. If either one feels an orgasm is imminent, they must stop temporarily and resume the act after some time has passed. Yoga adepts recommend rolling back the tongue against the palate to stop or delay the male orgasm. The intention of the ritual is to escalate pleasure tenuously, letting it peak without physical relief. Eventually the physical pleasure is transcended and the partners begin to experience *extasis* on the spiritual plane. It is at this moment that union with the Godhead is achieved.

Like Tantra and Kabbalah, Alchemy also aims at the sublime union of the human spirit with the divine. All the obscure jargon used by the alchemists and their talks about the transmutation of metals and the Philosophers' Stone hid under its murky symbology a search for the divine. The Materia Prima was in reality the human body; the secret Fire or First Agent was sex. In alchemical terms, the Materia Prima is placed in a mortar, pulverized with a pestle, mixed with the secret Fire and moistened with dew. The resulting "compost" was enclosed in a tightly sealed vessel or Philosophic Egg which was then placed in the Athanor or furnace of the Philosophers. The Athanor was devised in such a way as to keep the Egg at a constant temperature for long periods of time. The alchemists cautioned that "the outward fire stimulates the action of the inner fire and therefore must be restrained, otherwise, even if the vessel does not break, the whole work will be lost." This was a covert advice to the initiate that the sexual act must be controlled and the mind kept on its spiritual aims, otherwise, even if orgasm was not reached, the union with the Godhead would not be achieved. The end of the Work was similar to the sacred marriage of the kabbalists. Thus the early alchemists spoke of "the King reunited in the Fire of Love with his blessed Queen." The red sulphur fixed the white mercury, and from their union the ultimate perfection was effected and the Philosphers' Stone was born.

The alchemists also cautioned those who sought to practice their secret art for material purposes. In the Middle Ages, many took literally the teachings of the alchemists, and tried to find the physical counterpart of the Philosophers' Stone, with which they believed they could transmute common metals into gold. Not aware of the fact that the common metal was matter and gold was the spirit, they built intricate laboratories and mixed many unknown substances in their fruitless search. But their efforts were not lost entirely, because while searching for the Philosophers' Stone they unknowingly laid the foundation of organic chemistry.

The kabbalah, like the other systems I have mentioned, has as its central aim the union with the Godhead. The basis for this union is purity of intention and perfect acts for the love of God. Because of God's unifying essence, the sexual act is, to the kabbalist, the most perfect of all acts of worship. In sexual love, mankind transcends its human condition, and becomes One with God.

16 The Structure of the Psyche

Power of mind as an Absolute has been the subject of study of many schools of philosophy, and still eludes the comprehension of modern psychology, which reluctantly accepts the fact that it has barely begun to grasp the complexities of this awesome giant.

Although many new insights have come to light during the past decade, the basis of modern psychological thought is rooted in the theories of Alfred Adler, Sigmund Freud and Carl Gustav Jung. Of these three great psychoanalysts, only Jung had the vision to recognize that *mind* is an expression of a cosmic process that transcends the realm of the physical. It is therefore with the Jungian view of the mind that we will deal here.

To Jung, the human psyche or mind is composed of three levels. These are the consciousness, the personal Unconscious and the Objective or Collective Unconscious. The Conscious aspect of the psyche is the Ego or Persona, the everyday familiar "I" with whom we readily identify, the decision-making, active and *aware* part of the personality. The Unconscious is the source of all the fundamental symbols and other psychic contents and ideas that emerge daily into the Consciousness. Among these are repressed memories, feelings, instincts and desires, as well as intuition and an immense wealth of knowledge, which is, for the most part, a closed door to the Consciousness. Some of these unconscious contents surface to the conscious aspect of the personality from time to time, particularly in the form of dreams. The Collective Unconscious is the largest part of the psyche, and Jung conceived of it as the underlying portion of an iceberg, the uppermost tip being formed by the conscious Ego. The largest body of the iceberg, hidden from view by the water surface, is the Collective Unconscious. The Unconscious is therefore the largest and most important part of the human mind. It is a level of psychic contents that is deeper than both the Consciousness and the Unconscious. It is called "collective" because it is generically present in all human beings. That is, it contains materials which are held collectively by everyone regardless of race, creed and place of origin. These pyschic contents have existed since the early beginnings of the human race and some of them may even transcend human experience.

The three levels of the personality, both conscious and unconscious, are composed of the *libido* or psychic energy. This energy is released to the Consciousness through the constant tension between pairs of *opposites* in the deep Unconscious. The psyche is a non-physical space within the personality, where "psychic phenomena" takes place. The libido moves within this space in a variety of movements, up and down, forward and backward, inward and outward. This "space" is the totality of the human personality, a kind of inner cosmos. We cannot define what the libido or psychic energy really is. All we can say is that *it is*, it exists, and it can be seen under two aspects. One of these is energy manifested on the cosmic level of life, energy as a whole. The other is energy expressed specifically in the human psyche.

The principle of opposites is a main characteristic of the psyche. To Jung, everything subsists as a phenomenon of energy. But without the pre-existence of an antithesis there could be no energy. There must always be height and depth, heat and cold, positive and negative so that the order of equalization—which is energy—can take place. All life is energy, and this energy depends on forces held in opposition. The greater the tension between the pairs of opposites, the greater will be the energy that is released. This energy is generated through conflict within the person and is the active force within the psyche, being dissipated in activity and recreated by newly emerging tensions between the opposites.

The energy released by the opposites can create a *progression* or a *recession* within the psyche. That is, it can be of a positive or a negative nature. The progression phase of the psychic energy or libido happens when all is going well within the psyche and the energy can express itself in a creative way in the external world. At this point, the individual experiences an exhilarated feeling of well-being and all he does turns out well. The psychic energies are moving upwards and outwards at these times. But should an obstacle appear, the flow of the libido is reversed and the balance between the opposites cannot be maintained. The feeling of well-being is transformed into one of depression and confusion. All seems suddenly dark and without hope. Instead of harmony and joy, there is only discord and internal friction. The opposites, no longer in harmonious union, break apart and begin to oppose one another. The conflict creates new energy, but this energy is no longer moving forwards but rather downwards into the deep unconscious. This is the regression phase of the libido which causes it to expend itself within itself. The energy moves further down into the lower levels of the psyche from where it emerges in a variety of negative manifestations.

The processes that take place in the Collective Unconscious by means of the libido are manifested through the psychic forms known as *archetypes*. These are forms or images of a collective nature which occur all over the earth as parts of myths and at the same time, as independent and individual products of unconscious origin. These patterns of symbol formation recur throughout mankind in the various mythologies of the human race. Archetypes have existed since the early beginnings of humanity and for that reason they are based on the most fundamental structure of the psyche. What is most important to consider is that archetypes occur independently of Consciousness, almost as if they had a life of their own. In fact, they are concentrations of psychic energy that are representations of certain human and suprahuman personalities or traits, and they exist entirely on their own. The gods of the Greek and Egyptian pantheons are good examples of archetypes. So are the forces of the Tree of Life.

In themselves, the archetypes are only tendencies, potentialities, and they do not become significant in the life of an individual until they emerge outwardly in a specific form. Archetypes present themselves as facts, and when we come face to face with one, we are observing an outpouring of psychic energy manifested in a material way.

The tension that is created in the psyche as a result of the interaction between opposites is beyond the control of the individual. For this reason it is said to be autonomous; that is, independent of the guidance of the Consciousness. The energy released has the power to attract and gather together various psychic contents into constellations or "complexes." These Jung called *autonomous complexes*. They are so strong and individualistic that they function as small personalities within the total personality. In dreams these psychic systems appear in personified form, sometimes as a man and in others as a woman. The best known of the autonomous complexes are the persona, the Shadow, the Animus and the Anima. The persona is the conscious aspect of the personality, the mask that the individual presents to the world and with which he or she identifies. Because it represents the person's conscious attitudes, it must perforce rest solidly on the Unconscious, of which it is the diammetrical opposite. The negative qualities repressed by the individual, his antisocial urges and lack of discipline are concentrated into the Shadow, which is invariably identified with the weaker part of the personality. All the blunders that an individual makes which he cannot explain, all the negative, impulsive actions that create havoc in a human life are the result of the Shadow's inner work.

As the balancing element in the psyche, there is a feminine side in every man and a masculine side in every woman. In the man the feminine side is personified in the Unconscious as the Anima. In the woman the masculine side is personified as the Animus. In dreams, men see the Anima as a woman, while women see the Animus as a man. In contrast, the Shadow is always perceived as a figure belonging to the same sex as the dreamer.

The Anima expresses itself in daily life as inexplicable moods of a petty, catty nature. The Animus, on the other hand, expresses itself in arbritary, belligerent opinions. What is involved in either case is the assertion of the undeveloped side of the personality. For this reason, the Anima and the Animus are not really negative aspects of the personality, but an attempt of the Unconscious to balance it.

When an individual dreams of the Shadow, he sees it as a threatening figure that is trying to harm him in some way. The figure is always of the same sex as that of the dreamer. The Anima and Animus are seldom threatening. They in fact seem always to try to assist the dreamer in some way. They always manifest as persons of the opposite sex. Dreams of the Shadow or the Animus or Anima indicate that these autonomous complexes are being activated in the psyche of the individual for the purpose of integration into the conscious personality. The process of integration was called, by Jung, Individuation.

The Individuation process can only be accomplished through either the Animus or the Anima since they represent the personification of the Unconscious in the male and the female. In this sense the Animus and Anima, as the symbol of the Unconscious and of all the archetypes, has the largest concentration of libido energy in the Psyche.

Before the Individuation process can be completed and the personality be fully integrated, the forces of the Shadow and either the Anima or the Animus have to be recognized and reconciled with the indivudal's Conscious ness. At this point the person realizes that his persona is, in reality, a very small part of his psyche, and that most of his attitudes and traits are masks he wears to impress the world. He then comes face to face with his inner reality and becomes transformed in the process. Fundamentally, the aim of Individuation is to rid the personality from the false wrappings of the Persona and from the suggestive influence of the Anima or Animus.

When the Anima or Animus—as the Unconscious— becomes integrated into the Consciousness, its energies are transformed and act as a bridge between the conscious and unconscious parts of the psyche. Here the opposites that act within the psyche become integrated into a unified personality. This new force is known as the emerging Self.

The Self has been defined as an inner guiding factor that is different from the conscious personality and can be best grasped through the investigation of dreams. The now integrated Self appears in dreams as a superior being of the same sex as the individual. It becomes the regulating center that creates a constant extension and maturity of the personality. Its emergence may be very slight, or it may develop quite fully during a person's lifetime. How far it develops depends on how much the Ego is willing to listen to its messages. Those who do so become more complete human beings. But it must always be remembered that it is the Ego that serves to light up the psyche. The Self can prod the Ego, but only the Ego can reach the full potentialities of its own psyche.

In order to bring the Individuation process into reality, the individual must be willing to surrender consciously to the power of the Unconscious. Instead of trying to determine what he should do in a given situation, the person should simply *listen*, in order to learn what the Self—the inner totality of the psyche—wants him or her to do in each particular situation.

The subjective experience of Individuation gives the feeling that some supernatural force is actively interfering in the individual's life in a positive and creative way. Sometimes it seems as if the Unconscious were leading the way in accordance with a secret design. But for this to take place the individual has to realize that to fulfill one's destiny is the greatest of human achievements, and material considerations must always take a back seat in the development of the psyche.

To Jung, dreams seemed to follow an arrangement or pattern. It was this pattern of dreams that he identified as the Individuation process. Since dreams produce different scenes and images every night, if we are not careful observers of our dreams we fail to perceive their patterns. But if we watch our dreams over a long period of time, we will find that the same symbols keep on reappearing. If we then attempt to interpret the dreams' imagery, we will begin to observe hidden regulating tendency at work which creates a slow but discernible psychic growth. This growth is what Jung called the Individuation process.

The integration which is the result of the Individuation process is achieved in kabbalah through work in the Tree of Life, which is a symbol of the integrated Self. Adam Kadmon or the Cosmic Man is both God manifested on the cosmic level and the perfected human being in Malkuth or the material world.

As we have seen, work on the Tree must be accomplished through the balancing of opposite spheres. The tension between these opposites is what releases the psychic energies necessary to bring about changes in the material world. These changes, which first take place within the individual's psyche, are released through the power of the archetypes symbolized by the forces of the Tree: the Divine Names and the various angelic beings. These forces exist in the human Collective Unconscious and predate the conscious aspect of the personality. They are as real as the world around us, or perhaps more real, because they are not mere parts of the Persona of the world, but the basis of our very soul.

The imagery of dreams takes place in what is known as the Astral World. As we saw earlier, the Astral is the world of mind, and therefore its substance is the libido or psychic energy. This is the same imagery that is used in meditation and on all work on the Tree. Therefore, practical work in kabbalah is a conscious effort to contact the archetypes and autonomous complexes of the Collective Unconscious. It is then an Individuation process conducted by the conscious part of the personality instead of the Unconscious, which works mostly through dreams. That is why work on the Tree must be devoid of selfish intentions, as it then simply adds to the confusion and stagnation of the Persona or conscious Ego. Material considerations can only be used in conjunction with the Tree when they help in the spiritual development of the individual. Otherwise, the Qliphotic forces of the Tree, which can be equated with the sinister influence of the Shadow, will then come into being.

Man's personal god as the Adam Kadmon is therefore his own Self, an intrinsic part of his own soul, which flows outwardly from within the Unconscious to enrich his life and give it true meaning. Once the Self has emerged into the conscious personality, the now integrated Consciousness can use the vast symbology of the mind to make things happen according to his will. At this point, he will be one with the Self; that is, with the God within, and all the powers of that infinite force will also be his to wield.

Mind happens in a space-time continuum that exists beyond physical reality. All human events take place along different segments of this continuum. They co-exist in time but on different points of space. That is, past, present and future blend in the continuum and extend into infinity. The Self, being eternal and the overseer of Mind, can perceive all events happening along the continuum in their proper segment of time and space. Its infinite vision allows it to see both the beginning and the end of the universe simultaneously. When the Self has been fully integrated into the outer Consciousness, it can project through to the individual what is going to happen and when. This is the power we know as clairvoyance and clairaudience.

Apparent coincidences are points of contact between the Unconscious of one person and the Unconscious of another. When you dream about a person you have not seen in a long time and meet her the next day, or when you are thinking about someone and the telephone rings and that person is on the other end of the line, you are facing a "meaningful" coincidence. That is, your Unconscious and that of the other person came in contact with each other before your actual meeting or conversation. The force of the contact was so strong as to work its way through to the conscious mind. That is why you thought about or dreamt with that person. Jung called these "meaningful" coincidences, *synchronicity*, that is, synchronized events engineered by the Unconscious. Hunches, premonitions and wishes that come true are all synchronzied events.

Because the Self functions freely along the space-time continuum, it is not concerned with past, present and future.

To the Self, things are simply what they are. And because it has at its disposal most of the energies of the psyche, it can make things happen and change them at will. Affecting present and future events to the Self is simply a matter of transforming psychic energy into material happenings.

The urge towards Individuation and the integration of the psyche is present in all individuals. It may find expression in a variety of ways. Religious feeling is only one of these expressions. Art, the unity of the family, and all creative instincts are part of this urge. In those individuals who are deeply influenced by the Shadow complex, this urge becomes perverted and is often expressed in a violent or destructive form.

One of the most common ways that the need for Individuation expresses itself in an individual is through an overwhelming love for another person. In fact, when passion goes beyond the natural measure of love, its ultimate aim is the mystery of becoming whole, and that is why when a person falls deeply in love, he or she feels that the only worthwhile thing in life is becoming one with the object of their love. Very often, the individual that is loved is the physical counterpart of his or her lover's Anima or Animus, reflecting that particular archetype's intrinsic qualities. When this happens, it is said that the two lovers are *soul mates*; that is, that they are perfect complements of each other's souls. Human soul mates are the counterparts of the Shekinah and Her divine spouse, and when they meet in this world their union is full of joy and spiritual fulfillment.

Working towards spiritual development in kabbalah can be equated with the Jungian Individuation process. But while Individuation can never be influenced directly by the conscious personality, kabbalistic work is solely in the hands of the individual practitioner. The Unconscious still serves as a guide, but it is the Consciousness that steers the course. This is a significant difference that underlines once more the importance of judicious care in the practical kabbalah.

17 Correspondences With Other Systems

The Creative Force, dual and electromagnetic in essence, manifests itself in myriad ways throughout the created universe. The kabbalah is not the only system that expresses the view of a pair of cosmic opposites—male and female—that unite for the purpose of manifestation. This concept has been expressed in every religious and magical system that has ever existed. Because of the noumenous nature of mind and its infinite essence, this knowledge has been shared by all of mankind regardless of race, creed or place of origin. That which Jung called the Collective Unconscious, and which is an intrinsic part of every human psyche, has at its very roots this concept of opposites united for the purpose of manifesting their essence. This intuitive knowledge has come to mankind, not just through the historical process that gave birth to our modern societies, nor through the hereditary genes that gave us life, but through the indestructible atoms that formed part of the original creation of the universe. The first hydrogen atoms that composed the original substance from which the universe was created carried within them the secret of creation and the pattern of the cosmos. For the hydrogen atom was also created as a pair of opposites, proton and electron, positive and negative, male and female, united for the manifestation of matter. All of creation rests on the simple structure of the hydrogen atom, including ourselves. This consciousness of the hydrogen atom, imbedded in our souls, gave us the awareness and the understanding of the eternal opposites, forever united.

The instinctive understanding of the Creative Force permeating the universe caused mankind to search for it in nature and natural forces. Primitive societies, more attuned with the inner forces through their ready acceptance of the miraculous, were soon able to make the identification between the cosmic forces and nature. Fire and water, thunder and lightning, oceans and rivers, the wind and the forests, the sun and the moon, and everything in existence was seen as expressions of the one Creative Force. More civilized societies, deprived of their innocence by the demands of material considerations, slowly lost contact with the soul of nature and with the cosmic beat that gave them life.

When primitive man identified God with nature, he deified natural forces and worshipped them in an attempt to tap through them some of the divine energies with which they were invested. The raw forces that were evident in fire and lightning, in the ocean waters, in the forests and the mountains and in the earth itself were obviously concentrations of a tremendous energy, an energy that could be of great use if it could only be made available to man. To accomplish this, primitive man conceived the idea of *contacting* the forces of nature. This he set out to do by means of complex rituals and invocations. This is how the first religions were born. Today we pray in churches, temples and synagogues to the same forces worshipped by our primitive ancestors in groves and caves and forest clearings. That we call these forces by different names is of little importance because the Force is only one.

As he sought to contact natural forces, primitive man also saw a correlation between them and his own personal endeavors. The violent power of fire, for example, he identified with raw passion, both in love and in war. Water, on the other hand, because of its life-giving qualities, he identified with fertility and women. In this manner he proceeded to find a point of union between himself and natural forces, between the human and the divine.

All the gods and goddesses of the early religions shared a dual nature. They were all identified as natural forces and as protectors of different human concerns. The Babylonians, the Egyptians, the Greeks and the Romans all saw their gods in this dual light. The Jews, who introduced the concept of monotheism with the One Living God, also saw Him manifested in various aspects, which were grouped in the schema called the Tree of Life. The most important difference between the earlier religions and that of Judaism is that while the gods of the other pantheons were conceived as independent of each other, the sephiroth of the Tree of Life were seen as the manifestations of the same energy and the same God. But the central idea of contacting these divine forces was shared by all religions. That is why there are so many direct correspondences between the spheres of the Tree of Life and the gods and goddesses of other religious systems. (see Table 12.)

The term *avatar* is generally used to designate the various forms through which the same cosmic or divine force becomes manifested. The Egyptians were familiar with this concept, although they did not use the same term. But several of their deities became transformed through various processes, changing their names and their personalities in so doing. The Hindu gods, particularly Vishnu and Shiva, also undergo many transformations into different avatars. This peculiarity is also shared by the deities of the Voodoo pantheon, especially Legba and Aida Wedo.

The phenomenon of the avatar is a transmutation of the same energy into a different manifestation for a specific purpose. This purpose invariably concerns a redirection of energy to satisfy the order of things. It also usually involves

Table 12

Correspondences Between the Sephiroth, the Planets and Various Pantheons

Sephira	Planet	Egyptian Pantheon	Greek Pantheon	Roman Pantheon	Scandinavian Pantheon	Hindu Pantheon	Haitian Voodoo Pantheon	Afro-Cuban Santeria Pantheon
1. Kether	First Swirlings	Osiris	Aither	Aether	Ymir	Brahman	Dambhalah Wedo	Olofi
2. Chokmah	Zodiac	Thoth	Uranus	Coelus	Odin	Vishnu	Maraca	Obatala
3. Binah	Saturn	Maut	Rhea	Magna Mater	Frigga	Bhavani	Brigitte	Oddudua
4. Chesed	Jupiter	Ptah	Zeus	Jupiter	Balder	Rama Chandra	Adoum-Guidi	Orunla
5. Geburah	Mars	Seth	Ares	Mars	Loki	Shiva	Ogou-Ferraille	Oggun
6. Tiphareth	Sun	Ra	Apollo	Helios	Thor	Indra/Surya	Ogou-Chango	Chango
7. Netzach	Venus	Hathor	Aphrodite	Venus	Freyja	Sita	Erzulie	Oshun
8. Hod	Mercury	Anubis	Hermes	Mercury	Freyr	Hanuman	Legba	Eleggua
9. Yesod	Moon	Isis	Artemis	Diana	Sif	Lakshmi	Aida Wedo	Yemaya
10. Malkuth	Earth	Nephthys	Demeter	Ceres	Nerthus	Ganesh	Zaca	Orisha-Oko

a lesson for humanity. When Shiva manifests himself in the avatar of Nataraja, the master of the dance, he does so to teach men the element of constant change which is an intrinsic quality of the cosmic energy. When Erzulie transforms herself into the avatar of La Sirene, she symbolizes the Sacred Music, the *sound* which is necesssary to bring about changes in the cosmic energy. Both Nataraja and La Sirene are different manifestations of the same force, and they are both concerned with *changes in consciousness*.

A change in consciousness is a movement from within the psychic energies of the individual and is invariably caused by an archetypal force. This helps the individual during the Individuation process and brings him closer to the integration of his psyche. This is what happens when an archetype changes form—an avatar—as when the Shadow merges with the Anima and the Anima becomes the Self. The gods of the various pantheons and the sephiroth of the Tree of Life are all archetypal forces working within the Unconscious to bring about the integration of the psyche.

The Virgin Mary has been identified with the lunar avatars of many religions. Artemis, Diana, Isis, Dione, Melusine, Cerridwen, Isis, Arianrhod, and Astarte are all moon goddesses worshipped by a variety of cultures. Mary, as the perfect woman and mother, is usually represented with a half moon at her feet. The moon has been a symbol of womanhood since the beginning of time, and for that reason, all the religions have thought to identify it with their central female deity. In the Tree of Life, Yesod is associated with the sphere of the moon, and Mary is seen by Christian kabbalists as the personification of Yesod. But she is also identified with the Shekinah in the sphere of Binah, also known as the Dark Mother, Mara of the bitter waters. This is a reference to Mary's suffering and her mourning over the death of her son. Jesus himself has also been identified with one of the spheres of the Tree of Life, the sephira Tiphareth, where his title is The Son, and where the magical image of the sephira is a sacrificed god.

Perhaps through the influence of Christianity, Jewish elements have found their way into two African-based religions in the Caribbean: Voodoo and Santeria. The kabbalistic influence can be noticeably appreciated in both religions. That there should be kabbalistic elements in Santeria should come as no surprise since the religion is a combination of the beliefs of the Yoruba People and those of the Catholic faith. It is well-known that Spanish kabbalists, such as Moses de Leon and Moses Cordovero, were responsible for the kabbalistic renaissance of the 13th century. Some of the kabbalistic practices could have easily found their way from Spain to the New World during the Spanish Conquest. To the Spanish and their descendants in the New World, the kabbalah is very familiar ground. There is even a Spanish word—*cavilar*, which means to meditate profoundly— whose roots are clearly influenced by the word *cabala*, which is Kabbalah's Spanish version.

The Spanish colonizers obviously brought with them, not only their Catholic beliefs, but also a healthy store of kabbalistic knowledge. These elements were fused with the religio-magical beliefs of the Yorubas and the result was the birth of Santeria.

The Jewish and kabbalistic elements in Santeria are many. The identification of the various deities—like the sephiroth—with angelic or divine forces; lying on the floor to worship the deity; ritual swaying and chanting to evoke the deity; ritual cleansings with fowl (Yom Kippur) which are then sacrificed to the deity; blood sacrifices to the deity where the meat of the animal is later on eaten by the community. These are all practices which are shared by Santeria and by Judaism in general and kabbalah in specific. All the deities of Santeria are—like the sephiroth—the manifestations of One God.

Like Santeria, Voodoo also has many traces of kabbalistic and Jewish influence. The *veves* or ritual diagrams used in Voodoo to invoke the gods or *loas* are formed of different elements, such as wands, cylinders, serpents, stars and crosses. The wands represent the Creator. There are two wands in a veve to symbolize the dual nature—male and female—of the Creator. Intertwined by two serpents, they symbolize Dambhalah Wedo and Aida Wedo, the cosmic masculine and feminine elements which are the Creative Force of the universe. The cylinder of the veve corresponds to the Hebrew letter Shin, while the dual snakes correspond to the letters Tzadde and Lamed. The gods Legba and Erzulie are Dambhalah and Aida Wedo on a lower plane, yet with the same basic potentialities. The marriage between Legba and Erzulie symbolize the fire of heaven and is represented by the axis of the veve. This mystical marriage is identified by Voodoo practitioners with the marriage between the Shekinah and Her divine spouse.

When the houngan or Voodoo priest traces a veve, he is calling down the power of the loa represented by that particular diagram. The energy released is called the "crisis of loa" and is likened to the spiritual man descending to the physical man for the purpose of manifestation. Dambhalah Wedo, the Adam Kadmon of Voodoo, is also known as Roi-Youda (King of Judah).

The correspondence among the various religious systems stress the subtle yet powerful links that interconnect the foundations of all human thought. What the kabbalah symbolizes, and which is echoed by all the other religious and magical systems, is this essential unity. The force that is the Collective Unconscious and which is shared by all mankind is the manifestation of the dynamic force underlying the created universe: two opposites in harmonious union, symbolizing the oneness of all things. The lesson of the practical kabbalah is the synthesis of all opposites, and the objective is not power or wordly achievement. The objective is the merging with the universal mind, the integration of the psyche, and the realization of the unity of the human race. Ultimately, the objective is love.

Part
IV

THE KABBALAH
OF WISDOM

On Chaos, Dark Matter,
Black Holes and the Face of God

18 The Machinery of the Universe

On April 23, 1992, a team of researchers at Lawrence Berkeley Laboratory and the University of California at Berkeley, led by astrophysicist George Smoot, convulsed the scientific world with reports that they had detected broad "wrinkles" in the fabric of space. After analyzing data from the Cosmic Background Explorer satellite (COBE), they detected faint temperature fluctuations in microwave radiation echoing from the first moment of creation. Although the fluctuations were not larger than a hundred thousandth of a degree, they signaled primeval variations in the universe's topography about 300,000 years after its explosive birth. These variations were large enough to create the gravity needed to attract large amounts of matter and form increasingly expansive clumps, which ultimately were to become our galaxies and solar systems.

The importance of the discovery was such that it was immediately hailed by cosmologists around the world as the most important finding of the twentieth century. The main reason for all the excitement was that until this discovery, the theory of the Big Bang had been under increasing scrutiny and growing skepticism. Many of the world's best known cosmologists, especially those involved in quantum mechanics, had begun to doubt the Big Bang theory as the source of the universe. As we discussed in the first part of this book, this theory proposes that the universe came into being as a result of a gigantic explosion at "zero time;" at the very beginning of creation. But the findings of the Berkeley team gave the strongest possible support for the theory, for it is now believed that the density ripples picked up by the COBE satellite were created immediately after the Big Bang.

Dr. Smoot, who announced the findings at a meeting of the American Physical Society in Washington, said: "What we have found is evidence for the birth of the universe and its evolution." He added that the findings not only strengthened the Big Bang theory, but also gave evidence of the accuracy of two other hypotheses, those suggesting an inflatory model of the universe and the existence of cold dark matter, supposedly made of invisible subatomic particles believed to constitute about 90% of all the matter in the universe. Said Dr. Smoot, basking in the glow of discovery: "It's a mystical experience . . . it's like finding the driving mechanism of the universe. And isn't that what God is? If you're religious, it's like looking at God . . . "

A few years ago such a statement from a scientist would have been unthinkable. Modern science has traditionally stayed away from religion and mysticism, in an effort to use strictly empirical methods in its pursuit of scientific truths. Until quite recently, any mystical or supernatural leanings in a scientist would have branded his work suspect and his reputation would have suffered accordingly. Even men of Einstein's stature, who flirted with certain mystical concepts, were quick to deny any religious or mystical practices or beliefs. Einstein was fond of using God as a symbol of the universal laws. So he made statements such as "God does not play dice with the universe," and "God is subtle but he is not malicious." Once he expressed the whole of his scientific aim by stating tersely: "I want to know the thoughts of God. The rest are just details." But he persistently denied that he was religious in the strict sense of the word and explained these tantalizing statements as simple similes where the word "God" symbolized the universe and its mysteries.

Robert Jastrow was one of the first astrophysicists who cautiously voiced his belief in the existence of God and a divine plan behind creation. In his book *God and the Astronomers*, published as early as 1978, he had this to say:

> For the scientist who has lived by his faith in the power of reason, the story ends like a bad dream. He has scaled the mountains of ignorance; he is about to conquer the highest peak; as he pulls himself over the final rock, he is greeted by a band of theologians who have been sitting there for centuries.

But even Jastrow, in spite of this courageous statement, was careful to note at the opening of his book that he is an agnostic in religious matters. Because, he said, tongue in cheek, "When an astronomer writes about God, his colleagues assume he is either over the hill or going bonkers."

Today, this is no longer the case. Many scientists are still cautious about openly admitting a belief in an Ultimate Cause behind the creation of the Universe. But increasingly large numbers are beginning to express, not only a belief in a Creative Force, but also in the need for a more mystical approach to the subject. Paul Davies, a Professor of Mathematical Physics at the University of Adelaide in Australia, and one of the most brilliant exponents of astrophysics in the world today, had this to say in his book, *The Mind of God:*

> I cannot believe that our existence in the universe is a mere quirk of fate, an accident of history, an incidental blip in the great cosmic drama. Our involvement is too intimate. We are truly meant to be here.

And earlier in the same section he says:

> In the end a rational explanation for the world in the sense of a closed and complete system of logical truths is almost certainly impossible . . . If we wish to progress beyond, we have to embrace a different concept of "understanding" from that of a rational explanation. Possibly the mystical path is a way to such an understanding.

What prompted world famous scientists of irreproachable professional standing to turn a wondering gaze towards a possible Creative Force behind the Universe? The fact that such a Creative Force is leaping at them from every angle of the telescope and from every quantum equation ever conceived. George Smoot's discovery of broad wrinkles in the fabric of space is further evidence for an Ultimate Cause because it supports the Big Bang theory, which in turn supports the possible existence of God.

At the time of the Big Bang, there was a point of infinite compression known as a "singularity." Roger Penrose and Stephen Hawking proved such a singularity was inevitable as long as gravity remained an attractive force under the extreme conditions of the primeval universe. This agrees with Einstein's Theory of relativity according to which space, time and matter are related.

Scientists now believe that at the time of the singularity space must have shrunk until it disappeared. Because space, time and matter are linked irrevocably, this means that time and matter must have disappeared also. Therefore, the material singularity was at the same time a space-time singularity. Since all laws of physics are formulated in terms of space and time, all physical laws break down at the singularity. In other words, there was no time, no space and no matter at the time of the Big Bang, and physics cannot tell us what actually happened. Time, space and matter came into being simultaneously with the Big Bang. But scientists are quick to remind us not to conceive of the universe as "becoming" but rather as just "being." In other words, the universe just IS.

What happened before the Big Bang? Nothing, because the laws of physics did not exist then. There was no time so there can be no specific date attached to this momentous event. And if you ask a physicist where did it all happen, he will simply say EVERYWHERE, because there was no space, either.

The concept of an eternal universe has also been proven wrong by the second law of thermodynamics which forbids heat to flow spontaneously from cold to hot bodies while permitting it to flow from hot to cold. This tendency towards uniformity, where temperature evens out and the universe settles into a stable state, represents a maximum molecular disorder known as entropy, a "heat death." But the fact that the universe is still here and has not "died" yet, implies that it cannot have lasted for all eternity.

There is also Olber's Paradox, which says that if the universe were infinite in space and age, light from an infinity of stars would be shining constantly on earth and the sky would not be dark. But if the universe is not eternal, if it had a beginning, we can then only see the light of those stars whose light had time to travel to us from the beginning of the cosmos. This indicates the universe is not infinite. The Big Bang theory effectively refutes the concept of an eternal universe because if it began it cannot be eternal.

Saint Augustine of Hippo, writing in the 5th century, knew that time was part of the physical universe, but placed God as the Creator, outside time. In other words, he conceived of a Creative Force outside the universe, a concept that agrees with the conditions of the universe at the moment of the Big Bang when there was no time, no space and no matter. If this Creative Force was "outside" the universe, then "It" was in a perfect position to "create" space, time and matter through a singularity, a compressed point from which the Big Bang and the universe came into being. This singularity can be equated with the Kabbalistic concept of the AIN SOPH AUR, the primordial point of light emitted by God at the time of creation.

The concept of God creating the universe outside Himself is similar to that of an artist creating a work of art. He must do this outside Himself, for how can He create anything that he is a part of? How can a painter or a sculptor be inside his creation? He must work at it from the outside, carefully adding detail after detail, to perfect it in every way he can.

Of all the various scientific disciplines physics is the one that ultimately will answer all the gnawing questions that humanity asks constantly about its origins and ultimate destiny. For that reason physicists must attempt to reconcile their theories with the cosmic laws and find irrefutable proofs for all their premises. Only then can they be absolutely certain that they are treading on firm ground. That is the reason many physicists balk at the concept of a Creator, a Primum Mobile, behind the origin of the universe. Such an idea is beyond proof, at least for the time being. And proof is what physics is all about. Therefore, Smoot's recent findings must have caused a great deal of puzzlement and consternation to many physicists who were doing their best to find answers to the origin problem without having to resort to "metaphysical" speculations. But such speculations refuse to go away quietly, and the concept of a Creative Force continues to grow in strength with each new scientific discovery.

The main problem with the Big Bang is that it appears to be an event without a physical cause, which contradicts the law of cause and effect. But there is a possible explanation, and this can be found in quantum mechanics. The very core of this branch of physics is Heisenberg's Uncertainty Principle, according to which there are unpredictable fluctuations in the values of measurable quantities like energy and momentum. This implies that the microscopic world of atomic and sub-atomic particles is indeterministic. In other words, quantum events are not determined absolutely by the principle of cause and effect. The probability of an event may be known, but the "actual" outcome is neither known nor knowable. Because cause and effect are negligible in terms of quantum processes this allows physicists to speculate that there is no origin of the universe. This is precisely what famous quantum physicist Stephen Hawking and his colleague James Hartle have argued. According to Hawking, if the universe is self contained, as it appears to be, having no boundaries or edges, it would have neither a beginning nor an end. Ergo, no origin. This is in accordance with Einstein's theories, who believed that the universe is finite but unbounded. But although Hawking's concept suggests that the universe has no origin, it also states that it has always existed. How did it come into existence? According to quantum physics, it could have simply created itself.

The concepts of quantum mechanics do not imply that the universe is irrational. Although there is no certainty about the future states of quantum processes, the relative probabilities are still determined. This means that on a macroscopic scale, in the visible world where quantum effects are not noticeable, nature appears to conform to the laws of cause and effect and determinism. One could effectively argue that the indeterminism in the atomic and subatomic scale leaves the door wide open for creativity and change, as well as continuing evolution. This thought has occurred to many theologians who believe that the indeterminism of quantum physics allows God the freedom to continue the creation process without interfering with the laws of physics.

The concept of a "rational" world is based on the fact that it is ordered. Events follow each other according to immutable physical laws. The cycles of day and night and the very motion of the stars are ruled by these laws. This interrelation of events is what is known as causality. And closely tied to causality is the notion of determinism. This simply means that each event is entirely determined by an earlier one. Directly in opposition to determinism is indeterminism, or chance. This is exemplified by the throwing of a die or the tossing of a coin. This is the realm of quantum mechanics.

Therefore, we have a universe which is immensely complex and ruled by laws of cause and effect on a macrocosmic level, but at whose core lies the indeterminism that rules the atomic and subatomic particles on a microcosmic level. The universe is an interconnected whole where the fall of an apple is affected by the position of the moon. But not all systems function so predictably. There are also processes known as chaotic which exhibit no regularities. Their behavior appears to be entirely random.

There are far more chaotic systems in the universe than science thought at first. Among these we recognize fibrillating hearts, dripping faucets, turbulent fluids and a driven pendulum. Chaotic systems are extremely sensitive to outside disturbances. It is that property that makes them so unpredictable. The concept behind chaos is that the smallest interference or error will bring about minute changes in a chaotic system which will grow swiftly at an escalating rate until the system is thrown out of synchronicity and control. The most typical example is that of a pendulum that is swinging normally until someone touches it slightly. The pendulum will then give way to chaos, with the bob swinging erratically first one way then another in a completely random manner.

Chaos becomes of even greater importance during predictive calculations such as computer predictions. Any predictive computation must perforce include input errors because we cannot measure physical quantities with unlimited accuracy. Because the smallest error may bring about a chaotic response, this may affect the ultimate outcome of the prediction. And although most systems are deterministic and accurate in their final outcome, chaos must always be taken into consideration and herein lie the laws of chance and indeterminism, as well as randomness in nature.

Non-chaotic systems are both predictable and mathematically true because of their qualities of linearity and locality. A linear system "obeys" the rules of addition and multiplication associated with straight line graphs such as the laws of electromagnetism. Linear systems are neither chaotic nor sensitive to small external disturbances.

The quality of locality has to do with the fact that in most cases the behavior of physical systems is determined in its entirety by forces in its immediate vicinity. But there are situations where non-local effects can come into being. In quantum mechanics, two subatomic particles can interact locally and then move far apart. But even if they end up in the opposite sides of the universe, they must be still treated as a whole and their behavior will continue to affect each other in spite of the immeasurable distances that separate them. This fact is of great importance in the understanding of the universal forces and how they act as they do.

If we are to deepen our understanding of the universe, we have to take into consideration the concepts of contingency and necessity. Something is said to be contingent if its existence or the fact that it is the way it is depends upon something else, something beyond itself. On the other hand, something that is necessary does not depend on anything else for its existence. It contains the reason for its existence within itself and is totally independent from other things.

It is easy to see from the above concepts that everything in the universe is contingent upon something. How about the universe itself? Is it necessary or contingent? It is contingent if it could have been something else other than what it is.

Many physicists believe that eventually all the various laws of physics will be found to be linked together. The four main laws are those of the strong force, the weak force, the gravity force and the electromagnetic force. Already the weak nuclear force and the electromagnetic force have been found to be two aspects of a single electroweak force. Physicists are now looking for a superforce, a completely unifying superlaw that may be "necessary." This possible convergence would lead to a Theory of Everything, and indeed many scientists believe they may be on the brink of such a discovery. The currently popular superstring theory is the most recent attempt to unite all the fundamental forces and particles of physics into an all-embracing whole.

While physicists struggle with their attempts at a unified theory that may prove to be "necessary," the fact remains that the world is undeniably contingent. That is, all its components are dependent upon each other. It is also logical, rational and stable, in spite of all the randomness of chaos and the indeterminism of quantum physics. It is also not compelled to be as it is. It could have evolved otherwise. Why is it the way it is and not any other way?

The fact that the world is both rational and intelligible may be expressed as the principle of sufficient reason. This states that everything in the world is as it is for some specific reason. What is the reason for the world to be the way it is? If it is contingent, as it seems to be, it cannot have within itself an explanation of its existence. Only necessary things can do that. But the principle of sufficient reason demands an explanation for the world's existence. There has to be one. Therefore, this explanation must be outside the universe.

The overall organization of the universe has suggested to many astronomers an element of design. James Joyce, for example, has said that the universe seems to have been designed by a pure mathematician and begins to look more and more like a great thought rather than a great machine. And Albert North Whitehead, who co-authored *Principia Mathematica* with Bertrand Russell, believed that God is responsible for ordering the world, not through direct action, but by providing the potentialities that were then actualized by the physical universe.

But if God is not contingent upon anything else, He may be then said to be necessary. And how can a necessary being create a contingent universe? Before we attempt to find an answer to that question, we have to consider an even more important question. What or who is God? Can the answer be found in the dark matter that is said to permeate the cosmos?

All the stars and galaxies in the universe account for less than 10% of the mass of the universe. Most physicists believe that the rest must be some kind of invisible or dark matter whose nature has yet to be determined. Some of it may be formed by very dim stars known as brown dwarfs and others may be accounted for by black holes. But most of it is believed to be some form of "exotic" subatomic particles such as neutrinos, axions or wimps. These latter are considered to be the most likely candidates because of their cold properties. Scientists now theorize that wimps are everywhere and that billions of these subatomic particles pass through a human body on a daily basis. This cold dark matter may be detectable through temperature changes in ordinary matter, and presumably in a human body. Of course, these are all speculations and neither the wimp nor the elusive cold dark matter have been found by science, but the search is on, and scientists are sure that the dark matter exists and that it is only a question of time before it is finally located. It is also speculated by scientists that when it is finally found, dark matter may prove to be entirely different than anything we know of.

Kabbalah tells us that in the beginning, before Creation, there was only AIN, NO-THING, a Force, unknowable and indefinable, that was everywhere. It was from AIN, that AIN SOPH, matter in potentiality, and AIN SOPH AUR, the actual creation, came into being. This is a concept that very much agrees in principle with the idea of dark matter.

Closely linked to the concept of dark matter is the existence of black holes. A black hole is a region of space, or space-time, within which the gravitational field has become so strong that even light cannot escape from it. Black holes are said to form when a star explodes into a supernova and then collapses inwardly due to the gravitational pull of its inner core. Everything within the black hole is torn apart by the intensity of the gravitational pull within. Molecules, atoms, and even subatomic particles are totally disintegrated. According to Stephen Hawking and Roger Penrose, space-time singularities such as the one existing at the time of the Big Bang are inevitable in the conditions present in a black hole. But while in the black hole all matter, as well as space-time, is destroyed; in the Big Bang, matter and space-time were created. But, is it possible that there can be a reverse direction of time in the black hole? Can the singularity or single point created by the collapse of a star result in the eventual emergence of a universe such as ours? Are there other universes at the end of every black hole in our cosmos? Is our universe at the end of a black hole in another universe outside our own?

From what we have discussed so far in this chapter we can easily see a distinct correlation between the "singularity" which existed at the time of the Big Bang with the Kabbalistic concept of AIN SOPH AUR—the point of light emitted by the Creator for the purpose of Creation. From this light was formed the world of archetypes—Adam Kadmon—or body of God, which may be likened to the differentiated energy that existed in the primordial moment. But as we saw in the beginning of the book, this initial energy was still too powerful for the creation of matter, so it was necessary for four additional worlds to be emanated, each denser in quality, until the world of matter came finally into being. These four archetypal Kabbalistic worlds can be equated with the various states of subatomic particles which are the realm of quantum physics.

The elusive dark matter is part of these worlds. This implies that there are still an infinity of sub-subatomic particles, ad infinitum, which are yet to be discovered by physics, all of which form part of the four Kabbalistic worlds. Beyond these sub-subatomic particles lies the AIN SOPH AUR, the One primordial point of light whence Everything came into being. When science discovers this primordial point, it will know who and what God is.

The most stunning conclusion along Kabbalistic lines is that not only the material world, but also the spiritual world can be explained through the laws of physics. Since all that is came into being with AIN SOPH AUR, which is at the core of the physical universe, it follows that the spirit of Mankind is also of a physical nature. It is not visible because it is composed of subatomic particles but it is part of the World of Action, which according to Kabbalah, is the material world. It may very well be that the cold dark matter hunted by science is the world of spirit, the world of supernal Mind. Hinduism teaches that in the air we breath there is an invisible substance they call prana which is the essence of existence. Prana may be equated with spirit, with pure Mind, the World of Formation— Yetzirah—in Kabbalah, which is associated with the element of Air.

A well-known astronomer said recently that he believed God to be the sum total of all the laws of the universe. Not so, according to Kabbalah and to the Big Bang theory. For at the point of singularity that existed at the Big Bang there was no time, no matter and no space. All laws of physics broke down at the Big Bang. They simply did not exist. This means that the Creative Force who brought the universe into being must have been outside the universe at the time of Creation. Therefore, He/She must have been outside the laws of physics as well and could hardly be the sum total of those laws. The Creator has to be greater than His/Her Creation. The principle of sufficient reason tells us that.

The principles governing black holes also adhere to Kabbalah. The black hole is conceived in physics as a type of funnel where the entrance, or event horizon, is circular. At the end of the funnel there is a singularity or primordial point where all matter issuing from the black hole has been condensed. If there is a reversal of time, the singularity behaves as the Big Bang, resulting in the eventual emergence of a universe. Kabbalah tells us that prior to the emanation of the AIN SOPH AUR, the AIN SOPH, or Bestowing Vessel, withdrew Herself from the AIN, or Eternal Light, and formed a perfect circle through which the primordial point of light traversed to create the universe. This implies that there is another universe outside our own, completely different than ours, for it is a universe formed of pure light. It also implies that black holes in our universe could give birth to other universes.

Earlier in this chapter we discussed contingent versus necessary things, and we saw how necessary things are a unity unto themselves while contingent things are dependent upon each other. One of God's names in Kabbalah is Eheieh Asher Eheieh, meaning I Am That I Am. This, as we saw in the first part of this book, is better translated as Existence is Existence. Existence is the Absolute of reason. It exists by Itself and because It exists. This name of God tells us then that the Creator must perforce be necessary. How could He/She create a contingent universe? By creating it outside Himself/Herself, and thus investing it with the qualities He/She knew such a universe needed for its preservation and evolution.

All of this means that the universe, far from being a machinery, is an evolutionary process, where matter or the particles that form it are undergoing radical changes at a subatomic level. Such changes are Kabbalistically explained as the eventual return of all matter to the source of light which is the Creator.

19 Mind Over Matter

One of the most baffling enigmas of science is the mystery of Mind. Many attempts have been made to decipher it, but we are still unable to explain its functions and indeed its existence in physical terms. And although it is assumed that Mind is responsible for our reasoning processes, there is no definite evidence that this is actually so. Most neurophysiologists will insist that brain and Mind are irrevocably linked, but they cannot actually explain how this mythical link works, nor exactly where does the Mind connect with the brain.

Perhaps the most misleading concept is the one linking Mind with consciousness. If we conceive of consciousness as simple awareness, which is the most accepted definition, we can readily see that we are talking about two entirely different things, for Mind does not necessarily have to be "aware" to function. The Deep Unconscious is not aware and yet it works perfectly well without this quality.

Most scientists, when confronted with the concept of Mind, will refer to physiological processes within the body and the brain, and point our the sensors, the neurons and dendrites that control the physical body and its functions. But even the seat of consciousness, let alone the Mind, is a subject of much conjecture at present. Some scientists believe it to be the reticular formation of the brain, while others ascribe it to the hippocampus or to the cerebral cortex itself, but no one can say where for sure.

In the face of this controversy, some scientists are arguing that maybe the Mind does not "reside" in the brain at all, nor is directly connected with it. They prefer to think of Mind as a series of processes whose origins are still unclear.

One of the most eminent neurologists to join the revolutionary ranks of the scientists departing from the materialistic concept of Mind as a part of the brain, was Wilder Penfield. In his book, *The Mystery of Mind*, written shortly before his death in 1975, Penfield said that "There is no good evidence that the brain alone can carry out the work the mind does." He also warned scientists not to draw a final conclusion in the study of Man until the nature of the energy responsible for Mind action was discovered. At present, most realists espousing a relationship between Mind and brain acknowledge the fact that they may never come to know the energy responsible for Mind. All that they can hope to do is to make "best guesses."

Australian physiologist Sir John Eccles has said that the materialistic concept of brain action generating consciousness is patently absurd. He contends that any theory of consciousness must deal not only with the brain's effect on the mind, but also with the mind's impact on the brain. In his controversial book, *The Mind and Its Brain*, co-authored with philosopher Sir Karl Popper, Eccles maintains that in addition to brain states determined by physical laws, there are also mental states, which fall outside the boundaries of the material world yet interact with it.

But interestingly enough, it is physics, the "hardest" science of all, which has most readily embraced the concept of Mind outside the brain, and indeed of a Universal mind. The famed physicist Sir Arthur Eddington once said that "The idea of a universal Mind or Logos would be a fairly possible inference from the present state of scientific theory; at least it is in harmony with it." And Erwin Schrodinger, undoubtedly one of the greatest physicists of this century, believed in a collective unconsciousness or group mind for all mankind, which he called the One Mind. Schrodinger's famous wave equations form the foundation of quantum mechanics.

Writing as early as 1958, at a time when no scientist would dare voice a belief in mysticism, Schrodinger said that "Some of us should venture to embark on a synthesis of facts and theories, albeit with second-hand and incomplete knowledge of some of them, and at the risk of making fools of ourselves." He wrote this in the introduction to his book, *Mind and Matter,* which became one of the most widely acclaimed books on the subject. Continuing his courageous assault on materialism, Schrodinger concluded that:

> We have entirely taken to thinking of the personality of a human being . . . as located in the interior of its body. To learn that it cannot really be found there is so amazing that it meets with doubt and hesitation.

Openly admitting that he found his inspiration in the study of the Vedas and the Upanishads, Schrodinger went on to say that:

> There is obviously only one alternative, namely the unification of minds or consciousness. Their multiplicity is only apparent. In truth there is only One Mind.

With this idea, Schrodinger went beyond the individual personality to propose that Mind is not localized to each person but rather is transpersonal, universal, collective. In other words, it is non-local. It is shared.

Schrodinger not only proposed the concept of One Mind, but also advanced his belief that the mind is indestructible because it has what he called "a peculiar time-table." In other words, Mind is always Now. There is no before or after for the Mind. Since it cannot be affected by time, then it follows that Mind is eternal, it cannot be destroyed.

This holistic approach to consciousness has been espoused by increasing numbers of scientists in modern times. One of the most exciting hypotheses to be presented recently was advanced by neuroscientist Karl Pribram, head of Radford University's Center for Brain Research and Information Sciences in Radford, Virginia, and physicist David Bohm, Professor Emeritus of theoretical physics at Birkbeck College in the University of London.

In the early stages of his career, Pribram was a convinced materialist, but he slowly began to realize that the Mind had to be more than the result of simple brain activity. He became interested by the science of holography by means of which images can be created using laser beams. These images are known as holograms, and are formed by splitting the light of the laser into two beams. One beam is directed toward the object to be photographed and the other toward a mirror. Both beams then reflect onto a photosensitive plate or film.

When the hologram is illuminated by a laser beam, the image of the object appears in three-dimensional form.

The principle behind the hologram inspired Pribram to conceive the idea that the brain stores information in the same way, not only in creating a three-dimensional version of the world from electrochemical impulses, but also in spreading information across the entire system. On the heels of this idea, came the conviction that the universe also functions as a hologram.

Around the same time that Pribram was toying with the idea of a holographic brain, David Bohm had already made a rather convincing case for a universe based on the principle of the hologram. According to Bohm, the deep reality of the universe is enfolded, invisible to observation by scientific means. Like Schrodinger, Bohm found in the Hindu concept of Brahman of Godhead what he called an "Intangible, invisible flux of inseparable interconnectedness." He blended these mystical concepts with mathematical models and analogy and concluded that the idea of a stable world of normal consciousness is an illusion. The universe, in his opinion, is a kaleidoscopic and dynamic unity, a state of being he called the "holomovement" or "holoverse." In an interview with *Omni* magazine in 1987, Bohm said that:

> Deep down the consciousness of mankind is one. This is a virtual certainty because even in the vacuum, matter is one; and if we don't see this it's because we are blinding ourselves to it. If we don't establish these absolute boundaries between minds, then it's possible they could unite as one mind.

Pribram learned by chance of Bohm's studies paralleling his own and immediately seized the opportunity to blend his idea of the holographic Mind with Bohm's concept of a holographic Universe. In this manner he was able to formulate a theory of consciousness with deep metaphysical implications where science and mysticism unite as one. Consciousness, he proposed, is an extension of a larger, hidden reality. Mental properties are in reality "the pervasive organizing principles of the universe, which includes the brain."

As we saw earlier in this book, Kabbalah recognizes two classes of manifested reality. These are the Noumenal or Spiritual Plane, and the Phenomenal Plane of the objective or physical realm. The spiritual Plane is equated with pure thought—Shamaym or Heaven—and is the origin of the various kinds of phenomenal energies that comprise the material world.

The first three sephiroth of the Tree of Life are known as the Neshamah or World Soul, where the experience of Oneness with the Godhead is realized. This triad can be seen as the Self or human spirit, God in Man.

The next six sephiroth in descending order are divided into the Higher and Lower Ruach, and can be identified with the Unconscious, with Mind.

The last sephira is further divided into the Nephesch and the Guph. The Nephesch is identified with sensations, instincts and desires, while the Guph is the physical body as well as the entire material world.

In this Kabbalistic concept, the brain, as part of the body, or Guph, functions through the Nephesch, the Soul, which is equated with consciousness and the vital force of life. The brain is also a receiver through which the Mind communicates the insights it receives from the Self which is the Divine spark in Man. It is clear from this concept that the Mind is outside the body, as is the Nephesch, which envelops it like a garment. This is in accord with Schrodinger's concept of the One Mind and Bohm's perception of holographic universe, with its "Intangible, invisible flux of inseparable inter-connectedness."

From this we can see that Man has many "bodies." The Physical Body is surrounded by the Soul or Etheric Body, which in turn is surrounded by the Mind or Astral Body and ultimately by the Self or Spiritual Body. It is the Self which is Man's true nature and the sum total of his being. When a person dies, all his other "bodies" are eventually dispersed, and only the Self remains. This Self is a spark, a ray of light from the One Creative Force, with which it must inevitably merge in a glorious synthesis of Spirit. When Schrodinger and Bohm spoke of "Mind" they were actually referring to the Self, the Spirit which is One with the Godhead.

The question of death on physical terms is a subject of much debate for humanity. It can be focused from many angles, philosophically, religiously, mystically and scientifically. But of all the arguments on this highly controversial subject, the scientific and the mystical are the ones most irrevocably linked.

In reality, science and mysticism are not apart from each other. They are simply two aspects of the Mind of Man: the one part of his Mind that believes intuitively (Chesed—Synthesis) and the speculative part (Gebruah—Analysis) that wants to substantiate belief with proof. All the discoveries in the various scientific fields, all the technological advances in the history of civilization, have been the direct result of Man's quest for his identity and the ultimate cause of his existence.

Science is the vehicle Man uses to silence his doubts and validate his beliefs. But in order for science to succeed it must be pragmatic, irreproachable, immaculate. It has to be holy because it is the vehicle of a holy cause.

As we have seen, many scientists, especially physicists and cosmologists, are becoming increasingly aware of this link with mysticism and are seeking to blend science with metaphysics at the most basic levels. This is because they know intuitively that it is in the world of spirit that they will find the answers to the most gnawing questions about the material world. And that is also the reason why mysticism itself must seek to blend with science its highest spiritual wisdom.

In Kabbalah, death is seen as a transformation, an unveiling of the Spirit, the Self, from its material garments. The Physical Body "dies" and returns to the dust whence it came. But the Spirit, the personal awareness of the individual, survives because it is eternal.

Science tells us that matter can neither be created nor destroyed. If the Spirit is part of the created universe, as a manifestation of the AIN SOPH AUR, it follows that it must also be composed of matter, albeit on a subatomic or sub-subatomic level. And if matter cannot be destroyed, Spirit as a form of matter cannot be destroyed, either.

If we consider the question of the survival of the personality from the viewpoint of natural selection, we must ask ourselves why did nature choose the evolution of Mind in the human being. The vast majority of animal life on earth functions quite successfully without the benefit of sophisticated mental processes. Surely there must be a reason, however hidden from obvious view, for such a decision. Granted that the workings of Mind have allowed Mankind to lord over all other living forms on the planet and advance by leaps and bounds into the fields of science and technology to his obvious advantage, but why evolve other less practical qualities of Mind, such as inspiration, compassion and imagination? More important still, if natural selection has seen fit to develop Mind in Mankind, and Mind has proven to be the most valuable asset in the evolutionary process, why seek to destroy it through death? After all, nature always preserves valuable traits and highly adaptable species. Is there anything more valuable in nature than the human Mind? Why destroy it through death? Why bother to develop it through millions of years of careful evolution only to discard it with the disintegration of the body? This makes no sense, particularly if we take into consideration nature's meticulous thriftiness in the conservation of energy. If Mind is unbounded energy, unbounded in the sense that it is a separate entity from the body, then it must surely be preserved when the body itself disappears.

The idea of a disembodied Mind immediately presents us with the paradox of how it can have any type of sensorial experience when it is no longer associated with a brain with a complex sensorial apparatus. How can it see, hear, feel, when it has no physical senses? But if we accept that the Mind exists independently of the brain, then the paradox is solved. Because then we can ascribe conscious states to the disembodied Mind. If Mind and brain are conceptually distinct, then there is no problem in accepting that there may be cognitive activities such as thinking, imagining, believing and feeling in the absence of a brain. One may still ask how the disembodied Mind can have perceptual experiences without sense organs and a nervous system. The answer maybe found in the dream state. When we dream we seem to see with our eyes closed and hear even though we are surrounded by silence. Lame Deer, a Sioux Medicine Man, said that "What you see with eyes shut is what counts." He was referring to the landscape of the Mind, the world we perceive in dreams, which has no parallels in the world of the senses. This dream world with its own conceptual reality may be seen as the world of the Mind, the astral world described by the mystics.

But one may still ponder the fact that the dreamer is still very much alive and that his dreams may be accounted for by the activity of his brain. Yet when we sleep stimuli from the sense organs are cut off or, at any rate, fail to have the same effects upon the brain.

If we conceive of the world of dreams as the world of the Mind, does that mean that the disembodied Mind cannot perceive the physical world after the death of the body? To aid us with this problem we can consider the many reported cases of persons who have found themselves outside their bodies while awake. During this apparently spontaneous occurrence, a person can see his or her own body and its surroundings without using the physical senses. These people report a strong sense of awareness while they remain outside their bodies. Most of the time they seem to be floating above it and can feel the same sensations that are natural in their embodied states. Many of these cases are reported by persons who have had serious illnesses or accidents, but some seem to occur for no special reason, when the individual is feeling healthy and comfortable. It is almost as if the part of the person who left the body is the real personality, the true Mind, while the body itself is simply a shell, left temporarily by its occupant. I had a similar experience many years ago, while I was still living in Vienna. I was feeling quite well, at great peace with myself, and there was no reason for what actually happened. I had gone to bed and was settled comfortably with several books that I wanted to finish reading, when I suddenly found myself floating over the bed near the ceiling. I was not alarmed at all at this extraordinary occurrence, but I remember thinking that I had probably died. My Mind was completely clear and I was able to see and hear as if I were still in my body. As I hovered over the bed, I felt an irresistible force drawing me toward a corner of the ceiling and I heard a rushing sound like a loud rattle in my ear. The force pulled me out and away into a dark vacuum where I was no longer conscious of my surroundings. I do not know how long I remained away, but suddenly I was back in the room. I looked at my body, immobile in the bed, with great longing, and all at once I was back in the body, as if I had never left it. I remember my body felt strangely cold and quiet, as an empty house may feel after you have left it for many months. I cannot forget the feeling of "entering" into my body, of inhabiting it, as one would a house. This experience only happened once but it served to convince me of the reality of Myself as other than my physical body.

If the Mind has a separate existence as out-of-body experiences seem to indicate, then presumably it does not only perceive the physical world but also inhabits a separate reality in a world of images akin to the world of dreams.

The concept of a disembodied Mind that survives physical death invites the tantalizing speculation of its return to the physical world in another body through reincarnation. This idea forms an intrinsic part of most Eastern religions, but in fact it is a widely held view.

Rebirth, transmigration, reembodiment and metempsychosis are variations of the same theme. The most common objection to reincarnation is that the great majority of human beings do not remember any previous lives. And even those who are able to recall past lives through hypnotic regression are often accused of simply possessing very vivid imaginations.

But memory is a definitive quality of the human brain, not of the Mind. When a child is born his memory is a clean slate upon which existence will write in vivid letters the experiences of a lifetime. Yet, it is not farfetched to conceive of the entire history of mankind impressed in the human genes through heredity. Every human experience must perforce be encoded in the depths of the human brain and such knowledge does come to the fore sometimes in the form of precognitive flashes and atavistic behavior. We can say, without stretching credibility, that we have lived myriad existences through the miraculous process of evolution. Mind simply records this knowledge and assimilates it with each consecutive existence. For it is experience itself in the world of matter that the Self seeks. It gathers it through Mind and fuses it with the Eternal Creative Force of the universe.

Material experience is identified with the concept of karma in Tibetan Buddhism, where a soul is said to live many lives to cleanse itself of accumulated negative actions, or karma.

Kabbalah teaches that when the Godhead created the universe through the emanation of the AIN SOPH AUR, the light emitted was so powerful that the vessels used to contain it broke under the strain. The pieces of the vessels, or shells, fell to the world of matter where, deprived of the lost light, they became enveloped in darkness. This is the Kabbalistic cause for the negative actions of mankind and the "evil" in the world. It is the work of Mankind to retrieve the lost light and return it to its original Source. Reincarnation would allow Mankind through Mind to purify the individual spiritual essence and complete the mission on earth. Through successive existences, he or she would learn to divest the vestiges of the shells and the past negative actions. This concept agrees in principle with the Buddhist idea of karma.

Suffering in the world is explained by Kabbalah as the forced separation of the Shekinah, the feminine aspect of the Godhead, from Her beloved. As long as the light is dispersed, there will be evil in the world and spiritual synthesis will not be completed. That is why Mind is necessary. For Mind is the perfect vessel for the gathering of the light. But in order for Mind to transform dark matter into light, it must purify itself through many lives and many experiences. Only then can the Shekinah unite with the AIN for all eternity. One may ask where the individual fits into this eternal bliss. Kabbalah answers by saying the concept of the individual is an illusion. We are all One with the Universe, and Together, We are the Shekinah.

20 The Face of God

As we saw earlier, the trajectories of particles that end up inside a black hole end in a single, infinitely condensed point known as a singularity. Such particles cannot emerge in this universe. As a result, if such "wormholes" exist, they must connect to another universe.

The concept of other universes is the subject of much animated controversy among cosmologists. After all, if there are millions of black holes in our universe, as it is estimated to be, and there are singularities at the bottom of each black hole, these could presumably result in cosmic events like our own Big Bang, giving birth to other universes. Those universes would in turn have millions of black holes, ending in singularities and other Big Bangs, ad infinitum. But where did it all begin? Which was the first universe to be created? And how?

If we follow the creation process along kabbalistic lines, which so far adhere in principle with cosmological findings, then this universe was the fourth one to be created. We know this because when the Creator emanated His/Her Light in the form of the AIN SOPH, the Light had to be divided into two extensions, one representing the will to impart and the other representing the will to receive. Because God is complete within Himself/Herself, He/She has nothing to receive and can only impart. However, the Creation must be able to receive the gift of the Creator, and therefore there must be a transformation in God's Light. In order for this to happen, the Light had to extend itself several times, and each time its will to impart gave way to the will to receive.

The two extensions were doubled in intensity, forming four gradations in God's will. The fourth grade or stage of the will is what is known as the AIN SOPH AUR, the Middle Point of the Endless, and the final and complete vessel of recipiency. These four gradations are known as the four Kabbalistic worlds, the World of Emanation (Atziluth), the World of Creation (Briah), the World of Formation (Yetzirah) and the World of Action (Assiah).

This Kabbalistic concept explains why God is a necessary being while the created universe is contingent. Furthermore, it explains how God being necessary could create a contingent universe. He/She did this by the transformation of His will to give, to impart, into the will to receive through a subtle process where His/Her Light became progressively more dense until it became the single point whence the universe came into being. The creature then must desire to receive the bounties of the Creator, but in so doing it departs further from Him/Her because there is no will to receive in God. In order to come closer to the Godhead, Mankind must therefore try to sublimate the desire to receive and learn to give of himself, to impart, which is God's central characteristic. It is the unbounded desire to receive without giving that separates humanity from God and is the root of all evil in the world.

Therefore according to Kabbalah, the world of matter in which we live, this universe is the fourth emitted from God. That means that there are three other universes encompassing the one we inhabit, and beyond them there is the infinite Light that is God, AIN.

From the preceding we may further infer that our universe is not infinite but bounded by limits, and furthermore that it is circular in shape. This we know because the light of the AIN SOPH—the Endless World—was restricted in the form of a circle to indicate that it had no beginning and no end. The circle in Kabbalistic thought is the perfect geometrical form because it is equal in all its points. That is the reason why the various sephiroth or spheres of the Tree of Life are also conceived as circular.

Outside our universe, finite and circular, lies the Creator, pure and infinite Light, unknowable yet All Knowing. But our world is only one of many, according to the Kabbalah, so many in fact as to be deemed innumerable.

Kabbalah teaches us further that as the Creator is unknowable, that is far beyond our human ken to comprehend His/Her essence, and therefore what lies Outside our universe can never be known. This is also in accordance with the findings of modern cosmology which tell us that all the laws of physics break down, that is, they stop working, at the singularity that caused the Big Bang. This singularity, as we have already seen, is known in Kabbalistic terms as the AIN SOPH AUR.

When we think of multiple universes arising from this one, we must also consider the world of subatomic particles and the fact that there seems to be a hierarchy of organizational levels where higher levels can act downwards on lower ones. In other words, the body is composed of molecules, which in turn are composed of atoms, which are composed of electrons and protons, and so on into the subatomic and sub-subatomic levels, ad infinitum. This is explained in Kabbalistic terms as the Light travelling downwards from the original point that is the AIN SOPH AUR.

This means that there are many universes in the macrocosmos of the visible as well as in the microcosmos of the invisible. As the Light Itself is eternal and infinite, its course downwards must perforce be infinite and eternal.

Is there life in those other universes? Is there life in this universe other than our own? Kabbalah tacitly implies there is. The fact that the Godhead created us as thinking, feeling beings on this planet does not preclude that there are other beings in other worlds. Kabbalah speaks of the love the Creator has for His/Her creatures, but does not say that we are the only creatures He/She has created. Many scientists are increasingly embracing the Anthropic Principle which states that the universe could not exist by itself with all its grandeur if there were no creatures such as ourselves to be aware of its existence. In other words, the universe exists for our sakes.

In the Kabbalistic concept of the four worlds, there exists an existence before existence which is known as Adam Kadmon. This is the pure Light of God, unrestricted and undefined, and is for that reason known as the Body of God. This is a symbolical term as God has no form. It simply represents the will of God to impart. From this emanated the four Kabbalistic worlds.

As we already saw, Atziluth is the world of archetypes, Briah is the world of archangels, Yetzirah is the world of angels and Assiah is our universe. According to this Kabbalistic concept each universe or world is populated with sentient beings, albeit on different spiritual levels. It therefore follows that other universes emanated from our own must be populated as well. This is a very sobering and humbling notion because it implies that not only we are not unique, but also that there are other forms of life in a much higher state of spiritual evolution than our own.

The notion of archetypes is linked to the world of ideas, the very essence of thought and the realm of Mind, but in reality archetypes are beyond Mind. They are the molds upon which our Mind grows and evolves. They may be perceived but never fully comprehended because they exist in a world far beyond our own. Archangels and angels, on the other hand, belong to the sphere of feelings and emotions, and are more accessible to us while still existing on a higher spiritual plane. Because they are closer to God, we are encouraged by Kabbalah to enlist their aid in our search for union with the Creator. But even archangels and angels are not in total union with God. They are still separated from the Infinite Light by the creative process. They are closer to God than we are, but still long for a more perfect union. As long as they desire to receive, they must remain apart from the Creator. And strangely enough, it is Mankind with all our defects, that must complete the process of synthesis through which all the emanated worlds, even the higher ones, will be once more united with the Infinite Light. That is the reason why all the creatures of the higher worlds must help Mankind in its spiritual quest.

We are living in extraordinary times and are immensely privileged to be the witnesses of the wondrous blending of Mind and Matter, Body and Spirit, Science and Mysticism. Jung believed that there were no coincidences, only synchronized events, and it is in no way a coincidence that God should have chosen these present times to make His/Her reality quite plain for all the world to see. For we are approaching the millennium, a time during which, according to Kabbalah, God will finally show His/Her face to the world.

A Kabbalist, preparing for that momentous event, would create a special ritual, a daily ceremony, through which s/he would seek to effectuate the union that should be the goal of existence. One might decide to make a circle of 12 white quartz crystals, and sit within, dressed in plain white clothing, holding a single white candle in his hands. The light of the candle would represent the Light to which he aspired and the circle of quartz the yearly revolution of the earth around the sun. But he would not ask for anything. Instead, he would give himself to the Light in his totality and will to impart his very Essence to the Source whence he came and be One with It.

A hundred years ago Walt Whitman wrote a poem called "Passage to India." The words he put down on paper expressed, as only he could, humanity's desperate longing to achieve that ultimate union:

O Thou transcendent,
Nameless, the fibre and the breath,
Light of the light, shedding forth universes, Thou center
    of them,
Thou mightier center of the true, the good, the loving,

Thou moral, spiritual fountain—affection's source—
      Thou reservoir,
O pensive soul of me—O thirst unsatisfied—waitest not
      there?
Thou pulse—Thou motive of the stars, suns, systems,
That, circling, moving in order, safe, harmonious,
Athwart the shapely vastnesses of space,
How should I think, how breathe a single breath, how
      speak, if, out of myself,
I could not launch, to those, superior universes?

Bibliography

Achad, Frater, *Q.B.L.*, New York, 1969.

Agrippa, Cornelius, *De Occulta Philosophia*, New York, 1971.

Anderson, P.R., *Science in Defense of Liberal Religion*, London, 1933.

Anon., *The Cloud of Unknowing*, New York.

Anon., *The Golden Verses of the Pythagoreans*, London.

Apocrypha, The, New York, 1936.

Aristotle, *Metaphysics*, R. Hope, Transl., New York, 1952.

Aude Sapere, *The Chaldean Oracles of Zoroaster*, New York.

Asimov, I., *The Universe*, New York, 1966.

Bardon, F., *The Key to the True Quabbalah*, Austria, 1971.

Belchem, R.F.K., *A Guide to Nuclear Energy*, New York, 1958.

Best, S.B., *Genesis Revised*, London, 1964.

Bible, The, "Genesis."

Brill, A.A., Ed., *The Basic Writings of Sigmund Freud*, New York, 1938.

Boehme, Jacob, *The Signature of All Things*, London, 1969.

Bohm, D., *Wholeness and the Implicate Order*, London, 1980.

Campbell, J., *The Power of Myth*, New York, 1988.

Capra, F., *The Tao of Physics*, Boulder, 1975.

Charles, R.H., Transl., *The Book of Enoch*, London, 1980.

Child, J.M., *The Early Mathematical Manuscripts of Leibniz*, London, 1920.

Churchland, P.M., *Matter and Consciousness*, Cambridge, Mass., 1988.

Cuny, H., *Albert Einstein*, New York, 1965.

Darwin, C.R., *The Origin of Species*, London.

Davidson, G., *A Dictionary of Angels*, New York, 1967.

Davies, P., *God and the New Physics*, New York, 1983.

d'Olivet, Fabre, *La Langue Hebraique Restituèe*, Paris.

_____, *The Hebraic Tongue Restored*, N. Redfield, Transl., New York.

Dossey, L.M., *Recovering the Soul*, New York, 1989.

Durant, W., *The Story of Philosophy*, New York, 1953.

Eccles, J.C., *The Human Psyche*, New York, 1980.

Eddington, A., "Defense of Mysticism, " in *Quantum Questions*, Boston, 1984.

Einstein, A., *Ideas and Opinions*, New York, 1954.

Einstein, A., *The World as I See It*, New York, 1949.

Fodor, J.A., *The Language of Thought*, London, 1976.

Fortune, D., *The Mystical Qabalah*, London, 1935.

Franck, A., *The Kabbalah*, London, 1926.

Gaer, J., *How the Great Religions Began*, New York, 1954.

Gamow, G., *The Creation of the Universe*, New York.

Gaster, T.H., *The Dead Sea Scriptures*, New York, 1964.

Ginsburg, C.D., *The Kabbalah*, London, 1863.

Gleick, J., *Chaos*, New York, 1987.

Green, A. and Holtz, B.W., *Your Word is Fire*, New York, 1977.

Hahn, E. and Benes, B.L., *Breath of God*, New York.

Hall, C.S., *A Primer of Freudian Psychology*, New York, 1954.

Hannay, A., *Human Consciousness*, London, 1990.

Hawking, S., *A Brief History of Time*, New York, 1988.

Heidegger, M., *Being and Time*, New York, 1962.

Hoyle, F., *Astronomy and Cosmology: A Modern Course*, 1975.

Huxley, A., *The Perennial Philosophy*, New York, 1962.

Jastrow, R., *God and the Astronomers*, New York, 1977.

Jeans, J., *The Mysterious Universe*, New York, 1948.

Jung, C.G., *The Archetypes of the Collective Unconscious*, New York, 1959.

_____, *The Structure and Dynamics of the Psyche*, New York, 1960.

_____, *Mysterium Coniunctionis*, New York, 1963.

Kant, I., *Prolegomena to Any Future Metaphysics*, New York, 1951.

Knight, G., *A Practical Guide to Kabbalistic Symbolism*, London, 1965.

Krakovski, L.I., Rabbi, *Kabbalah, The Light of Redemption*, Israel, 1970.

Leakey, R., *Origins*, New York, 1977.

Leibniz, W., *Monadology*, London, 1890.

Leslie, J., *Universes*, London, 1989.

Levi, E., *Key to the Mysteries*, London, 1969.

Lully, R., *The Tree of Love*, London, 1926.

Lund, D.H., *Death and Consciousness*, North Carolina, 1985.

Luria, Isaac, Rabbi, *Ten Luminous Emanations*, Rabbi L.I. Krakovski, Transl., Jerusalem, 1969.

Luzzatto, M.C., Rabbi, *General Principles of the Kabalah*, New York, 1970.

Lycan, W.G., *Consciousness*, Cambridge, Mass.

Maimonides, M., *The Guide to the Perplexed*, New York, 1956.

_____, *Mishneh Torah*, New York, 1974.

Mathers, S.L.M., *The Kabbalah Unveiled*, New York, 1971.

_____, *The Key of Solomon the King (ed.)*, New York, 1976.

Myer, I., *Qabbalah*, New York, 1970.

Ouspensky, P., *Tertium Organum, A Key to the Enigmas of the Universe*, New York, 1968.

Petuchowski, J.J., *Understanding Jewish Prayer*, New York, 1972.

Penfield, W., *The Mystery of the Mind*, New Jersey, 1975.

Penrose, R., *The Emperor's New Mind*, New York, 1989.

Pfeiffer, C.F., *The Dead Sea Scrolls and the Bible*, New York, 1972.

Plato, *Phaedo*, New York, 1942.

Platt, R.H., *The Forgotten Books of Eden*, New York, 1980.

Popper, K. and Eccles, J.C., *The Self and Its Brain*, Berlin, 1977.

Progoff, I., *Jung, Synchronicity and Human Destiny*, New York, 1973.

Regardie, I., *A Garden of Pomegranates*, Minnesota, 1970.

_____, *The Tree of Life*, New York, 1972.

_____, *The Art of True Healing*, London, 1966.

Russell, B., *The ABC of Relativity*, London, 1958.

_____, *The Analysis of Mind*, London, 1921.

Sagan, C., *The Cosmic Connection*, New York, 1973.

Saint Augustine, *Confessions*, London, 1982.

Scholem, G., *Major Trends in Jewish Mysticism*, New York, 1954.

_____, *On the Kabbalah and Its Symbolism*, New York, 1965.

Schrodinger, E., *What is Life?*, London, 1969.

Sheldrake, R., *A New Science of Life*, Los Angeles, 1981.

Shipman, H.L., *Black Holes, Quasars, and the Universe*, Boston, 1976.

Straughn, R.A., *Meditation Techniques of the Kabalists, Vedantins and Taoists*, New York, 1976.

Suares, C., *The Cipher of Genesis*, Berkeley, 1970.

_____, *Sepher Yetzirah*, London, 1968.

Trachtenberg, J., *Jewish Magic and Mysticism*, New York, 1961.

Voltaire, *Philosophical Dictionary* (See *Genesis*), Middlesex, 1971.

Waite, A.E., *The Holy Kabbalah*, New York, 1960.

Watson, L., *Supernature*, New York, 1967.

Weiner, H., *9 1/2 Mystics, The Kabbala Today*, New York, 1969.

Westcott, W.W., ed., *The Sepher Yetzirah (The Book of Formation)*, London.

_____, *Aesch Mezareph (The Purifying Fire)*, New York.

Whitman, W., *Leaves of Grass*, New York, 1961.

Zohar (The Book of Splendour), G. Scholem, ed., New York, 1949.

THE COMPLETE BOOK OF
AMULETS & TALISMANS
Migene González-Wippler

The Pentagram, Star of David, Crucifix, rabbit's foot, painted pebble, or Hand of Fatima … they all provide feelings of comfort and protection, attracting good while dispelling evil.

The joy of amulets and talismans is that they can be made and used by anyone. The forces used, and the forces invoked, are all natural forces.

Spanning the world through the diverse cultures of Sumeria, Babylonia, Greece, Italy, India, Western Europe and North America, González-Wippler proves that amulets and talismans are anything but mere superstition—they are part of each man's and woman's search for spiritual connection. This book presents the entire history of these tools, their geography, and shows how anyone can create amulets and talismans to empower his or her life. Loaded with hundreds of photographs, this is the ultimate reference and how-to guide for their use.

0-87542-287-X, 304 pp., 6 x 9, photos, softcover   **$14.95**

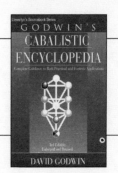

GODWIN'S CABALISTIC ENCYCLOPEDIA
David Godwin

One of the most valuable books on the Cabala is back, with a new and more usable format. This book is a complete guide to cabalistic magick and gematria in which every demon, angel, power and name of God ... every Sephiroth, Path, and Plane of the Tree of Life ... and each attribute and association is fully described and cross-indexed by the Hebrew, English, and numerical forms.

All entries, which had been scattered throughout the appendices, are now incorporated into one comprehensive dictionary. There are hundreds of new entries and illustrations, making this book even more valuable for Cabalistic pathworking and meditation. It now has many new Hebrew words and names, as well as the terms of Freemasonry, the entities of the Cthulhu mythos, and the Aurum Solis spellings for the names of the demons of the Goetia. It contains authentic Hebrew spellings, and a new introduction that explains the uses of the book for meditation on God names.

The Cabalistic schema is native to the human psyche, and *Godwin's Cabalistic Encyclopedia* will be a valuable reference tool for all Cabalists, magicians, scholars and scientists of all disciplines.

1–56718–324–7, 832 pp., 6 x 9, softcover **$24.95**

SIMPLIFIED MAGIC
A Beginner's Guide to the
New Age Qabala
Ted Andrews

In every person, the qualities essential for accelerating his or her growth and spiritual evolution are innate, but even those who recognize such potentials need an effective means of releasing them. The ancient and mystical Qabala is that means. A person does not need to become a dedicated Qabalist in order to acquire benefits from the Qabala. *Simplified Magic* offers a simple understanding of what the Qabala is and how it operates. It provides practical methods and techniques so that the energies and forces within the system and within ourselves can be experienced in a manner that enhances growth and releases our greater potential. A new reader Qabala could apply the methods in this book with noticeable success!

The Qabala is more than just some theory for ceremonial magicians. It is a system for personal attainment and magic that anyone can learn and put to use in his or her life. The secret is that the main glyph of the Qabala, the Tree of Life, is within you. The Tree of Life is a map to the levels of consciousness, power and magic that are within. By learning the Qabala, you will be able to tap into these levels and bring peace, healing, power, love, light and magic into your life.

0-87542-015-X, 208 pp., mass market, illus. **$4.99**

THE MAGICIAN'S COMPANION
A Practical and Encyclopedic Guide to Magical and Religious Symbolism
Bill Whitcomb

The Magician's Companion is a "desk reference" overflowing with a wide range of occult and esoteric materials absolutely indispensable to anyone engaged in the magical arts!

The magical knowledge of our ancestors comprises an intricate and elegant technology of the mind and imagination. This book attempts to make the ancient systems accessible, understandable and useful to modern magicians by categorizing and cross-referencing the major magical symbol-systems (i.e., world views on inner and outer levels). Students of religion, mysticism, mythology, symbolic art, literature, and even cryptography will find this work of value.

This comprehensive book discusses and compares over 35 magical models (e.g., the Trinities, the Taoist Psychic Centers, Enochian magic, the qabala, the Worlds of the Hopi Indians). Also included are discussions of the theory and practice of magic and ritual; sections on alchemy, magical alphabets, talismans, sigils, magical herbs and plants; suggested programs of study; an extensive glossary and bibliography; and much more.

0–87542–868–1, 522 pp., 7 x 10, illus., softcover   **$24.95**

To order, call 1-800-THE MOON
Prices subject to change without notice

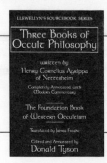

THE THREE BOOKS OF
OCCULT PHILOSOPHY
Henry Cornelius Agrippa, edited
and annotated by Donald Tyson

Agrippa's *Three Books of Occult Philosophy* is the single most important text in the history of Western occultism. Occultists have drawn
upon it for five centuries, although they rarely give it credit. First
published in Latin in 1531 and translated into English in 1651, it has
never been reprinted in its entirety since. Photocopies are hard to
find and very expensive. Now, for the first time in 500 years, *Three
Books of Occult Philosophy* will be presented as Agrippa intended.
There were many errors in the original translation, but occult author
Donald Tyson has made the corrections and has clarified the more
obscure material with copious notes.

This is a necessary reference tool not only for all magicians, but
also for scholars of the Renaissance, Neoplatonism, the Western
Kabbalah, the history of ideas and sciences and the occult tradition. It
is as practical today as it was 500 years ago.

0–87542–832–0, 1,024 pp., 7 x 10, softcover   **$39.95**

THE GOLDEN DAWN
As revealed by Israel Regardie

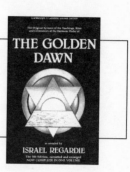

Complete in one volume with further revision, expansion, and additional notes by Regardie, Cris Monnastre, and others. Expanded with an index of more than 100 pages! Originally published in four bulky volumes of some 1,200 pages, this 6th Revised and Enlarged Edition has been entirely reset in modern, less space-consuming type, in half the pages (while retaining the original pagination in marginal notation for reference) for greater ease and use.

Also included are Initiation Ceremonies, important rituals for consecration and invocation, methods of meditation and magical working based on the Enochian Tablets, studies in the Tarot, and the system of Qabalistic Correspondences that unite the World's religions and magical traditions into a comprehensive and practical whole.

This volume is designed as a study and practice curriculum suited to both group and private practice. Meditation upon, and following with the Active Imagination, the Initiation Ceremonies are fully experiential without need of participation in group or lodge. A very complete reference encyclopedia of Western Magick.

0–87542–663–8, 840 pp., 6 x 9, illus., softcover   **$24.95**

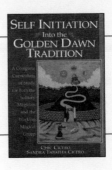

**SELF-INITIATION INTO THE
GOLD DAWN TRADITION**
Chic Cicero and Sandra Tabatha Cicero

Regardless of your magical knowledge or background, you can learn and live the magical Golden Dawn tradition with the first practical guide to Golden Dawn initiation. *Self-Initiation into the Golden Dawn Tradition* offers self-paced instruction by the established authorities on this magical order! Without massive amounts of complex information, Golden Dawn experts Sandra Tabatha Cicero and Chic Cicero present direction that's clear and easy-to-follow. Upon completion of this workbook, you can be a practicing Golden Dawn magician with knowledge of Qabalah, astrology, tarot, geomancy and spiritual alchemy. Other than a desire to learn, there is no prerequisite for mastering this highly sought-after magical curriculum.

Lessons in *Self-Initiation into the Golden Dawn Tradition* are enhanced by written examinations, daily rituals and meditative work. Become a Golden Dawn magician—without group membership or prohibitive expense—through the most complete, comprehensive and scientific system on Golden Dawn study to date!

1–56718–136–8, 800 pp., 7 x 10, softcover   **$39.95**